Gentry bade farewthe table. He went to th the bill. Then he walked

Turning left at the far end of the half-empty, unlit parking lot. No one had pulled into the spaces next to him. He wondered vaguely where Judi had parked her precious Corvette. The night dial on his watch read ten thirty-five as he climbed into his unlocked car, a small frown of concentration furrowing his brow as he thought of which liquor store on the way home would still be open. He could always stop at one of the all-night supermarkets in town, but Judi had to have the best of everything. A cheap brand of champagne would never do. Leaning slightly forward to reach the dashboard, he started the engine as he pulled on his headlights, as it was his habit to do.

He felt the explosion before he heard it as the roof of his car erupted like a mushroom . . . .

BODIES OF EVIDENCE

BODIES OF EVIDENCE

*The True Story of
Judias Buenoano
Florida's Serial
Murderess*

CHRIS ANDERSON &
SHARON McGEHEE

SMP
ST. MARTIN'S PAPERBACKS

Published by arrangement with Lyle Stuart

BODIES OF EVIDENCE

Copyright © 1991 by Chris Anderson and Sharon McGehee.

Excerpt from *Who Killed Precious?* copyright © 1991 by H. Paul Jeffers.

Library of Congress Catalog Card Number: 91-18458

ISBN: 0-312-92806-8

Printed in the United States of America

Lyle Stuart edition / July 1991
St. Martin's Paperbacks edition / April 1992

10 9 8 7 6 5 4 3 2 1

In fond memory of
Michael William Douglas.
The eagle has finally landed.

Contents

Acknowledgments

The authors wish gratefully to acknowledge the personal contribution of the following individuals to the completion of this book: Diana Adams, Doris and Ralph Adams, Dorothy Adams Anderson, Timothy Augello, Gerald F. Barnes, Bradford J. Brown, Esq., Nancy Cabannis, Emma Cappucci, Lt. Col. Paul D. Carmichael, Frank Chamberlain, Jerri Chamberlain, Ted Chamberlain, Robert E. Cousson, Robert Crongeyer, Esq., Michael W. Douglas, Assistant State Attorney Russ Edgar, Douglas Edie, Carey Flack, John W. Gentry, Mary Lucille Holland, Faye Johnson, James Johnston, Esq., David McGehee, Eileen A. McGehee, Galen McGehee, Gerald McGill, Esq., Avery Hunt Meyers, Lodell Morris, Assistant State Attorney Michael Patterson, Nelson Peacock, Judge Belvin C. Perry, Ed Ryan, Howard Sandum, Rick Steele, Superintendent Marta Villacorta, Dina Williams, Allan J. Wilson.

The authors wish to thank the following for their cooperation and services: Broward Correctional Institute, Pembroke Pines, Florida; Deputy General Counsel to the Governor of Florida; Escambia County Courthouse, Pensacola; Florida State Attorney's Office, Pensacola; Florida State Archives, Tallahassee; Florida State Prison Secretary for Operations, Tallahassee; Pensacola Chapter of Florida Motion Picture and Television Association; Pensacola Historical Museum; *Pensacola News Journal*; Pensacola Police Department; Pensacola Public Library; Santa Rosa County Courthouse, Milton, Florida.

Don't be fooled by me.
Don't be fooled by the face I wear.
For I wear a thousand masks, masks I'm afraid to take off,
And none of them are me.
Pretending is an art that's second nature to me,
But don't be fooled.
For God's sake, don't be fooled.
I give the impression that I'm secure,
That all is sunny and unruffled with me,
Within as well as without.
That confidence is my name and coolness my game,
That the water's calm and I'm in command,
And that I need no one.
But don't believe me,
Please . . .

—from Judias's scrapbook

Prologue

THREE-TIME CONVICTED murderess Judias Buenoano, alias Judy Ann Goodyear, alias Ann Lou Welty, sits in a tiny cell on Florida's death row at the Broward County Women's Detention Center and waits. She waits, as she has waited for the past six years, for the final life-or-death decision that will determine her fate. She waits and hopes and perhaps prays that her death sentence will not be upheld, that her final appeal to the United States Supreme Court for life imprisonment will not be denied, that her lawyers' final plea for clemency to Florida's governor will not be turned down, and that the hour of her execution will not finally arrive.

Should all of her hopes be denied, the prescription for execution by the State of Florida is precise and grim. In the slightly larger deathwatch cell, nine feet wide and fourteen feet deep, the condemned woman spends her final hours. She is served the traditional last meal of steak and eggs, orange juice, coffee, and hash brown potatoes. A small circle at the top of her head is shaved. She walks the thirty feet from her cell to the execution chamber. In the gallery twelve witnesses and twelve members of the press watch through a glass partition as she is strapped into the hideously medieval-looking electric chair. She is given the conventional four or five minutes for her last words. The death warrant authorizing her execution is read to her. Then a steel plate is fitted over the shaved spot on top of her head, a black veil is placed over her face, and an anonymous executioner pulls the switch. Two thousand volts and fourteen amps of electric current course through her body for the two minutes it takes her to die and pay her final debt to society.

How and why Judias Buenoano came to be on death row waiting to become the first white woman to be executed in Florida's electric chair in seventy years is a story that begins on a June night in Pensacola, Florida, in 1983, when a car exploded in a secluded restaurant parking lot and triggered a two-year police investigation that eventually unearthed a trail of buried victims, ranging over twelve years and across five states, and nearly a million dollars in life insurance policies.

To reach the end of the intricate maze of long-undiscovered murders, one must begin, as with Ariadne's thread, with the last intended victim.

1

A Small Kiss Good-bye

NESTLED AMONG THE PINE-GROVED SHORES of sheltered bays and brackish bayous, the port of Pensacola lies sequestered at the westernmost corner of Florida's panhandle, a mullet toss from the Alabama state line. Along that northwest coast of the Gulf of Mexico, tawny Alabama sands meet the hundred-mile stretch of glistening white quartz crystal beaches in the Gulf Islands National Seashore, known unofficially as the Redneck Riviera. A graceful three-mile-long Bay Bridge connects the Pensacola city shoreline with the jutting Gulf Breeze Peninsula, which is connected in turn to the narrow ribbon of Santa Rosa Island by the shorter Bob Sikes Bridge, humped high in the middle to allow tall-masted ships to pass. Where the western tip of windswept island dunes almost meets the mainland shore, the U.S. Naval Air Station guards the channel entrance to the deepest natural harbor on the Gulf Coast. Across the narrow channel stand the remains of a four-hundred-year-old Spanish fort, renamed Fort Pickens after a South Carolina hero of the Revolutionary War, and long known to tourists for the iron-barred brick chamber where the celebrated renegade Apache chief Geronimo was imprisoned for several years. The city of Pensacola, having lived under Spanish, French, British, American, and Confederate rule since its founding in 1559, was finally surrendered to the Union commander at Fort Pickens after a brief Confederate stand on May 10, 1862. Ever since, native Pensacolans have devoted themselves to serving the needs of their ever-expanding transient Yankee population and the Unit-

ed States Navy with saccharine smiles and honeyed phrases
of "Ya'll come back, ya hear?"

To John Wesley Gentry II, Pensacola had always been
home.

John Wesley Gentry II was delivered at home by a
midwife on June 16, 1946, when Ninth Avenue was still
a dirt road and the far north inland section of Pensacola
was called "Tater Town." He was the second eldest of
five brothers—the namesake of his paternal grandfather—
in the fourth generation of native Pensacolans. True to his
heritage—the family had been lumberjacks—John Gentry
II grew to a manly height of six foot three and a robust two
hundred pounds. A soft brow and neatly trimmed goatee
framed pale, honest eyes that matched the slow temper
and easy-going drawl. He was a member of the Mormon
faith. Missionaries from the Church of Latter-Day Saints
would come by the door. John considered himself a "sort
of very logical person," and what they said made sense to
him. At sixteen, he joined the church.

John Gentry still recalls every waking moment of June
25, 1983. That particular day remains vivid in his memory
because it was very nearly his last.

He recalls sitting around the breakfast bar in Judi's kitch-
en early on that sultry Saturday morning as they planned
the day hour by hour. He had told her he wanted to get
some new speakers for his car radio over at the flea market
on T and W streets. He figured on asking James if he
wouldn't mind installing them for him. Judi's son, just
seventeen, was very good at hooking up things. James had a
stereo system in his truck you could hear two blocks away.

Gentry remembers telling Judi he'd be home with the
new speakers by noon. He was to be at the Driftwood
Restaurant by seven-thirty that evening to greet the guests
for the party. One of Judi's female employees at her Fingers
N Faces beauty salon was leaving for nearby Fort Walton
Beach, and Judi was throwing a going-away bash for the girl
and about six of the other manicurists and their husbands
and boyfriends. Since Judi had to stay late at the shop, he

was to greet the guests and make sure they were properly
seated. And he was to be sure to park in the lot beside
the Driftwood Restaurant and not across the street near
the old Hotel San Carlos. The last time they were there,
a drunk had come up and tried to bum a buck. Judi didn't
want to be hassled again. That made sense to him, but
she needn't have been so adamant about it. Besides, he
would have done whatever she wanted anyway. It was
her party, and he wanted to accommodate her, and that
was that.

It was just eight forty-five as Gentry headed toward town
on the Pensacola Bay Bridge in his 1981 Ford Futura.
His sunroof was open wide to the refreshing gulf breeze
that danced across the glittering silver-blue water, already
reflecting the unbroken glare of the morning sun in mid-
summer. His favorite Kenny Rogers ballad bleated from his
worn-out speakers.

A few minutes later he turned off the wide boulevard
at the foot of the Bay Bridge toward the old East Hill
section of town and onto a quiet residential street shaded
by century-old gnarled oaks. Parking before a weathered
clapboard house with a covered Southern-style veranda,
he bounded up the wooden steps and entered through
the worn screen door. He had invited his mother to the
dinner party and wanted to see if she was ready for him to
pick her up that night. He had mentioned to Judi that he
might bring his mother along. To his surprise, Judi hadn't
objected. She always tried to keep a straight face about it,
but he knew Judi had never cared for his mother at all. His
mother made no bones about not liking Judi.

Lucille Gentry was a stern, strong, independent woman
of German stock and Alabama birth. She was used to hard
work. But twenty-five years of shifts at the St. Regis paper
mill and raising six kids on her own had taken their toll. A
resigned weariness had taken permanent hold of her deeply
lined, weatherbeaten face. She'd taken leave from the mill
the day before and still didn't feel very well. No, she didn't
think she'd go to Judi's party, but he could stop by on his

way and see if she felt up to it. At sixty-something, she didn't need to be pushed.

Gentry had always admired his mother. His attitude toward his father was different. He really couldn't say that much bad about his father. Hubert L. Gentry was a good man at heart, but like many other local men, he had two major weaknesses—alcohol and irresponsibility. Sometimes he would leave home for two or three years and suddenly show up again, all the worse for wear and time spent in jail for bad checks, drunken and disorderly conduct, and general rowdy behavior. But his wife still loved him. They stayed married for thirty years and were together when he died in 1969. Hubert quit drinking one day, and he died three weeks later. Gentry always figured his father's system just couldn't adjust to the shock. That's probably why he was never a big drinker himself.

It was eleven-thirty before Gentry returned to Judi's two-story white clapboard home in Gulf Breeze with his newly purchased speakers in the trunk. He entered the house to find James where he had left him earlier that morning—slumped in the same chair by the door leading into the kitchen. Kimberly, Judi's fourteen-year-old daughter, was busy on the couch necking with her boyfriend and smoking cigarettes. He had made an agreement with Judi when they first got together that neither would interfere in the other's personal affairs, and no matter what Judi allowed her daughter or son to do, he considered that none of his business. But it sure wasn't the way he would raise his kids.

Politely, he asked James if he would mind installing his new speakers that afternoon. "No problem," James mumbled. Together they opened the trunk of his car and unwrapped one of the speakers. "No problem at all," James repeated.

Gentry was surprised to see Judi's shiny new white Corvette pull up the driveway. He hadn't expected to see her until the dinner party that evening. She had said something about lending her car to the girls to go out on the town after the party and driving home with him. What was she doing home now? She waited until James sauntered back into the house; then, leaning against the closed trunk of Gentry's car, she announced, "I saw the doctor this morning, and I'm pregnant."

Gentry felt his jaw drop. He didn't know if he was elated or just dazed. He had never got to raise the two sons from his first marriage, and he had always wanted another son. Judi knew how much he wanted to be a father again. He couldn't tell whether she was happy or not. She'd been so touchy lately, he was almost afraid to embrace her. She suggested they take the afternoon off and celebrate together. She wanted to go to University Mall, take in a movie, have lunch, do some shopping. She needed to pick up a gift to present to her departing employee that night. The mall was one of the few places in town where she could purchase Players, her imported British cigarettes.

Leaving his car for James to work on, Gentry hopped into the passenger seat next to Judi, and they took off in her high-powered sports car.

The bridge traffic heading toward the island strip of cooling gulf beaches was beginning to back up on the south-bound lanes as they cruised along unimpeded in air-conditioned silence toward the sun-baked mainland. Traffic was sparse on the massive new Interstate 10 as they continued the twenty-minute drive to the North Davis exit and negotiated the sprawling, always crowded parking lot of the giant University Mall, one of the latest to crop up on the northeast outskirts of greater Pensacola near the new campus of the University of West Florida.

There were plenty of empty seats in the intimate dark interior of the mall's four-theater cinema complex as Gentry slid in next to Judi in a center row. Refusing his offer of popcorn with a shake of her head, she kept her gaze on the screen before her. Gentry sat quietly munching his popcorn and tried to concentrate on the film. Ordinarily he would have enjoyed it—a political drama in which his favorite actor, Martin Sheen, played a candidate for President.

Gentry's stomach was grumbling from the hard kernels of salty popcorn as they exited into the painful glare of mid-afternoon. He was glad Judi had suggested Morrison's for lunch. Like most of the local businesses, Morrison's Cafeteria—once a fixture of Southern hospitality in downtown Pensacola—had followed the general exodus to the suburbs in recent years. Resisting the automated efficiency of its Northern counterparts, Morrison's retained a flavor of Dixie-style leisure. An unhurried line of smiling, aproned servers patiently handed choice cuts of carved roast beef, Southern fried chicken, fresh broiled snapper, and an endless variety of gelatin salads, overcooked vegetables, rich pecan pie, and frothy cream pies over the glass-partitioned display. Morrison's had always been a treat. As a child Gentry had pressed wide-eyed against the protective pane, clutching his grandparents' hands as they moved through the serving line. The cafeteria still evoked comforting feelings of innocent well-being deep in the pit of his stomach.

They joined the long line of tray-bearing lunch-goers with few words and went to a Formica-topped table in the center of the noisy dining room. Gentry watched as Judi coolly arranged her lunch on the table and set the empty tray aside. He knew better than to ask if she was serious about being pregnant. Judi rarely joked about anything. All his feelings about splitting, and now this. Two years they're together and she's not pregnant, and now all of a sudden, she is. And Judi was forty, a couple of years older than he. . . .

It was February 1981 when he first saw her, at a new roadhouse out on Nine Mile Road and Mobile Highway that featured the latest female mud-wrestling fad.

The Merry Go Round was a huge lounge spanning fifteen thousand square feet with a three-ring circus of bands and entertainment separated by wooden railings. The female mud wrestling was set up in the center ring. It was impossible to distinguish the jumble of amplified music and shouting emcees from the din of the raucous, beer-drinking singles crowd. He was leaning back against one of the railings with a bourbon and Coke, feeling overdressed in his jacket and tie, when he noticed a woman in black standing behind him. He turned around and did a double take. She was staring intently at him.

"Do you know what the prime rate is?" she asked.

Being a businessman, he told her, leaning slightly toward her large-boned, five-foot-seven frame and catching a heavy dose of her pungent perfume. He didn't find her attractive in the usual sense, but she knew how to make the most of what she had. All decked out in her low-cut black dress, flashy jewelry, and spike heels, she looked out of place among the beer bottles and sawdust. She was certainly no country girl who dipped snuff and walked around barefoot. There was a certain pride and intelligence about her that impressed him. He figured, if a woman takes pride in herself, she takes pride in everything she does. She gave him her number. He called her for lunch the following day.

They met at El Palacio, the Mexican restaurant with the giant sombrero where North Palafox joins Mobile Highway on the way out to the endless strip of car lots known locally as Car City. He paid the bill. She said, "I guess I owe you." Jokingly, he told her, "You owe me ten thousand jelly beans." That evening he returned to his apartment and found in front of his door a glass jar three feet tall and eight inches across containing ten thousand jelly beans. Six months later he moved in with her and the kids.

For the first year and a half it remained a whirlwind romance. Everything was good, including the sex. He was single and making excellent money in his carpet and wallpaper business, and she seemed to have a healthy bank account to go along with her first-class appetite. They went on cruises and trips to New York, ate out at expensive restaurants six nights a week, went shopping for five-hundred-dollar dresses. The more money he could spend on her, the better she liked it. Then suddenly, right after Christmas, when he got sick with a stomach ailment and spent two weeks in the hospital, she turned off like a light switch. Everything went from a ten to a two practically overnight. They didn't plan things together like they used to. She would come home and he would come home and she would go to sleep and he would go to sleep. He didn't figure on being around much longer. . . .

Here she was sitting across from him, going on about getting married by the ship's captain on that world cruise they'd planned. She'd even called the cruise line. It had sounded like fun before. Now all he could think about was the baby. Then she mentioned something about an abortion. A front-page headline from the *Pensacola News* back in January flashed through Gentry's mind. "Locally, Seven Abortions for Every Ten Births." It had set off a ferocious debate among the three-hundred-odd Assembly of God, fundamentalist, and charismatic Christian churches in Pensacola. Some church-goers had even started picketing the town's four abortion clinics. But he knew better than to try to talk religion to Judi. If anything, she was a devout atheist. She wouldn't allow any crosses on the walls, no picture of the Last Supper. He'd tried to buy her a gold cross on a chain once, and she'd refused it. The last thing he wanted to do was make her angry. He told her it wasn't what he wanted, but he couldn't stop her from having an abortion. It was her decision, and he would stick by whatever decision she made. But he hoped she would have the child.

As they were leaving the restaurant, Judi handed him a small bag of marijuana, telling him to give it to James when he saw him. It wasn't the first time she had given him pot for James. It happened all the time. He put it in his pocket and forgot about it. They walked around the mall a bit. Judi purchased a present for her employee at a jewelry boutique and stopped at the tobacconist for her Players cigarettes; then they drove home across the Bay Bridge in Judi's Corvette.

They reached the house around four-thirty. Judi remained in the car. It was getting late, she said. She had to get back to the shop to write out payroll checks. She would change into her party clothes there and meet Gentry later at the Driftwood. She repeated his parking instructions and drove off.

Gentry's car stood in the driveway where he had left it. The trunk was closed. James's truck was nowhere around. He went immediately into the house. No one was home. His new speakers stood beside the chair James had occupied that morning, still in their boxes. He figured James had not had time and would get around to installing them later. He put the speakers away on a shelf in the laundry room, showered, dressed, and left the house in his own car by six o'clock.

Crossing the Bay Bridge for the fifth time that day, Gentry turned north the short distance to Tenth and Brainerd, stopping again before his mother's house. His younger brother Albert was home, cleaning the backyard pool in the early summer dusk. He had brought Albert into the Wallpaper Mill Outlet, his discount carpet and wallpaper store, a few months before and given him a third of the business. Ever since their father had died, Gentry had tried to look out for Al. The business was growing steadily, but they were at a dangerous point of expansion. Gentry had left his large, glass-paneled corner store in Town and Country Plaza Friday afternoon and dropped in at the bank next door, where he had applied for a twenty-thousand-dollar line of credit. His banker had assured him that the loan was approved. All he had to do was come in Monday morning and sign some papers. He had returned to his store and written out some checks to his creditors. He hadn't dropped in on Judi's Fingers N Faces salon just six doors down as he usually did. He had been slowly disengaging himself and his business from Judi. She had lent him a few thousand to start his business the year before, and he'd paid her back. Money was very, very important to Judi. He didn't want her thinking he owed her anything. Something had told him not to involve her in his loan transaction. Something else told him not to mention anything to his mother or Al about Judi's being pregnant just yet. He asked his mother if she felt well enough to come to the party with him. She didn't. He had better go on without her. By seven-fifteen he had left his mother's house and was headed for the Driftwood Restaurant.

A dusky haze filtered the fading pink, blue, and gold sky as Gentry swung onto Palafox Street and cruised slowly down the wide boulevard toward the heart of old Pensacola. A few blocks south the four-lane artery narrowed to a one-way main drag on its way to a waterfront dead end. Along either side, half-deserted in the encroaching twilight, stood rows of houses with restored New Orleans-style façades, recently abandoned for the sprawling parking lots of suburban shopping malls where the integrated city buses didn't go. In the shadows, too, beckoned the forgotten Woolworth's five-and-dime. There, not so long ago, pale waitresses in dirty pink uniforms stood with arms folded in sullen silence behind darkened whites-only lunch counters while the unsung sisters of Rosa Parks sat overflowing on tiny, cracked red stools, silently demanding to be served. There, too, an old Creek Indian wrapped in a warm blanket once huddled outside, as perennial, stiff, silent and ignored as his wooden cigar store likeness.

At the corner of Palafox and Garden, deep in the musty heart of the city, loomed the ghostly landmark of the Hotel San Carlos, a faded, streaked, eight-story square stucco edifice reminiscent of the Spanish heritage of this aged City of Five Flags. Opened on February 1, 1910, and billed as one of the most modern hotels in the South, she was once the proud grande dame whose tiny wrought-iron balconies displayed applauding local officials and their ladies in antebellum costumes surveying the delighted crowds and gawdy fiesta floats parading by below. Closed in 1981, she seemed an old abandoned mistress, her boarded windows and littered hollow lobbies sheltering local derelicts, panhandlers, and prostitutes. Catty-corner across Garden from the San Carlos stood the Driftwood Restaurant, sandwiched discreetly between the modest Pensacola Savings and Loan and the sedate white stucco Chamber of Commerce. A lone surviving tribute to traditional Southern hospitality in downtown Pensacola, the Driftwood was known no less for its posh pink decor than for its expensive Greek cuisine.

It was close to eight o'clock, but the lazy summer sun still blazed above the horizon as Gentry maneuvered his car into the Driftwood parking lot, as Judi had instructed. He pulled into the southwest corner of the largely empty lot, about thirty feet from the sidewalked curb. Grateful for a chance to unwind with a few drinks before Judi and her entourage arrived, he entered the cool, dim interior of the Driftwood.

Most of the fourteen guests were seated by the time Judi strolled in at a quarter to nine and took charge of the affair. Gentry knew she had been having some problems with returned checks at the bank lately, but it didn't cramp her style. The champagne was plentiful. She presented a diamond pendant to the employee she was honoring. Then at about ten-twenty, with the party still in full swing, she turned to Gentry, telling him that she and the girls wanted to go out for a few more drinks and finish off the evening. He was to go home ahead of her, if he didn't mind, and deliver the packet to James that she had given him at lunch. He could pick up some more champagne, and she would join him later for a private celebration of their own. She gave him a small kiss good-bye.

Gentry bade goodnight to the party guests and left the table. He went to the front of the restaurant and paid the bill. Then he walked out to his car.

Turning left at the near corner, he approached the far end of the half-empty, unlit parking lot. No one had pulled into the spaces next to him. He wondered vaguely where Judi had parked her precious Corvette. There was no gleam of white in the shadowy darkness. The night dial on his watch read ten thirty-five as he climbed into his unlocked car, a small frown of concentration furrowing his brow as he thought of which liquor store on the way home would still be open. Most of the package stores downtown closed early to avoid holdups. Once he crossed the Bay Bridge into Gulf

Breeze, he'd be in Santa Rosa—a dry county. He'd have to cross the island bridge to the beach in Escambia County to find another liquor store. He could always stop at one of the all-night supermarkets in town, but Judi had to have the best of everything. A cheap brand of champagne would never do. Leaning slightly forward to reach the dashboard, he started the engine as he pulled on his headlights, as it was his habit to do.

He felt the explosion before he heard it. Suddenly he was back in Vietnam on Marine patrol a second after he stepped on that land mine. His nostrils burned with the same distinct, sweet-acrid odor. He had that same ringing sensation of suddenly being thrown down a forty-foot tunnel. At first he had no idea what had happened. Then he thought his battery must have exploded. The roof of his car erupted like a mushroom. Everything turned black and smudgy. He felt a sharp twinge in the back of his neck. He put his hand there and brought it back covered with blood. He looked down to open the door. Both his shoes were blown off his feet. He struggled out the door and tried to walk, his six-foot-three frame bent double as he staggered toward the street. Someone was trying to force him to the ground. He told him to leave him alone; he was going into the restaurant; he had to get to Judi. . . .

He collapsed on the sidewalk. When he looked up, a crowd of people was gathered around him. Two men in white uniforms were cutting the charred remnants of his clothes away from his bleeding torso.

Judi was standing over him, screaming hysterically. "My god, my god! What happened? Jackie Morgan did this—I know it— It was Jackie Morgan!"

What the hell was she talking about? The last thing he saw as they lifted his wounded body into the back of the ambulance was Judi, swooning back into the crowd.

He almost never knew what hit him.

2

"Is the Poor Bastard Dead?"

DETECTIVE TED GERONIMO CHAMBERLAIN stumbled out of a deep sleep and, cursing under his breath, fumbled in the semidarkness of his barren bachelor apartment in blind pursuit of the persistently ringing phone he had stashed earlier that night in the seldom-used dishwasher. Startled cockroaches scattered in all directions as he flipped on the kitchen light and grabbed for the instrument.

"Geronimo, I just got a call. Got a car downtown that blew up with a guy in it."

The excited drawl over the phone belonged to Rick Steele, Chamberlain's recently assigned partner on the Pensacola detective squad. A polite, quiet, by-the-book guy from a local middle-class family, wouldn't say shit if he had a mouthful.

"Is the poor bastard dead?" Chamberlain mumbled, reaching automatically for the pack of extra-long, dark More cigarettes on the kitchen counter.

"Not yet. He's on his way to the hospital."

"The AFT [Alchohol, Tobacco and Firearms] and lab boys'll be crawling all over the place by now. You're personnel. Check it out. Make sure they get pictures of every vehicle parked in the area. There's nothing much I can do on the property end until they impound the car—what's left of it. I'll meet you first thing in the morning over at the felony garage."

Chamberlain hung up, hesitated, then shoved the phone back in the dishwasher, shutting the door with a determined thud. Grabbing the last beer from the nearly empty refrigerator, he sat down on the edge of the worn couch in the sparsely furnished room and, popping open the can, took a long, practiced swig. He took another swig and swallowed hard, his rugged, leonine features tensing as he resisted the familiar impulse to grab his holster with its semiautomatic and eight-clip of hollow-point bullets, pull on his short leather boots with his backup .38 snub-nosed shoved inside, and head out the door. Always the first one in . . . His trained mind's eye pictured the scene of the crime—police barricades, red lights, ambulances, and official vehicles spilling over the sleepy street corner where a few hours before he had driven routinely by, mesmerized by the false façades of dreamy decadence.

Pensacola had seemed an exotic setting twelve years before, when Chamberlain quit his tactical police unit and the cold, mean streets of Boston to join his retired detective father and ex-cop brother on the sun-kissed sands of West Florida. It hadn't taken him long to adjust. He interned for a year with his father's polygraph business, joined the Pensacola Police tactical squad, and volunteered for the SWAT team. Full Cherokee on his mother's side, French and English on his father's, Chamberlain always did like a challenge. All told, he had about twenty years of police experience under his belt. He had started off on a walking beat up in Attleboro, Massachusetts, that first winter. If he could make it through that, his father told him, he'd make a cop. "You'll make a good cop—you've got a lot of hoodlum in you." He'd made it to the tactical squad in Boston, then the riot squad. He had even started a special rescue unit of sky divers before he headed down south. They had a lot of street crime, a lot of violence up North. Down South, the criminals were more middle-class, and more treacherous too. Like that mild-mannered chemist who poisoned his obese wife and hid her body in a storage freezer for three months. He knew from the results of the polygraph test the guy was guilty as hell, but all he could do was watch and wait and stay on the trail until the suspect finally cracked and led him to the evidence. It seemed that as the years increased, so did the crime. He knew one thing—he'd never be out of a job. As times got worse, his business got better.

Pensacola had its share of shootings, stabbings, and strong-arm robberies. In 1983, according to statistics assembled by the Federal Bureau of Investigation, Florida's Escambia County ranked fourth in the nation in assaults, fourteenth in rape, and twelfth in violent crime generally. But car bombings just weren't its style. Leave that for the drug rings up North. The only bomb threats they'd had in Pensacola were from overzealous right-to-lifers who believed it their divine right and duty to dynamite local abortion clinics. The Pensacola tactical force didn't have a bomb squad. They called in the boys from nearby Eglin Air Force Base to dismantle any suspected explosives. Most often the call for the local SWAT team was a response to a barricaded house. The team would rush from the back of the unmarked windowless van in their camouflage fatigues armed with high-powered rifles, machine guns, and grenades and surround some poor bastard who'd been pushed over the edge and wanted to commit suicide but didn't have the nerve to do it himself. So he'd hole up inside his house with a gun and take potshots until the SWAT team put him out of his misery. In Chamberlain's seven years on the Pensacola SWAT team, they'd had a 100 percent no-kill record. A good team could lob tear-gas grenades from room to room until they pinned the guy where they wanted him so he could be taken in and Baker Act-ed—mentally evaluated for treatment and rehabilitation. He figured at least half the criminals in Pensacola could use some evaluation and rehabilitation. Too bad the state couldn't afford it.

Chamberlain took a last hungry drag on his cigarette and tossed the butt into the cheap metal ashtray on the makeshift table he'd put together from some odd scraps of wood. Always the first one in. . . .

Back in '66, in Vietnam, he'd volunteered for special forces reconnaissance—go in, secure the area, and set up to bring the helicopters in. Never knew what they were getting into. . . . He probably had Uncle Joe to thank more than anyone else that he'd made it back in one piece. Uncle Joe was an amazing old man. Liked living alone, kind of like a hermit. Didn't like anybody on his land fuckin' with him. That crazy old Indian taught him everything he knew—how to shoot a bow and arrow, throw a knife, use a hatchet, hunt, track. He got a lot of good sense from Uncle Joe. . . .

After draining the last of his beer, Chamberlain added the can to the growing collection of empties stacked in the corner. He figured there was six months' worth of empties—a row for each month he'd spent alone since he separated from his second wife, Jerri, and moved into the Lamplighter, an apartment complex that resembled a cheap motel. He couldn't really blame Jerri for wanting the separation. She'd said when they got married she'd try to handle it—never knowing when he'd be home, watching the evening news and calling the station to see if he was the cop that had been shot. She was a good woman and a good mother. Worked hard as a nurse. Well, give her some time. Maybe she'd come around.

He missed his six-year-old stepson Bradley the most. . . . Seven years on the SWAT team, and one day he just walked into the captain's office and quit. It happened on Christmas Day. Whenever he got a chance, which wasn't too often, he tried to spend some time in the woods with Bradley—to teach him how to get water from the dew on the leaves, how to tell time in the sand with a stick, how to survive on his own. They were just getting started when the damned beeper went off. They had had to pack up, hop in the pickup truck, and head back to town. Halfway there he got a 10-22 on the radio—a "cancel out." He kept on driving. At the station he marched in and told the captain, "It's Christmas, damn it! I quit!" "I guess you've done your turn on the barrel, Geronimo. Suppose it's time we put you on investigations," the captain had drawled. Now he had damned-near regular hours, but he figured the change had come a little too late. It had been a while since he'd had the chance to take Bradley out to the track to watch him race . . . trying to be the first one in. . . .

Chamberlain glanced at his watch. It wasn't even midnight, but it felt like four in the morning to the overworked muscles of his lean, compact body. He was eagerly anticipating the early morning hours of driving practice laps in his lucky "45," a rebuilt Monte Carlo stock car, but the desire had drained from him now. This Sunday morning would only bring a fresh set of problems, questions, facts, and details to be patiently, endlessly tracked down, examined, sorted out, compiled, filed, and reexamined until they all fit into a neat, clean case report with no loose ends and a positive conviction. Exhausted, Chamberlain stretched back on the couch, promising himself an afternoon soon with Bradley. He slipped into a dreamless sleep.

3

"Not Your Average Drug Kingpin"

THE EARLY MORNING OF JUNE 26, Chamberlain stood with arms akimbo behind the open trunk of the 1981 two-door Ford Futura at the Pensacola felony garage and let out a low whistle. From the trunk the bomb had exploded forward through the backseat, blowing out the front and rear windshields and lifting the sunroof up like a teepee.

"Looks like the sunroof saved the guy's ass. Whatya find so far, Buddy?"

Chamberlain gave Bob Cousson a sharp glance. He'd worked with the tough Irish special agent from the Federal Bureau of Alcohol, Tobacco, and Firearms before and knew him to be a no-nonsense hard worker who liked to get things done.

"Two sticks of dynamite in the trunk under the left backseat. It was rigged pretty good. The wires were connected to the taillights so it wouldn't go off till after dark. We thought at first it was hooked to the ignition. Since he was long-legged and short-bodied, he must've leaned forward and turned on the ignition and the lights at the same time. That might've saved his life. A two-inch piece of shrapnel went right through the headrest, shot through two layers of sheet metal, and lodged in the frame of the sunroof. If he'd been leaning back, it would have gone right through the back of his skull. The word's already out on the street that it was some kind of Mafia drug deal. Anything for a headline."

"Probably some local jerk with a screwdriver, some wire, and a grudge," Chamberlain joked grimly.

"And a connection for dynamite," Cousson added. "Right now we can get into this case on Title 2 of ATF. If we've got somebody putting together bombs and going interstate, we go to Title 11. It was an amateur job, though. There wasn't enough dynamite to do the job properly. A pro would've connected to the gas tank and left the paraphernalia for the explosion."

"What's left for us to go by?"

"Two pieces of multistrand wire. Looks like they were used to connect the leg wires of the blasting cap to the taillights. Fragments from the blasting cap. Residue from the explosives. Some black electrician's tape we can check for fingerprints. We'll have a complete list of exhibits in a couple of days."

Chamberlain examined the two foot-long strands of orange-and-white plastic-coated wire Cousson handed him.

"Looks like some color-coded stuff used by auto manufacturers. Not that easy to come by. Let's check these babies out," he commented, handing the evidence back to Cousson.

Detective Rick Steele, sporting a casual plaid jacket, madras tie, and regulation brown oxfords, strolled over, a large manila envelope pressed under one arm.

"Whatya find out, partner?" Chamberlain greeted him, getting down to business.

"I got there right after I called you, about eleven-thirty. The crime scene officers had already boarded off the area. The victim, a John Gentry, white male, thirty-six, had already been taken to Sacred Heart Hospital. When I got to the emergency room, the victim was back in X-ray."

"Who'd you talk to?" Chamberlain interjected.

"The victim's brother, Albert Gentry, and the girlfriend, a Judias Buenoano. They were sitting in the waiting area there. I asked them who they thought would want to hurt Mr. Gentry. The brother came up with a lady they had been in business with in Mobile—a Jackie Morgan. The company was Wallpaper Mill Outlet. Evidently there were two of them, one in Mobile and one in Pensacola.

The Gentry brothers decided to pull out of the one in Mobile, and shortly afterward the business folded. There were suits and countersuits, and Ms. Morgan recently lost a civil suit to the Gentrys. Albert Gentry said he couldn't think of anybody other than Jackie Morgan who would have been upset enough with his brother to have done anything to him."

"What about the girlfriend?" Chamberlain asked.

"She didn't come up with anybody. She said they'd gone there for dinner, that it was a going-away party for one of the young ladies that had been working for her. Also, that it was a kind of celebration. She had found out she was pregnant and had just told Mr. Gentry that afternoon. The dinner was over, they decided to leave. Since they had come in separate cars, he was going to leave first and meet her back at the house they both shared. It was her home. He lived there. She said she was still inside the restaurant and heard the explosion. When she came out, Mr. Gentry had already exited the car and was lying on the sidewalk. She was very upset and crying. Evidently she had fainted at the restaurant."

"Did you think she was sincere, or was she going the whole nine yards for your benefit?"

"Seems she could've been. Sincere, I mean."

"What about the victim? Did you talk to him?"

"I got to talk to him for about three minutes in between some X-rays. I asked him how he was doing and how he felt. He could hardly hear me, because of the explosion, I guess. I asked him if he had any idea who could have done this. He said he had absolutely no idea. He was, of course, in my opinion, still in shock. When they came back and said they had to have him, I just let him go."

Steele handed Chamberlain the manila envelope he had been holding.

"The crime lab sent these over this morning. The property records on the victim and some photos taken at the scene of the bombing."

Chamberlain reviewed the official list of John Gentry's personal effects: "One white shirt, front pocket containing one pack Joker rolling papers; one pair blue slacks with black belt; right front pocket, wrist watch, Orient 21-jewel, $30.48 cash; left front pocket, one plastic baggie of suspect marijuana; left rear pocket, blue cloth wallet with driver's license, SS card, four Braves baseball tickets; one blue coat containing checkbook, right inside pocket; one pack Merit cigarettes and Bic lighter, left inside pocket; one black-and-red necktie; one right shoe."

"This tells us he likes baseball, smokes Merits, and rolls an occasional joint. Not exactly your average drug kingpin," Chamberlain remarked, handing the reports back to Steele. He studied the series of 8 x 10 black-and-white glossy photographs in silence.

"I told 'em to be sure and get all the vehicles parked in the area, like you said," Steele inserted.

"Wonder why he parked in the parking lot down the street when there were plenty of empty parking spaces right in front of the restaurant?" Chamberlain mused aloud.

"Lucky for passersby that he did. Shrapnel flew for two hundred yards in all directions," Cousson remarked.

"Whose white Corvette is that parked in front of the San Carlos?" Chamberlain directed the question to Steele.

"Mrs. Buenoano's. ATF held it to check it out. Thought there might be explosives hidden in her car, too."

Chamberlain looked at Cousson.

"It was clean," Cousson said.

"Why'd she park almost two blocks away from the restaurant where the bums hang out instead of in the parking lot next to her boyfriend? If it was my car, I wouldn't leave it there," Chamberlain said rhetorically. "Let's go pay Mr. Gentry a visit, partner. I got a feeling he's got a lot to tell us."

4

She Was Insistent

OF THE MAJOR HOSPITALS serving the city of Pensacola, Sacred Heart boasted the newest and most modern facilities. It had been built in the early sixties on the expanding northeastern outskirts near the equally new Pensacola Junior College to replace the crumbling stone Gothic structure in the shady old East Hill neighborhood, where the cream of Pensacola's crop of Catholic baby-boomers had been born. The new breed of younger doctors preferred the bright, sterile setting of Sacred Heart to the darker, postwar edifice of Baptist Hospital, which was patronized by the older generation of Pensacola's Protestant physicians. Baptist was situated on the border between a traditional white middle-class neighborhood and an encroaching enclave of poor local blacks. No one chose to go to Escambia General. It was situated near the county jail, which it closely resembled, in the northwest industrial section. It was reserved for injured prisoners, welfare recipients, and the bloodier emergency cases of automobile accidents, shotgun wounds, and serious stabbings. Shortly before midnight on the evening of June 25, 1983, the EMS ambulance had sped the semiconscious John Gentry ten miles along Ninth Avenue to the Sacred Heart Hospital emergency room.

Early on the morning of June 27, Detective Ted Chamberlain clicked his way down the shiny tiled lobby of the intensive care unit of Sacred Heart Hospital, Detective Rick Steele striding briskly slightly behind him. Chamberlain tried to ignore the queasiness that hospital settings never failed to excite as he approached the station desk to inquire about John Gentry's condition and his ability to undergo questioning. Police guards stationed at the corridor entrance and flanking the door to Gentry's room reflected the growing suspicion of local law officials that the car bombing had been perpetrated by underworld drug dealers. They might make a second attempt on Gentry's life with a bomb planted somewhere on the hospital floor. Gentry was a "noninformation" patient; the hospital would not confirm to anyone but authorized personnel that Gentry had been admitted.

Upon presenting his detective's shield to the head nurse, Chamberlain was briskly informed that John Gentry remained in stable but guarded condition in intensive care and could receive no visitors until further doctor's orders. The medical report read like that of a wartime casualty:

MULTIPLE FRAGMENT WOUNDS SECONDARY TO A BLAST INJURY: X-rays revealed multiple metal fragments contained within the posterior chest, flank and scalp, some secondary to fragment wounds sustained by the patient while in Vietnam. There were multiple large fragment wounds of the right flank with intraabdominal penetration. The wounds were found to contain large metallic fragments measuring up to 7 to 8 cms in diameter, as well as multiple fragments of foam rubber, plastic, and cloth. There were lacerations of the posterior scalp measuring 6 cms in length and a laceration of the left posterior ear containing a metallic fragment. The entire right colon had been severed by a metallic fragment contained within the abdominal cavity. The same fragment passed through the lower pole of the right kidney and lacerated the lower lateral third of the kidney. The wounding fragment also lacerated the right transverse mesocolon as it passed into the abdominal cavity. There were multiple bleeding vessels in the base of the right transverse mesocolon. The patient underwent abdominal exploration with debridement of multiple blast wounds, a right hemicolectomy, terminal ileostomy, exploration of a lacerated right kidney, debridement of multiple fragment wounds of the posterior chest, abdomen, scalp, and left ear. Estimated blood loss

was 1500 cc and patient received 1000 cc replacement.
The patient tolerated the operation well and was returned
to the Intensive Care Unit.

Chamberlain and Steele retraced their steps through the
hospital corridor to the elevator, anxious to continue their
preliminary investigation with a visit to Albert Gentry
at the Wallpaper Mill Outlet in Town and Country
Mall. They were not prepared for the image of female
beguilery that appeared when the elevator doors opened
before them.

Posed in a seductive slouch, she wore a long white
off-the-shoulder Mexican peasant dress meant to enhance
her large-boned, middle-aged figure. Her narrow black eyes,
from between the low bangs of her closely cropped dark
hair and the high ridge of her prominent rouged cheek-
bones, flashed with a strange intensity. A sudden whiff of
her pungent perfume got Chamberlain right in the gut.
Chamberlain rated his women by six packs. One six pack—
pretty good. Two—okay. This one was a two-caser—he'd
pass out first.

Recovering, Steele drawled a polite introduction to John
Gentry's fiancée. Judias Buenoano extended her heavily
bangled arm, returning Chamberlain's strong grip with
a weak gesture of her perfectly manicured, cold, damp
hand, adorned with long red diamond-tipped nails and an
assortment of heavy rings.

"Detective Chamberlain," she acknowledged with a coy
nod.

"Ma'am," Chamberlain nodded back. He began with the
standard line: Did she know of anyone who might have
wanted to harm her fiancé?

Her voice was surprisingly high-pitched, an emphatic
mixture of Southern and Midwestern accents delivered in
rapid bursts of self-assurance.

"Well, I really don't know, but he was getting these
threatening calls from Jackie Morgan, the woman over
in Mobile he was involved in these lawsuits with. I really

can't say, but maybe she had something to do with this. It's really such an unfortunate thing. I'm dreadfully upset over the whole situation, you know."

"Uh-huh," Chamberlain nodded. "What is it you do, ma'am? Do you have any interest in Mr. Gentry's business?"

"Heavens no. I've owned my own business since 1980—Fingers N Faces. It's a beauty boutique for ladies in Town and Country Mall. I have degrees as long as my arm. I make five hundred thousand dollars a year." She smirked a tight-lipped scarlet smile.

"Is that a fact?" Chamberlain grinned back. "That's a lot of fingernails."

The smile disappeared into a tight, thin line.

"Unless you have any more questions you'd like to ask me. . . ."

"No, ma'am, that'll be it for now. We'd appreciate it if you'd keep yourself available," Chamberlain concluded, returning her level gaze.

"Of course. You have my business address. Now if you'll excuse me, I want to check with the doctor on John's condition. He's lucky to be alive, you know."

With a parting shrug, Judias Buenoano pranced off down the hall, her high heels echoing metallically after her as Chamberlain and Steele took the next elevator down.

"There's something wrong with that honey," Chamberlain remarked to no one in particular.

That afternoon Chamberlain and Steele interviewed John Gentry's brother, Albert Gentry, at the Wallpaper Mill Outlet in Pensacola's Town and Country Mall. Albert Gentry confirmed that Jackie Morgan had brought numerous lawsuits against John Gentry and that she had lost one of them within the past three weeks. He also gave them the name of Gentry's attorney in Mobile, Alabama. After driving the sixty miles to Mobile, Chamberlain and Steele interviewed Gentry's attorney. He said that Morgan felt John Gentry was the cause of her business failure in Mobile and that she might want to ruin Gentry financially. He did not feel that she would want to kill his client. Then he requested that his name not be mentioned in connection with the case. They contacted the Mobile Police Department Bomb Squad to see if any similar bombing incidents had occurred in the Mobile area. None had. Chamberlain and Steele returned to Pensacola with no leads, no match, and no connections.

"Work this case till you come up with something," Sgt. John Baldwin told them. "This sort of thing doesn't happen in Pensacola. The captain wants this mess cleared up in a hurry."

On June 29, 1983, four days after the bombing, Chamberlain and Steele interviewed John Gentry in the intensive care unit of Sacred Heart Hospital. Later transcripts recalled the following conversation:

"Do you have any idea who could've done this to you, Mr. Gentry?" Steele asked.

"Naw, no idea. I can't think of anybody who'd be mad enough at me to want to kill me." A pale, weak John Gentry rasped his answer around the nasogastric tube.

"We talked with your brother, and he told us about this Jackie Morgan in Mobile who had some lawsuits against you. You think she might have hired someone to kill you?"

"No. She's mad at me, but I don't think she'd try to kill me over it. No—no way," Gentry said emphatically.

"Who would benefit from your death? Any heirs, life insurance policies, things like that?" Chamberlain stepped in as Steele continued taking notes.

"Judi and I have this life insurance policy together. . . ."

"What are you talking about? How much is it?" Chamberlain pressed.

"Five hundred thousand apiece," Gentry drawled.

Chamberlain looked hard at Steele.

"That's a lot of money. You're not even married to her."

"Well, Judi and I were planning on getting married, and whenever you have two businesses, you want to make sure that if something happens, it's taken care of. So we went down and saw Barbara, my insurance agent." Gentry coughed and looked away. "The thing is, we had to tell the insurance company some things that weren't quite true. We had to say that we had an insurable interest in each other's business so that if one of us should die, the other would need insurance to cover their losses. The insurance agent wrote a covering letter to that effect, because we weren't married, and the insurance company accepted it."

"When did the policy go into effect?"

"We applied sometime in late October or early November. We were talking fifty thousand dollars. I figured that was enough to take care of whatever debts would be left over and to get buried. She wanted to up it to a hundred thousand. I said okay, that's reasonable, and we left. I asked Judi about it on a couple of occasions, and at one point she said the insurance company wasn't acting fast enough, and she went there and told them to cancel it. That was fine by me. But the other day, Friday I think it was, I called the insurance agency about something else with my business, and I asked them about the policy, how come Judi didn't like it. They told me not only did she like it, she upped it to five hundred thousand. It'd been in effect since last November. So I guess Judi never did cancel it. I just let it ride. Who cares about something like that?"

"Yeah, maybe she just neglected to tell you about it," Chamberlain concurred. "Tell us exactly what you did on the day of the bombing."

Gentry shifted uncomfortably in the half-reclined hospital bed, a twinge of pain from his internal injuries registering on his bandaged face. Breathing heavily, he recounted the events of June 25, 1983.

"What time did you arrive at the restaurant?" Chamberlain intervened.

"I guess I got to the parking lot just about eight."

"What parking lot was that?"

"Well, Judi told me to be sure and park the car in the parking lot down from the Driftwood, on the corner of

Garden and Baylen. Said she didn't want the panhandlers from the San Carlos bothering us. She made a big thing out of that. I don't know why, 'cause I could've just as easily parked on the street directly in front of the place."

"You mean she told you not to park in front of the restaurant?"

"She was just real insistent that I park in that particular parking lot."

"Do you always do what she tells you?"

"I don't know. I guess I pretty much do."

"That's mighty white of you, buddy. Did you use your lights? Did you have to turn on your headlights before you got to the parking lot?"

"I don't think so. I really don't remember. I remember the ambulance ride, and X-ray. I remember asking the doctor if what happened to me was life-threatening. He said yeah. I said, 'Well, see ya when I wake up.' I thought my battery had exploded. I didn't know that my car was blown up till I woke up in intensive care with the cops and my mother and brother around me. You know, my mother was supposed to go with me that night, but she got sick at the last minute. What if she'd been in the car, too?"

Chamberlain and Steele made their way through the crowded hospital parking lot in silence.

"Somethin' ain't right," Chamberlain mused, lighting up a cigarette.

"What do ya mean?" Steele asked.

"Ya got the broad tellin' him where to park. You got the car left with her son workin' on it all afternoon. You got her tellin' us she makes five hundred thousand a year, and turns out she's got an insurance policy on the jerk for that amount. Doesn't that sound a little weird to you?"

"Yeah, I guess I can see your point," Steele replied, sliding into the passenger seat of the unmarked police car.

"Hell yeah, you can," Chamberlain muttered, gunning the engine. "We'd better start lookin' into this."

5

Her Kind of Town

On the morning of June 30, Chamberlain pulled into the modest parking lot of the nondescript offices of John Broxson and Associates insurance agency at 672 Brent Lane in Pensacola. He had in hand a signed subpoena for John Gentry's insurance records.

Upon examination, the records confirmed that a Provident Life and Accident $500,000 mutual beneficiary life insurance policy between John Gentry and Judias Buenoano had been in effect since October 1982 and that Judias Buenoano had been making combined monthly insurance payments of close to two hundred dollars since that time.

Barbara Corwin, vice president of the life, health, and financial services department at Broxson and Associates, knew John Gentry as a previous property and casualty client. John Gentry and Judias Buenoano had dropped into her office the afternoon of August 25, 1982, and discussed a buy-sell agreement policy to fund their partnership in the Wallpaper Mill Outlet at 3300 North Pace Boulevard in Town and Country Plaza. Judias, according to Corwin's recollection, had done most of the talking.

When Corwin asked them how much insurance they were considering, fifty or a hundred thousand, Judias had said she thought it would be more equitable in the neighborhood of five hundred thousand, and at a later date to look at possibly going to a million. They had completed two applications that afternoon, one on Judias, with John as the owner and beneficiary, and one on John, with Judias as the owner and beneficiary. Judias had written a check on her Fingers N Faces salon account in the amount of $157.74 to cover the down payment. The policy could not be approved, however, without some proof that in the event of either partner's premature death, the business would actually suffer that much monetary loss. "The problem being," Corwin told Chamberlain, "that you just don't buy that much insurance without the reason for insurability and why that much." The insuring company needed to know when the partnership was established, how much in retail sales the business had been doing each month, and the projected annual income of the business based on pending sales and contracts.

Several days later Judias Buenoano had supplied the required information to Barbara Corwin over the phone. According to Judias, her partnership with John Gentry in the Wallpaper Mill Outlet had been established in June 1982. She had supplied the money to start the business and Gentry had supplied the expertise. Judias had said they were doing approximately $24,000 a month in retail sales, had pending contracts of $209,800, and projected an annual income of more than $400,000. They planned to open an additional location in a nearby city after the beginning of 1983. Barbara Corwin had supplied the information to the insuring company, and the policy was approved in October 1982. As Corwin was in the hospital at the time, her brother had informed Judias that the policy was in effect.

Chamberlain asked Barbara Corwin if she would be willing to repeat her information down at the state attorney's office, if necessary, at a later date. Corwin said she would be happy to cooperate with any police investigation involving one of her company's policies.

Chamberlain left the agency with a knowing smile on his face. It was beginning to look like John Gentry had unwittingly signed his own death warrant.

That hot, clear summer evening at approximately seven-thirty, Chamberlain traced the route John Gentry had taken to the Driftwood Restaurant the evening of June

25 under similar weather conditions. He did not have to use his headlights.

The morning of July 1, Judias Buenoano received a phone call from Detective Rick Steele of the Pensacola Police Department. Would she cooperate with the investigation into the attempted murder of her fiancé by coming down to the station and submitting to a polygraph examination? "All we're doing is eliminating people, ma'am. It's just routine," Steele told her. After some discussion as to time, Judias agreed to take the polygraph test. Twenty minutes later, Detective Steele received a phone call. "I'm Perry Mason," the male voice identified himself. "I'm Judi's attorney. She's not taking the test," the voice said, and abruptly hung up.

At six-fifteen on the clear Saturday evening of July 2, Officers Tucker and Patterson watched from their unmarked police vehicle in the Town and Country Plaza parking lot as Judias Buenoano left her Fingers N Faces salon and walked the short distance to her white Corvette. "White female, 5'6", 130 lbs., dark hair/dark complexion, not very pretty," Tucker noted on the surveillance log. The two Pensacola police officers waited as their suspect drove out of the crowded parking lot, then followed the white Corvette as it headed east across town on Fairfield Drive, up North Ninth Avenue, and turned into the visitors' entrance of Sacred Heart Hospital. At six twenty-five she got out of her vehicle and entered the main lobby of the sprawling red-brick hospital complex as the undetected surveillance team watched and waited.

Judias marched determinedly down the shiny sixth-floor corridor of Sacred Heart Hospital, an unopened pack of Players cigarettes clutched in one hand. It had only been three days since John had come out of the coma, but he had already had visitors—his mother and his brother, those two detectives. . . . According to the doctor's report, he could be discharged in a few weeks. She would convince him to come back home with her. With her nursing experience, who could take better care of him? She could always handle men like John. The bigger, the better. Big, honest, hardworking, hard-loving, hard-drinking good old boys who minded their mamas. . . .

Judias flashed a confident smile at the uniformed guard seated outside the door and breezed into the private hospital room. John Gentry, looking unusually frail in the rumpled hospital bed, managed a weak smile when she greeted him with a peck on the cheek. He averted his eyes under her scrutiny as she asked how he felt.

"I've been better," he joked lamely. He'd been lying there thinking about his talks with those detectives.

Gentry kept his gaze on the bedsheets, his voice wavering. "You know, these detectives have been here asking me these questions and all."

"What sort of questions?" Judias rummaged through her designer bag for a lighter.

"Oh, just about what I was doin' the day I got blown up, and how come you told me where to park, and how come you didn't tell me about the insurance policy. . . ."

Judias's voice rose sharply. "What are they trying to say—that I did something wrong? They're trying to poison your mind against me. They're trying to convince you that I did something wrong, and you know better. I'm the last person who would try to hurt you. Don't you believe me?"

Gentry stared at Judias as she lit one of her fancy cigarettes, her profile sharp and hard in the harsh fluorescent light. He didn't know what to believe anymore. In the two years they'd lived together, she'd told him she loved him once, maybe twice. She wasn't a very emotional person, except when she got angry. She had these huge mood swings. He always thought it had something to do with her childhood. She wouldn't talk about her past much. . . .

According to the insurance forms, she was born Judias Anna Lou Welty in Quanah, Hardeman County, Texas, just below the Panhandle, not too far south of the Oklahoma border, on April 4, 1943. Her father was Zia Jesse Otto Welty, an itinerant farm worker. Her mother, Judias Mary

Lou Northam, was a full-blooded Apache. Judias claimed the Apache chief Geronimo was her great-great-granddaddy. Her mother, like ten out of twelve of her siblings, died of tuberculosis. Judias was just two years old then, and her younger brother, Robert, was newly born. Her two older brothers were placed out for adoption, and she and Robert were sent out west to live with their grandmother.

When Judias was twelve and old enough to be sent to an orphanage, her father remarried for what she later said was about the seventh time, and she and her younger brother were taken to live with their father and his new wife and her children in Roswell, New Mexico. She and Robert were badly abused by their father and stepmother both—beaten, starved, burned with cigarettes, and much else. She was treated like a servant and forced to miss meals if even a spot of grease was found on the stove she had cleaned. She had to sit at the table and watch the rest of the family eat. One time, when she had missed seventeen meals in about two weeks, and her stepmother started beating Robert again, Judias blew up. She grabbed a pan from the stove, pouring hot grease on two of her stepbrothers, and got into a fistfight with her stepmother. She started swinging and kicking and throwing things at her father and stepmother until, she said, she "durned near killed them." She was fourteen, and she was taken and locked in a cell for sixty days with adult women, some of whom were drunks and others prostitutes. When the judge asked her whether she wanted to return home, she said she didn't. She was placed in a juvenile detention center at Foothills High School in Albuquerque, New Mexico, until she graduated in May 1959 at the age of sixteen.

John Gentry had believed most of what Judias told him. It was something that made him feel sorry for her. People weren't just born vicious—they had to be made that way. When he'd asked her about her brother, Robert, she'd said she didn't want to have anything to do with him. Her exact words were, "I wouldn't spit down his throat if his guts were on fire."

He'd believed her when she told him she'd gone to nursing school on scholarship, had Ph.D.'s in biochemistry and psychology from the University of Alabama, and had been head of nursing at West Florida Hospital. She sure seemed to know a lot about drugs and medicine, always consulting the big medical dictionary she kept on the kitchen counter. But he couldn't get over those photographs the police had shown him of her Corvette parked in front of the Hotel San Carlos that night—exactly where she had told him not to park. And she had sure lied about that $500,000 insurance policy. He remembered picking her up for lunch last December and asking her as they went through the drive-in window at the Taco Bell whatever happened to the policy. She'd told him it had been canceled. Maybe she'd even lied about being pregnant. She sure didn't look pregnant. She looked tired and worried and over forty.

"At the rate you're improving, you'll be back on a solid diet soon. I'll bring you some of your favorites—barbecued pork, you love that." Judias was plumping his pillows efficiently and chattering on as if nothing had changed. "In a few weeks, you'll be well enough to come home, where I can take proper care of you. I've got your room all prepared. The children won't disturb you, I'll see to that. I'll see that you're properly nourished too."

She stopped fussing with the pillows and stood close beside him. Her long red fingernails stroked his bare arm gently. "I miss you, John. I can't wait to get you back home again. This whole thing has taken such a toll on me and the children. I need you home with me."

Gentry stared at the ceiling. "Judi, I'd pretty much decided to stay at my mother's for my rehabilitation. I figure I could get better care and all there."

"How in hell can somebody give you better care than me!" Judias suddenly yelled, slamming her cigarettes onto the hospital foodstand and sending it spinning in circles away from the bed.

"Go ahead! Go home to momma! I never want to see you again as long as I live!"

Judias stormed out of the room, slamming the door behind her.

Gentry stared after her in disbelief. She'd acted that same way last November when he had refused to take any more of those vitamins she insisted he take that kept making him so sick. Stormed up and down the stairs. And when he had asked her to refill the prescription the doctor had given him for his blood pressure when he'd gotten out of the hospital last Christmas. He'd asked her if she had done it, and she'd said she hadn't. When he reached for the bottle, she'd gone into a near panic, grabbed the bottle from him, and put it in her purse and stormed out. He'd wondered what kind of a crazy mood she was in that day. And then there was that time in April when she'd made a great big bowl of his favorite Waldorf salad. Within fifteen minutes of tasting it, his vomiting and stomach convulsions had come back again. That salad sat in the refrigerator for three or four days till it was finally thrown out. Nobody would touch it. No, he sure didn't know what to believe anymore.

At 7:10 P.M. Judias was seen leaving the Sacred Heart Hospital parking lot behind the wheel of her Corvette. Turning right onto North Ninth Avenue, she merged into the hectic Saturday night traffic and headed south. Officers Tucker and Patterson followed several car lengths behind. Judias continued down Ninth, past the busy shopping malls and neon lit fast-food restaurants, past the Exxon station—which proclaimed a 10 percent discount on labor "to those whom Jesus loves"—and headed directly for the bay shore as the relentless Florida sun began to wane in the pale blue summer sky. She stopped in the left-turn-only lane for the traffic light at the junction of Ninth Avenue and the sweeping shoreline approach to the Bay Bridge and lit up a cigarette.

To her right, not far beyond the partially restored historical district of Seville Square and the abandoned waterfront warehouses, lay the city docks at the foot of South Palafox Street. Fleets of prosperous shrimp boats once cluttered the

busy debris-strewn harbor; now a few lonely workboats
stretched their empty nets from black cranes silhouetted
against the sky. Nearby beckoned the doors of Trader Jon's
and other sailor saloons of the once rowdy red-light district.
Their dark, boozy interiors harbored drunks, bawdy strip-
pers, and performing transvestites. Strolling shore patrolmen
watched for adventurous sailors who had strayed off base to
find a little action. The scene ended at the water's edge
with the Old Municipal Auditorium. The plain red-brick,
two-story edifice, built out over the water at the end of the
long city pier, was once the cultural center of town, where
Elvira DeMarko's School of Ballet had staged annual recitals
for the proud parents of would-be ballerinas. The elaborate
modern Civic Center built farther uptown off the new interstate connection drew local crowds to out-of-town music
concerts and sports events. The abandoned auditorium now
hosted the occasional local wrestling match. Farther west,
Main Street ran along the shoreline past warehouses and
railroad boxcars, past Joe Patti's seafood market, where
shy, hardworking Vietnamese immigrants labored on wet
wooden platforms in knee-high rubber boots, beheading
endless pounds of shrimp and cleaning nets full of bay
oysters, scallops, and snapper, heedless of the powerful
stench of dead fish.

The long back road merged into Barrancas Avenue as
it continued across the narrow mouth of Bayou Chico.
Past the sailboats of the Pensacola Yacht Club, a bastion
of white male supremacy since 1917. The club's female
members were yet to win the vote, and its black servants
of twenty-five years were being summarily dismissed in the
Republican tide of the eighties and hastily replaced by
blond unisex Yuppies in a halfhearted tribute to progress.
Once past the pungent Bayou Chico drawbridge, Barrancas
ambled past the fenced green-velvet golf course of the
Pensacola Country Club. There the ladies lunched between
their golf and bridge games, while the maid prepared dinner
at home, and waited for their husbands—doctor or lawyer
or insurance executive—to return after a few rounds with

the boys. At the intersection of Navy Boulevard, Barrancas ended abruptly in the midst of the sandy township of
Warrington.

Just beyond Bayou Grande armed sentries guard the entry
gates of the U.S. Naval Air Station. Established in 1825
to suppress the slave trade and stop Caribbean piracy, the
small naval base burgeoned into a major training center
for navy pilots with the arrival of an aviation unit from
Annapolis in 1914. Home to the USS *Lexington* aircraft
carrier and to the famous Blue Angels jet pilots, the base
commanded 5,800 acres overlooking Pensacola Bay and
nearly ten thousand navy personnel. For more than twenty
thousand Pensacolans, about a third of the city's population, the navy was boss. The naval air station became
known as the Cradle of Aviation and the Annapolis of
the South; Pensacola earned the nickname Mother-in-Law
of the Navy, as officer candidates dressed in whites courted
the cream of Pensacolan society—its debutantes—in the
reclining seats of their silver Corvettes and British racing
green Jaguars.

To the east of Palafox, Main Street rambled past the
shabby shanties of Niggertown—rickety wooden structures
with gaping holes and skewed porches. There half-clothed,
skinny-limbed black children had stood listlessly watching
the passing cars until the black population was relocated
to hastily erected single-story brick row housing further
inland. That made way for a waterfront renovation project
and a brand-new city marina and rows of pastel townhouses
facing the gently curved shoreline. In a town where seg-
regation was less an issue than a fact of life, the black
community obliged by remaining intact and largely invis-
ible. A few blocks north, not far from the unadorned
Pensacola Police Station, lay the *Pensacola News Journal*,
once a proud member of the conservative, right-wing Perry
Southern newspaper empire, now a recent inductee under
the corporate umbrella of Gannett Publishing Enterprises,
proclaiming in giant blue-and-white letters "Home of *USA
Today*."

This was a land of retired navy captains, plump, well-pensioned widows, used-car salesmen, hungry insurance agents, and idle, disenchanted youth. Here it was as easy to purchase a fifty-thousand-dollar double-indemnity life insurance policy as an over-the-counter .38 special at the local K-Mart. A bad check over $150 was a second-class felony, and the local sheriff's office was swamped with more than thirty-five thousand check-fraud cases a year. Here the average tour of duty was a two-year navy transfer, and year-round open season was declared on the Yankee tourist. As long as you were spending it in Pensacola, no one cared where your money came from; strangers were welcome friends and neighbors were often strangers. In this town, business was conducted at the leisurely pace of a more gracious era, when hypocrisy was an accepted way of life. The perverse pride of the Old South was reflected in the full shotgun racks of "big boy" pickup trucks and the smug faces of the self-righteous right. It was a town dedicated to the slow, serious pursuit of pleasure in a landscape of palm trees, church steeples, and oyster bars, amid bumper stickers shouting alternately, "Honk if you love Jesus!" and "Hell no, we ain't forgettin'!"

It was her kind of town.

Judias pressed her foot on the accelerator as the arrow signaled green and turned left onto the smooth double lanes leading to the Bay Bridge. The long rows of white lights stretched across the twilight horizon seemed to trace the vertebrae of a giant crouching reptile.

She was sorry she'd let her temper get away from her. She'd have to stay in control next time. John had to come home with her. It was a miracle that he was still alive. Now she'd even mortgaged her house to save his business. His brother, Albert, had come to her the Monday after the bombing, quietly desperate. John was still in a coma; no one knew if he would live or die. The bank had immediately canceled his line of credit, but not before he had sent out over ten thousand dollars in uncovered payments to his creditors. There could be felony charges. Albert had asked her if she would lend them the money to cover the checks. If she could, he'd appreciate it; if she couldn't, he'd understand. He knew John had left most of the business to her in his will. What else could she do? She'd bought the house in the Whisper Bay subdivision of Gulf Breeze in 1978 through a real estate agent—over the phone, sight unseen, fifty thousand, all cash. It had appreciated to at least seventy thousand by now. She told Albert not to worry, she would lend the business the money. She went out the next day and secured a mortgage on her house for twenty thousand dollars. She gave Albert ten thousand for the business and kept the rest. She needed some cash for herself. "We'll pay you back," Albert told her. She had made Albert promise not to tell John about the loan. The less he knew right now, the better.

Judias glanced into her rearview mirror. There were few other cars on the bridge. She'd noticed that same faded brown sedan with the telltale trunk antenna a slight distance behind her at the last light. She shifted into high gear as she ascended the midrise of the bridge, her speedometer approaching eighty miles per hour. The sedan kept pace behind her. "Stupid cops," she thought. She knew how to handle them too.

Judias slowed to the speed limit as she exited the bridge, cruising straight down Gulf Breeze Parkway past the brand-new pink-stuccoed condominium villages, through the small expensive township of Gulf Breeze with its souvenir and seashell shops, and under the overpass where the flashing neon dolphin lit the south turnoff toward the Miracle Strip of Santa Rosa Island's Gulf beaches. She continued down the lonely straight stretch of Highway 98, heading east across the long pine-forested peninsula for about four miles. Then she turned left into the discreet entrance of the Whisper Bay subdivision. She followed the narrow, winding road through the exclusive neighborhood of hidden ranch-style homes, turning into the driveway of a white two-story colonial with peacock blue shutters and a carved wooden plaque announcing "The Buenoano Family." She pulled her

Corvette next to a two-tone blue Ford 4 x 4 step-side truck parked in the drive and disappeared into the brightly lit house.

Officers Tucker and Patterson parked quietly among the bushes a short distance away, noted a 10–42 at 1930 hours on the surveillance chart, and waited.

An hour and a half later, the blue Ford truck that had been parked at the house screeched out of the driveway. Judias was at the wheel. Tucker and Patterson pursued as the truck turned left onto U.S. 98 and sped down the empty highway. After a few minutes, the truck suddenly turned into an obscure subdivision. Tucker and Patterson cautiously followed the winding suburban street past darkened houses, the truck nowhere in sight. The street made a final turn onto a dead-end road. Switching off their headlights, Tucker and Patterson moved slowly forward in the dark. Suddenly they were confronted by the glare of bright headlights. Judias had turned the truck around and was waiting for them. They'd been burned.

Patterson turned to Tucker. "It'll be interesting to see if she reports that someone was following her," he remarked with a sheepish grin.

6

Attempted Murder

On the morning of July 3, Chamberlain and Steele returned to Sacred Heart Hospital to confront John Gentry with additional questions and certain facts. Gentry, sitting up and in visibly better shape, was anxious and agitated.

"I've been up thinkin' all night," Gentry greeted them.

"What's eatin' at ya, buddy?" Chamberlain asked.

"Well, I been runnin' things through my head, and I just can't believe what I'm thinkin'. Judi was here last night, and I asked her how come she didn't tell me about that insurance policy, and come to think of it, how come she told me where to park that night, and how come she told me to leave the party early."

"Yeah, and what did she say?" Chamberlain prompted, keeping his face blank.

"Well, she just got madder'n hell. Said you were tryin' to poison my mind against her. Then she said she wouldn't see me anymore and walked out. I don't know, I just can't believe it. I was happy about the baby. . . . I thought she was, too. . . . I just can't believe it."

"Maybe she's got financial problems," Steele inserted.

"I don't know what the hell she's worried about. She knows she's in my will. Hell, she'd get half my business and my mother would get the other half. What more does she want?"

"How much cash money would that be?" Chamberlain asked.

"She'd stand to get about three-quarters of a million dollars."

Chamberlain looked at Steele and ran his hand through his thick salt-and-pepper hair.

"Tell me, when's the last time you were in the hospital?"

"Back in December, eighty-two, I got real sick and checked myself into Sacred Heart here. I was vomiting, had stomach cramps, dizzy spells. The doctors couldn't find out what was wrong with me, so they released me and I went home. But ya know, Judi had been giving me these Vicon-C vitamins, these orange-and-white capsules. I noticed that every time I took them I got sick. Judi kept insisting I take two capsules a day. She told me she had these degrees in psychology and pharmacology and all, and I figured she knew what she was doin'. When I got out of the hospital, she started givin' 'em to me again, and I got sick again. So I just started puttin' 'em in my pocket, and I stopped gettin' sick. I remember I took one more capsule just to see if I'd get sick again, and I did. Ya think that might've been it?"

"It's a possibility. You wouldn't happen to have any of those capsules now, would you?" Chamberlain asked.

"As a matter of fact, I saved a couple, thinkin' I'd have 'em analyzed someday to see if I was allergic to 'em or somethin'. They're still in my briefcase over at my office wrapped up in a little bag. If you want 'em, you can have 'em."

That afternoon Chamberlain met with Albert Gentry at the Wallpaper Mill Outlet, presenting a signed release form for the capsules contained in his brother's briefcase. Albert Gentry produced some additional capsules given to him by Judias Buenoano. He stated that on June 29, Judias had asked him if he knew whether she was in John Gentry's will.

Acting on information received from Resident Agent Dewitt Fincannon of the Bureau of Alcohol, Tobacco and

Firearms, Chamberlain began investigating a possible connection between Judias Buenoano and the Gambino organized crime family. Judias had told a girlfriend that Mario
Gambino was an "old family friend" who visited her regu-
larly in Pensacola, where she would "take care of him."
The girlfriend had been frightened of Judias's alleged mob
connections. Chamberlain called ATF agents in Miami and
New Orleans to determine if there were any connections
between the Gambino family and any recent car bombings.
The following day, Chamberlain received a phone call from
a representative of Paul Castellano, the acting head of
the Gambino family in Miami. The family lieutenant told
Chamberlain, "You don't need to be looking down here.
No way is there any connection with what you've got up
there. No way."

The orange-and-white capsules retrieved from Gentry's
briefcase were delivered to the Florida Department of Law
Enforcement laboratory in Pensacola for analysis. The
capsules, which were supposed to contain a high-potency
vitamin C compound, were found to contain instead an
unknown powder. The capsules appeared to have been
tampered with. Upon submission to the FBI laboratory
in Washington, D.C., for a poison scan, the capsules were
found to contain paraformaldehyde, a Class III poison with
no known medical use. Continued ingestion would cause
slow deterioration of the internal organs and eventual
death. The substance would not be detected in an autopsy
report.

On July 11, Chamberlain and Steele presented to Assistant Florida State Attorney Russell Edgar, Jr., what they
considered to be strong evidence in the case against Judias
Buenoano for the attempted murder of John Gentry.

Soft-spoken, clean-shaven, with penetrating blue eyes
and a quietly seductive manner, Russell Edgar, Jr., enjoyed a
growing reputation as a dedicated, winning special prosecutor in Florida's First Judicial Circuit and one of Pensacola's
most eligible bachelors. Having received his law degree in
1974 from Florida State University College of Law, Edgar

had been with Florida State Attorney Curtis Golden's office since his arrival in Pensacola in 1978. Edgar, who prided himself on his meticulous courtroom preparation, had recently completed a successful prosecution of a local arsenic poisoning case.

"I'm sorry, boys, but I just don't think you've got enough here for a conviction. You need to develop more on this particular type of poison. Let's say we go out on my sailboat this weekend, relax a little, and discuss the whole thing," Edgar replied, reclining in his high-back leather chair.

Chamberlain blew up. "What the hell do you want. A goddam confession? I'll get the warrant myself!" he charged and stalked out of the office.

"I wouldn't invite him out on your boat just now, if I were you. He'll throw you over," Steele told the amused attorney, and followed his hot-blooded partner out the door.

On the afternoon of July 12, Chamberlain and Steele arrived at the office of Dr. Richard Lucey on North Ninth Avenue, the physician who had treated Gentry during his hospitalization in December 1982. They presented Dr. Lucey with a medical record release form signed by John Gentry.

The discharge summary on John Gentry signed by Dr. Lucey on December 28, 1982, states:

> Thirty-six-year-old male initially admitted with anorexia, nausea, vomiting, and three-week history of productive cough. Initial evaluation revealed some mild abnormality of multiple liver enzymes, and it was initially felt that the patient had a mild resolving hepatitis. However, subsequent hepatitis profile was entirely negative. Upper endoscopy subsequent to epigastric pain entirely normal. . . . The need for discontinuing cigarette smoking as well as changes in life-style and increasing physical activity was discussed in detail . . . At the time of discharge, the patient was asymptomatic and it was felt that he may well have had a mild resolving viral hepatitis.

Dr. Lucey told Chamberlain and Steele that he could not make a clear determination of John Gentry's illness at the time. Upon his release he had prescribed a mild tranquilizer and antacid. He had not tested Gentry for any poison.

On July 15, John and Albert Gentry met with Assistant State Attorney Russ Edgar and Detective Chamberlain in the labyrinthine offices of the new Pensacola Judicial Center, squarely situated at the quiet junction of Spring and Main streets, just across the train tracks that run beside the bay. John Gentry, discharged from Sacred Heart Hospital's intensive care unit the day before, his wounds healed satisfactorily after a prolonged postoperative course due to continuous drainage from his lacerated right kidney, testified that Judias Buenoano had started giving him the orange-and-white Vicon-C vitamin capsules on or about December 1, 1982. She was giving him two capsules per day every day for two weeks. Each time he took a capsule, he would become ill.

On December 16, 1982, Gentry recalled, he had checked himself into Sacred Heart Hospital with dizziness, nausea, vomiting, diarrhea, and severe stomach pains. He was not given the capsules during his hospital stay and his symptoms stopped. During his hospitalization of approximately twelve days, he was medically tested, but no definite cause of his illness was found, and he was released on December 28. Upon his return home, Judias again gave him the Vicon-C capsules. Again, he became ill. He continued taking the capsules for approximately six days. He stopped taking the capsules for one day and his symptoms subsided. He took one more capsule the following day and his symptoms returned. He refused to take any more of the capsules. He threw away most of the remaining capsules, but kept two to be tested at a later date. They were the same capsules found by the FBI laboratory to contain paraformaldehyde.

The National Poison Center Network information card listed the symptoms for the ingestion of paraformaldehyde, a white solid polymer of formaldehyde, as immediate intense pain in stomach with ulceration or necrosis developing; nausea, vomiting, hematemesis (the vomiting of bright red blood), severe abdominal pain, and diarrhea; vertigo, convulsions, stupor, and coma; and respiratory or circulatory failure possibly resulting in death.

That afternoon, Assistant State Attorney Russ Edgar started a direct information file on his signature for the arrest of Judias Buenoano for the attempted murder of John Gentry by poisoning.

At 8:35 on the morning of July 27, 1983, one month and two days after the bombing, Chamberlain and ATF Special Agent Bob Cousson sat in an unmarked police car outside the home of Judias Buenoano at 2812 Whisper Pine Drive, Gulf Breeze, Santa Rosa County, Florida, and waited as she drove her white Corvette out the driveway and disappeared down the road on her way to her place of business. Then, along with a Santa Rosa County sheriff's deputy and two Pensacola crime scene investigators, they proceeded to execute a federal search warrant issued by U.S. Magistrate Robert L. Crongeyer for Vicon-C capsules and bombing paraphernalia. Simultaneously, Detective Rick Steele and a similar search party hit the Fingers N Faces beauty salon with a warrant issued by Judge M. C. Blanchard for paraformaldehyde, a substance used in the cleaning of salon utensils. Chamberlain had his front door.

Fifteen-year-old Kimberly and seventeen-year-old James Buenoano sat in sullen silence on the living-room couch as the team of investigators conducted their thorough, methodical search of the Buenoanos' three-bedroom, two-story, carpeted home, which was complete with a basement game room equipped with a regulation pool table, jukebox, and pinball machine.

Seized under the warrant was a piece of orange multistrand copper wire with two white stripes, similar to the wire used to connect the leg wires of the bombing device placed in John Gentry's car. It was found in James Buenoano's bedroom, along with a toolbox containing a roll of black plastic electrician's tape, a six-inch pair of wire cutters, and a pair of chrome fishing pliers. A bottle of Vicon-C vitamin capsules of the same type used in the attempted poisoning of John Gentry was found in Kimberly's bedroom. Also seized were a small quantity of marijuana and a short-barreled shotgun found in James's room. James Buenoano was immediately arrested for possession of marijuana and the illegal shotgun. To Chamberlain, things were looking good.

Within the hour, a very vocal and angry Judias Buenoano was placed under arrest upon her arrival at her beauty salon. She was charged with the attempted murder of John Gentry between December 1, 1982, and January 4, 1983, by poisoning.

Handcuffed and transported to the Pensacola City Police Department, Judias Buenoano was met by her attorney, James Johnston, an established Pensacola trial lawyer and former Florida state senator. Johnston had been a personal friend of the Buenoano family for the past several years.

Judias was asked by prosecutor Russ Edgar to make a statement concerning the charge against her.

"No, Judi, don't make any statement right now," Johnston told her.

"Book her on first-degree attempted murder," Edgar replied.

Judias was taken to Escambia County Jail, then transferred to the Santa Rosa County Jail beneath the courthouse in the middle of the small historic town of Milton. Milton, nestled on the banks of the Black Water River some twenty miles north of Pensacola and deep in the Florida panhandle, was the county seat of Santa Rosa County, where Judias had resided when the alleged poisoning of John Gentry occurred.

Judias was quickly arraigned. With her lawyer at her side, she pleaded not guilty to the charge of attempted murder. Johnston waived the Florida Speedy Trial Rule, which requires that a trial be granted within ninety days.

Judias's bond, set at fifty thousand dollars, was promptly posted by Robert Hill, owner of EZ-Rent of Pensacola, another married male friend of the Buenoano family.

Her trial was pending.

7

On the Dynamite Trail

"YOU OLD STILL-FINDER—you got us so far out here in the woods and the gas tank's bouncin' on empty. You sure you know where we're at?"

Chamberlain shoved his nearly empty cigarette pack into his shirt pocket and glared at Bob Cousson as the ATF special agent raced the unmarked, souped-up Camaro down the wooded back roads of lower Alabama on the way to Frisco City. Their target on this sticky afternoon of August 11, 1983, was the nearest dynamite dealer in the Pensacola area.

"Stop your whining. We'll be out of the woods here in a minute," Cousson replied with a good-natured grin. "You're the one who kept sayin', 'Let's go check out the dynamite.' We were supposed to be off at four. Steele went home to his wife an hour ago. You're the guy with the hard-on for this case."

"Can you believe this guy Gentry? He tells me Judi had him out looking for dynamite to blow up a stump in the backyard two weeks before the bombing. The fool goes around asking everybody he knows where he can get some dynamite to blow up a stump in Judi's yard. He can't find any. When we talk to Gentry's old tree-stumpin' buddy— this Les Miller—he tells us he told Gentry he didn't know where to get any dynamite. Then he tells us he was puttin' some carpet in Judi's home a week later, and he asks her about the dynamite. Judi tells him she didn't know why Gentry wanted the dynamite, 'cause the stump was removed from her yard long ago. Who do you think is lying?"

"I figure it this way. Gentry tells us about this 'Uncle Johnny' he knows as John Daniels from Brewton, Alabama, who's a good buddy of Judi and James Buenoano. They go hunting and fishing together, and he keeps them supplied with pot and whatever else."

"Yeah. Didn't you check out that trailer Judi was supposed to have somewhere in Alabama?"

"We talked to Jimmie Bryars, co-owner of this fishing camp at Hubbard's Landing up in Stockton. Judi Buenoano had a trailer parked there for the past several years. He told us Judi's son, James, and this John Rowell from Brewton had stayed at the trailer and fished just three weeks before. We checked out the Buenoanos' trailer, but it was clean of any explosives or devices. Seems to me that John Daniels and John Rowell are one and the same, and when we find 'Uncle Johnny,' we'll find the dynamite."

"Sounds good to me, buddy. Look here—a pit stop. Pull over. We can get some gas, and I need a pack of butts."

Cousson pulled off the remote backwoods highway into the dilapidated single-pump service station. Just up the road a barefoot kid stared from the rickety porch of a slanted shack surrounded by huge piles of chopped wood. Chamberlain climbed out of the Camaro, taking a long stretch in his leather boots, worn jeans, and de rigeuer plaid shirt, and strutted into the tiny station. The grizzled proprietor eyed him like he hadn't seen a customer in twenty years. Chamberlain asked for a pack of Moores Red.

"Uh, what's that?" the old man mumbled through the gap in his front teeth.

Chamberlain held up his empty cigarette pack. "These cigarettes right here."

"Ain't never seen none of them before," the old guy said suspiciously.

"So what ya got?"

"I got Pall Mall and Camel."

"I'll take the Pall Mall," Chamberlain said. He turned around and got back into the Camaro beside Cousson.

"Will you get me back to civilization? We've got an antenna. Let's get out of here before they think we're lookin' for stills!" he told the veteran federal agent.

"Yep, revenooers, that's what we were," Cousson mused aloud as he pulled back onto the deserted highway. "Started out in 1963 in Birmingham. All we did was look for moonshine stills and work a few sawed-off shotgun cases. They made basically a rum—a hundred pounds of sugar and a hundred gallons of water, a little bit of yeast and cornmeal, and just pour in some whiskey or rye. It's just like any other liquor if it's made right. But those people weren't makin' it right. They'd run it through truck radiators to condense it into beer, then they distill it into moonshine. Green whiskey is all it is. We used to average between twenty-five and thirty-five stills a month. Heard some shots, but they never shot at me."

"Yeah, I saw that picture in your office of you bustin' up a still out in the woods in your uniform. Just like in the old movies." Chamberlain grinned.

"That was a small one. Did about three hundred gallons a week. The legal industry runs every seventy-two hours with ideal temperatures and conditions. Out in the woods, it may take seventy-two hours to a week, depending on the weather and all. Most of the moonshiners didn't drink it themselves. They drank beer and wine. The biggest consumers used to be the large black and poor white populations of Birmingham and Atlanta. They'd go to the shot house and buy a shot of whiskey for fifty cents. We figured out for about five dollars worth of sugar, the moonshiner could make one hundred fourteen dollars profit. Now all the raw materials have gone up in price, and everybody's got more buying power to be able to buy vodka, and the new generation wants pot or somethin' else. We didn't really put 'em out of business. Most of the arrests came under the Internal Revenue Code: ten dollars and ten cents per gallon of whiskey was federal tax, and then all these fees. The moonshiners were a lot more cautious than your marijuana growers. If they saw one strange footprint around, they wouldn't come back, 'cause they didn't have that much of an investment. There's a lot more money in marijuana that there ever was in moonshine. Of course, the fines are heavier too."

"So are the growers," Chamberlain replied. "Most of 'em would make two of me. They take potshots at me, you better believe I'm gonna shoot back. This is one Indian they ain't gonna get!"

By dusk, Chamberlain and Cousson were at the home and business of D. L. Wiggins in Frisco City, Alabama, a federally licensed explosives dealer. They obtained a list of eleven individuals in the Brewton, Alabama, area who had purchased dynamite in the past two to three months. Chief Jim Holt of the Brewton Police Department verified that all of the dynamite purchasers were local residents known to purchase dynamite on a regular basis to blast stumps and beaver dams for timber companies—with one exception: Rayford "Ray" Odom of Brewton. Odom, also known as Ricky Dewberry, was a known associate of John Daniel Rowell of Brewton. Johnny Rowell, who used to work laying pipes for swimming pool companies but had been unemployed for the past five years because of a back injury, was known to the vice and intelligence narcotics units of Brewton and Pensacola as a suspected drug dealer and marijuana grower. Cousson and Chamberlain exchanged knowing glances. They'd found "Uncle Johnny."

Continuing to follow the dynamite trail from the trunk of Gentry's car to Brewton, Alabama, Cousson and Chamberlain contacted the dynamite purchasers on Wiggins's list. Each could account for the dynamite and blasting caps they had purchased, with the exception of Rayford Odom.

That week, Judias Buenoano's long-distance telephone records for her residence and place of business were subpoenaed. Examination of the records revealed that twelve calls were made to the home of John Daniel Rowell in

Brewton, Alabama, from the Buenoano residence and seven from Judias Buenoano's Fingers N Faces salon. There were two calls on June 13, 1983, and one call on June 17, 1983, the day Rayford Odom purchased explosives, from the Buenoano residence to Rowell's. And two calls were placed from the Finger N Faces salon to Rowell's residence on July 1, 1983, six days after the bombing of John Gentry's car.

On August 22, 1983, Detective Rick Steele and Special Agent Bob Cousson returned to the home of explosives dealer D. L. Wiggins and obtained the ATF form executed by Rayford Odom on June 17, 1983, for the purchase of fifty sticks of "Hercules 50%" dynamite, twenty nonelectrical Hercules blasting caps, six electrical Hercules blasting caps, and twenty feet of fuse cord. The elderly Mr. Wiggins remembered two men arriving together to purchase the dynamite on June 17. One man said he had forgotten his wallet, so the other produced his driver's license and signed the necessary forms. The man who had forgotten his wallet paid for the sale with seventy-five dollars cash. The man who produced his wallet and license was Rayford W. Odom.

Cousson and Steele drove the few miles from Frisco City to the police station in Brewton, Alabama. With the assistance of Captain Purnell of the Brewton Police Department, they located Rayford W. Odom, aka Ricky Dewberry, at his home on Travis Road. Odom, a skinny, pale, nervous fellow with a twelfth-grade education, admitted under questioning that he had purchased the explosives from Wiggins on June 17 and that Johnny Rowell had accompanied him. He had bought the dynamite to blow up some stumps in his yard, he said.

"*Did* you blow up any stumps with the dynamite?" Steele asked.

Odom stared out across the shadowy backyard, which was littered with discarded auto parts, old tires, and odd piles of wood. He nodded. "Yes, there's one blown up there."

"How many sticks of dynamite did you use?" Cousson asked.

"Well, I figure I blew up three stumps. Took three sticks and one cap for each charge," Odom drawled.

Cousson pressed on. "That's nine sticks of dynamite and three blasting caps. Where's the other forty-one sticks and the rest of the caps?"

"I really don't know nothin' about dynamite. I got scared of it and threw the rest of the caps into the river. We—I mean I—threw the rest of the dynamite into the river too," Odom stammered.

Odom agreed to take a polygraph examination to confirm his story.

That afternoon Ted Chamberlain met Steele and Cousson and the witness Rayford Odom at the Brewton Police Department. Accompanying Chamberlain was his father, a licensed polygraph examiner with over 30 years' experience in criminal investigation. Frank Chamberlain, a retired Boston police detective, had often assisted his son on criminal cases. He was an expert qualified to administer the carefully phrased yes or no questions that elicited the autonomic responses of breathing, pulse rate, blood pressure, and skin moisture that, when properly recorded and interpreted, provided a measure of a person's intent to tell the truth. More than a few defense attorneys had sent their clients out of town to Frank Chamberlain's Pensacola office for an unrecorded trial run before agreeing to allow their clients to take a polygraph examination, the results of which would be admissible in court only upon a stipulated agreement with the prosecuting attorney: if the client passes the polygraph, the results are accepted; if he doesn't, the results are not admitted. As Frank put it, "It's kind of like going to a plea bargaining—whichever way it goes, that's how they're going to plead the case."

At approximately five P.M., Frank Chamberlain administered a polygraph examination to Rayford Odom in a back room of the Brewton police station. During the thirty-minute examination, Odom showed deceptive results in several areas relating to the purchase and disposal of the dynamite. "He's lying," Frank Chamberlain reported; then he returned to the back room and confronted Odom with the negative results of his test. A few minutes later, Frank Chamberlain reemerged. "He's ready to talk to ya'll now," he told the waiting investigators.

At 6:28 P.M. on August 22, 1983, in the presence of Detectives Steele and Chamberlain and Federal Agent Cousson, Rayford W. Odom made the following statement:

> My real name is Rayford Wright Odom, but I have gone by the name of Ricky Dewberry most of my life. I am thirty-four years old, married, and work part-time for H & R Block. I was raised in Brewton, Alabama. I have never been arrested for a felony offense.
>
> I have known John Daniel Rowell most of my life.
>
> On June 17, 1983, in the afternoon, I was at the swimming hole at the Cedar Creek Bridge near Brewton when Johnny Rowell asked me if I wanted to ride to Frisco City, Alabama, with him to buy some dynamite. I told him that I would.
>
> I left Brewton with Rowell in his blue Ford car and we drove to a house near Frisco City, Alabama. Johnny Rowell went into the house to buy the dynamite, but the people would not sell any to him because he did not have a driver's license. Rowell came to the car and asked me if I had a driver's license. I told him I did, and he asked me to buy the dynamite for him, because he had left his billfold with his driver's license in it at home and did not want to drive all the way back to Brewton to get it.
>
> I went in the house and filled out a form to buy the dynamite. Johnny Rowell paid the man for the dynamite. Johnny purchased fifty sticks of dynamite, six or ten electric caps, twenty nonelectric caps, and I believe about sixty feet of fuse. Rowell went to the magazine with the man to get the explosives.
>
> Rowell and I drove back to Brewton, and he let me off at my truck. Rowell kept all the dynamite.
>
> Rowell told me he was going to use the dynamite to fish in private ponds, and he told me he would bring me

a mess of catfish. It was my understanding that he was
going to throw some dynamite in the ponds and when
it went off the fish would float to the top and he would
pick them up.

I did not get any of the dynamite, and I do not know
what Rowell did with it. I have not seen the dynamite
since Rowell and I got back to Brewton on June 17, 1983.

At six the following morning, Chamberlain, Steele, and
Cousson returned to the Brewton police station. The midnight shift commander informed them that John Rowell's
blue Ford was parked in front of his home. An hour later,
the team of investigators contacted the six-foot-four, 250-
pound, bearded John Rowell at his residence and asked him
to accompany them to the Brewton police station to answer
a few questions. Rowell agreed to do so.

When questioned about the dynamite purchase of June
17, 1983, Rowell confirmed that he had asked Rayford
Odom to accompany him to Frisco City to purchase some
dynamite for the purpose of blowing up some fishponds,
and that Odom had presented his identification for the
explosives purchase since he himself had left his billfold in
Brewton. Rowell stated that he had left the dynamite in the
back of his pickup truck and put the fuses under the front
seat. He said that on June 22 or 23, the dynamite and fuses
were stolen from his truck along with a 16-gauge shotgun.
He had not reported the theft to any law enforcement
agency and could give no reason why he had not. Rowell
admitted that he had been a close friend of the Buenoano
family for several years and that he had spoken to Judi and
James Buenoano on the phone and in person since June 25,
1983, but could not remember the dates. He further stated
that he had no previous knowledge of the fact that John
Gentry, whom he had met at the Buenoanos' home, had
been involved in a bombing incident.

Rowell declined a polygraph examination.

Convinced that John Rowell was not telling the truth
about the explosives, Chamberlain and Cousson interviewed Terry Gibson, a confidential informant working

for the Brewton Sheriff's Department.

"Terry, do you know a fellow by the name of John Rowell?

"Yes, sir, I do."

"When was the last time you saw him?"

"The last time I saw him and talked to him was the day that he and I went fishing down at Florella."

"Have you ever seen him in possession of any explosives?"

"Yes, sir, I have. He was in possession of two sticks of Hercules powder. I believe they were one-pound sticks. . . . They were a raised-grain [type] and they were between an orange and a yellow. Fuse with him, with a blasting cap. We were going fishing up above Florella, and Mr. Rowell showed me the dynamite. He took it out of the ice cooler and showed it to me—two sticks, looked like one-pound sticks, they were fifty percent nitro and they had a Hercules emblem, picture of a man standing on it. And I was scared, and I said, get it out of the truck. And he stopped and hid the dynamite beside the road. And on the way back from Florella was when he asked me, uh, he asked how would I use it if I was going to blow up something. I said what, and he said an automobile. I told him, if I were gonna blow up anything I would hook it to a spark-plug wire. He just laughed. We got on down the road and stopped and got the dynamite. He wrapped it up and put it in a lunch box with these Playmate tools. The last time I saw it, he took it and put it on the back of his truck, which was parked in the yard whenever I brought him home from fishing. Last time I saw it."

"Approximately what date was this?"

"It was the eighteenth day of June, 1983."

Cousson and Chamberlain prepared an order for the arrest of John Rowell on the charge of possession of unregistered destructive devices. They continued to seek further evidence linking John Rowell, Judias Buenoano, and her son, James, to the bombing of John Gentry's car.

The ATF laboratory report from Atlanta, Georgia, on the evidence submitted from the bomb scene and the materials seized in the search of the Buenoano residence revealed several facts. A Hercules electrical blasting cap had been used to detonate the destructive device. The orange-and-white plastic-coated wire found in James Buenoano's bedroom had physical characteristics identical to the wire used to connect the blasting cap leg wires to the taillights of Gentry's car. No comparison could be made between the ends of black plastic tape recovered from the bomb scene and the two rolls of tape found at the Buenoano residence. Efforts continued to trace the color-coded orange-and-white wire, believed to be used by automobile manufacturers.

The ongoing investigation into the background of Judias Buenoano revealed that she had met a Bobby Joe Morris in Pensacola in 1973. They began living together. Bobby Joe Morris grew up in Brewton, Alabama, with John Rowell. They were best friends and worked together in a pipeline and swimming pool construction business while Morris lived with Judias Buenoano. In 1977, Morris moved to Trinidad, Colorado, and was joined by Judias and her children six months later. Morris was living with Judias at the time of his death on January 28, 1978. Morris's unexpected death puzzled the attending physicians in Trinidad, Colorado, who could not determine the cause. Judias Buenoano had been working as a licensed practical nurse at the hospital where Morris died and had assisted in his case and care. She was the beneficiary of a thirty-thousand-dollar life insurance policy taken out by Morris in 1977.

Interviews with Judias Buenoano's employees and acquaintances also revealed that her first husband, James Goodyear, had died in Orlando, Florida, in 1971 from a mysterious disease he had contracted while serving in the air force in Vietnam. Her first-born son, Michael Goodyear, had been killed in a boating accident near Pensacola in 1980.

"Judi's had a really tragic life," one female employee volunteered sympathetically.

"Oh, really?" Chamberlain replied. He promptly sent for the army medical records on James Goodyear, Michael Goodyear, and the Trinidad hospital records of Bobby Joe Morris.

On September 12, 1983, Chamberlain and Steele again interviewed John Gentry at Sacred Heart Hospital. Gentry, readmitted on September 6 for additional abdominal surgery because of his blast injuries, was recovering satisfactorily from the closure of his ileostomy. He was anxious to see the detectives, he said, because Judi had visited him the previous evening. He had not seen her during his two-month convalescence at his mother's home. Not since he had sent an employee from his store to pick up his clothes and personal belongings from her house and Judias had thrown the boxes down the stairs at the unsuspecting messenger. Now she was back, trying for several hours to persuade him that the police did not have their facts straight about her participation in the bombing of his car. She tried to tell Gentry that he had purchased the orange-and-white wire found in James's bedroom and had used it as a television antenna by hooking it to a window screen. Gentry did not recall such a wire or using a wire for any such purpose. Judias told him that the vitamin capsules the police had analyzed for poison were brought into her home by Kimberly's boyfriend. She said that Johnny Rowell had told her everything the police had asked him concerning his purchase of dynamite and his relationship with her. They were conducting a witch-hunt, she said. They were trying to crucify her.

Gentry then said that James Buenoano had visited John Rowell in Brewton, Alabama, on June 23, 1983, two days before the bombing, in order to purchase some marijuana. James had returned that afternoon without the pot, claiming that John Rowell did not have any.

At the conclusion of the interview, Chamberlain informed Gentry that Judias's employee, Susan Williams, had said that a few weeks prior to the bombing, Judi had made plans for a world cruise for herself and her children. Gentry would not be going, Judi had told her, because he was suffering from terminal cancer and did not have long to live. Judias had reportedly told another employee just before Christmas of 1982, during Gentry's first hospitalization, that she could not "kick him out of her house" because he had a terminal illness. Keith Lewis, a friend of Gentry's who had visited him at Judi's home just before Thanksgiving of 1982, said he thought Gentry had cancer because Judias had told him that she discovered a letter from a doctor in Mobile informing Gentry that he had a terminal illness.

Chamberlain then informed Gentry that Judias's subpoenaed medical records revealed that she had undergone a tubal ligation prior to a removal of her right ovary in Baptist Hospital in Pensacola in 1975. Medically speaking, it was highly unlikely that since that time she had actually been pregnant with his or anyone else's child.

"No shit," Gentry said in awe.

Driving home that evening, Chamberlain pulled to a stop at a traffic light on North Ninth Avenue. In the lane directly to his right sat Judias Buenoano behind the wheel of her white Corvette. Chamberlain returned Judias's intense glare with a confident grin. As the light turned green, Chamberlain sped off with a friendly wave. Through his rearview mirror, Chamberlain watched as Judias jumped from her stalled car and frantically brushed the burning ashes of her dropped cigarette from the front of her charred white dress.

8

Arsenic

TED CHAMBERLAIN WAS RELAXING on the couch in his apartment with his feet up and a cold beer, enjoying a late-night rerun of "The Honeymooners." His rare moment of off-duty leisure was interrupted by a phone call from his estranged wife, Jerri. Her ex-husband was attempting to gain custody of her youngest child, six-year-old Bradley. Since the age of two, Bradley had called Chamberlain, his stepfather, "Dad," and considered him to be his real father. The strong feeling was mutual.

Suppressing his instinctive anger, Chamberlain did his best to reassure Jerri. Nobody was taking Bradley anywhere; he'd make sure of that. He'd never forget coming home from Vietnam to his first wife and a house full of idiot hippies, his three-year-old daughter asleep in the back room. He'd gone upstairs and found his wife in the sack with some guy. He came down, wrapped his daughter in a blanket, and headed out the door. Some creep said, "Where you going with that kid?" That did it. He lost his temper and knocked the son-of-a-bitch through a plate-glass window. He got a divorce a month later.

Jerri was far different from his first wife. He knew she was a good sport when they were first introduced by mutual friends at a local football game. She was a little shy and embarrassed at first. Her dancing blue eyes avoided his as he lit her cigarette. It was hard for him to believe that this woman, petite and blond, with dimples and a tender smile, was thirty-something and the mother of five children. Their brief courtship suffered from the chronic interference of well-meaning friends, and their Memorial Day wedding in 1980 turned into a free-for-all. His buddies on the police force had dragged him away, handcuffed, in the back of a van while the girls whisked Jerri off to a male-stripper nightclub. It was two in the morning when they were finally reunited at their planned honeymoon trailer camp out on Navarre Beach. He stood alone in the trailer door with a towel wrapped around his wet, bruised body after a final dunking in the Gulf by his squad of buddies. "Where the hell have you been?" he greeted his confused bride. They slept in separate beds in the rented trailer on their wedding night. He returned to duty the next morning. Two weeks later he started to work with the tactical squad, which went off duty at six in the morning. Jerri's nursing hours at the hospital were equally demanding—seven days on the night shift, seven days off. After two years of this constantly conflicting schedules, they felt like a pair of strangers. The separation had been a mere formality.

Something soft and vulnerable in Jerri's trembling voice suddenly touched him. "Okay, babe," he sighed. "Let's give it another shot for the kids."

Back together with Bradley and Jerri's two teenage daughters in a larger apartment in the Charleston Manor complex off Scenic Highway, Chamberlain and Jerri sat side by side on the couch going over the medical reports Chamberlain had received on Judias's deceased loved ones.

Bobby Joe Morris, a 220-pound, six-foot-three-inch, thirty-five-year-old white male, was admitted to San Rafael Hospital in Trinidad, Colorado, on January 4, 1978, in shock. He had felt great twenty-four hours before, but at five P.M. on the day of admission, he suddenly became very nauseated and started vomiting. He developed severe abdominal pain in the epigastric area associated with diarrhea that was eggshell in color. Upon examination, his amylase level was found to be elevated, but all other signs were normal. The cause of his shock was unknown. Since he had been in shock for several hours, his heart rate was increased and he had had no urine output in that period. He was also in metabolic acidosis.

Morris was treated immediately for shock. He was given an infusion of IV solution for his dehydration and Dopamine to bring up his blood pressure. He was placed in intensive care and his electrolytes were monitored closely. By January 6 he appeared to be clinically improving, but that evening he developed delirium tremens. (Morris had been a heavy drinker. His wife, Judias Morris, revealed to the attending physician that her husband had been drinking at least two cases of beer per day for the past several years.) He began having muscle twitching, hallucinations; he became disoriented and very difficult to manage. The patient was in full-blown delirium tremens; the doctors now felt that alcohol withdrawal was perhaps the cause of shock. Morris was given a shot of 100 mg of Librium every four hours, and started on Aqua Mephyton and Thiamine for possible liver problems. By January 7 Morris had become more agitated and belligerent; his talking was wild and confused, and he suffered horrible hallucinations. He remained in delirium tremens with fever, increased heart rate, and sweating. His metabolic problems included increased sodium, increased potassium, and increased chloride, with very low calcium. He was unable to tolerate oral medications. He became diabetic and was started on insulin. His metabolic acidosis continued and he remained dehydrated regardless of the amount of fluids he received. On January 9 he went into congestive heart failure. His delirium raged on. He developed severe respiratory distress and had to be treated with oxygen.

Later that day Morris started to come out of his delirium and was able to carry on a somewhat sensible conversation for short periods; however, he fluctuated in and out of hallucinations and agitation. His kidney status improved, but his calcium remained very low, as did his platelets. His amylase finally began to increase, confirming a probable diagnosis for the shock as severe pancreatitis. The next day he was more conversive, although still confused and disoriented. His congestive heart failure was improving, but the diabetes continued. Within a few days, Morris was lucid and his chest much clearer. By January 14 he was completely oriented.

On January 15 the patient developed a urinary tract infection and was started on intravenous Keflin. He developed a rash on his trunk, thought to be a possible reaction to the drug Keflin, which was discontinued.

Nevertheless, he was seemingly recovering. By January 16 the pancreatitis seemed resolved and he was started on clear liquids. In two days he was very stable, completely coherent. The IV was discontinued and his diet increased. By January 21 he was well enough to walk around the room, and Morris was discharged with a follow-up examination scheduled in a week's time.

The attending physician's final diagnosis listed delirium tremens, acute pancreatitis, alcoholic hepatitis, hypotension with shock, metabolic acidosis, acute renal failure, congestive heart failure, urinary tract infection, possible drug reaction to Keflin, and diabetes, completely resolved.

Two days later, on January 23, 1978, Bobby Joe Morris was readmitted to the ER at San Rafael Hospital, again in a state of shock for no apparent reason. According to his wife, the day after he returned home he had begun to vomit uncontrollably and to have severe diarrhea. The wife told the doctors she had not become concerned until he became very weak and fainted every time he tried to sit up. Upon admission, Morris's blood pressure was not audible either lying down or sitting up. His chest was clear, and his heart showed normal rhythm with very rapid rate. He was awake and oriented. He had had no urine output for the past twelve hours. He was treated as before for shock, with fluids and drugs to raise his blood pressure. By the following morning, he appeared to be doing fairly well, though his calcium remained low, a condition thought to be due to continuing pancreatitis.

On the evening of January 24, he began to go downhill very rapidly, with rapid heartbeat and severe metabolic acidosis. His blood pressure plummeted and he became swollen. Suspecting massive infection, the attending physician prescribed broad-spectrum antibiotics and steroids. The next day the patient seemed to respond, but on the twenty-sixth he again became very agitated and belligerent and needed to be restrained. He was taken from intensive care to a private room, where he continued to deteriorate rapidly. On January twenty eight he was tested for lupus with negative results. The metabolic acidosis—for which there was still no known cause—continued. On January 28, 1978, Bobby Joe Morris had severe arrhythmia. His heart stopped at seven-twenty A.M. Resuscitation was begun, but after all signs and symptoms of brain death, it was stopped at approximately seven-fifty-six A.M.

The final hospital report listed massive sepsis with septic shock, metabolic acidosis, possible hepatic encephalopathy, hypotension, and death. A chronic pancreatitis diagnosis was made upon autopsy. The cause of death was thought to be severe hypotension with lactic acidosis and arrhythmia secondary to the acidosis, resulting in cardiac arrest.

Bobby Joe Morris's death certificate, signed by his attending physician, Dr. Charles Raye, listed the immediate cause of death as cardiac arrhythmia and arrest due to metabolic acidosis as a consequence of possible systemic lupus erythematosis. The death certificate listed Morris's surviving spouse as Judias Welty; the informant was Mrs. Judias Morris.

An autopsy was performed by Dr. John Aultshulter, a pathologist called in from Denver, Colorado. His postmortem examination stated that all organs removed—heart, lungs, spleen, kidneys, pancreas, and bowel—appeared normal. Microscopic examination showed the organ tissues were normal and nonmalignant with the exception of the pancreas, which revealed extensive fibrosis and mild chronic inflammatory reaction. The tissue pathology report concluded: "The cause of death in this patient is as obscure as his clinical course during his terminal illness in the hospital. There are no anatomic lesions that would account for his death. One questions the possibility of some form of toxic-ity. . . . During the last few days of his life, the patient had toxicity screen performed, and phenothiazines were found to be present in the urine and blood. . . . At this time, the cause of death remains obscure."

Detective Rick Steele had contacted the attending phy-sicians and coroner for Bobby Joe Morris by phone in Trinidad, Colorado, in August 1983. According to Steele's report, Dr. Charles Raye had admitted that Bobby Joe Morris's death was suspicious and that no direct cause of death could be determined. Raye said that Thorazine was found in Morris's blood, though this drug was not given to him per doctor's instructions. Thorazine, he stated, causes a drastic drop in blood pressure in a normal person. Morris was in shock and had very low blood pressure both times he was admitted to the hospital.

Dr. Sally Fadec, an attending physician for Morris, told Steele that she suspected foul play from the beginning. She said she tried to keep an eye on Judias because she worked at the hospital at the time as a licensed practical nurse and assisted with Morris's care during his stay in the hospital.

The local coroner stated that Judias rushed him to release Morris's body so that it could be taken to Florida for burial.

Dr. Aultshulter remembered the autopsy of Morris very well. He had conducted the autopsy while the body remained in the coffin and after embalming. Aultshulter stated that it was impossible to do a proper autopsy under such conditions.

Chamberlain returned Bobby Joe Morris's medical reports to the pile of papers spread before him on the coffee table.

"Okay, babe," he said to Jerri. "Give me what you got on Thorazine."

Jerri, a nurse specialist at the Poison Information Cen-ter at Baptist Hospital, had brought home copies of the information sheets on various drugs and poisons at her husband's request. She read aloud from the list of clinical symptoms for the ingestion of the class of phenothiazines, of which chlorpromazine, or Thorazine, was a major derivative: " 'Acute toxic doses of phenothiazines is not well established in literature. In general, signs and symptoms of overdosage include hypotension, miosis, hypothermia, CNS depression, tachycardia, urinary retention and seizures. . . . The lethal dose is thought to be in the range of fifteen to a hundred and fifty milligrams per kilogram, depending on the individual agent.' "

"If Judi was giving Morris Thorazine, couldn't that have caused his low blood pressure and heart failure, especially since he was a heavy drinker?" Chamberlain asked.

"I guess it might have accounted for the hypotension and tachycardia, but that poor man suffered from everything from delirium and shock to metabolic acidosis, hepatitis, renal failure, and congestive heart failure. And it doesn't account for the sudden vomiting, diarrhea, and abdominal pain he checked in with both times. That sounds more like classic arsenic poisoning to me."

"Arsenic? What are you talking about, woman? Read me the effects of arsenic poisoning."

" 'Early symptoms within hours following exposure to arsenic include abdominal pain, vomiting, profuse "rice-like" diarrhea, pain in extremities and muscles and flushing of the skin; renal failure, jaundice, vertigo, delirium, and coma may occur; myocardial toxicity including ventricular fibrillation; toxic delirium and encephalopathy are complications of acute arsenic poisoning.' "

"That sure sounds like everything Morris went through. But wouldn't they have found arsenic in his blood with all the tests they did?"

"Not if they weren't looking for it. You'd be surprised how many calls we get at the Poison Center from doctors who don't know anything about poisons. Listen to what it says about clinical management of acute arsenic poisoning. 'The initial step in management is a suspicion of the possibility of arsenic poisoning; this may be a feat in itself, as the exposure may not be known to the patient, as in cases of attempted homicide. Patients who show gastrointestinal, neurologic, and subsequent renal involvement and have a history of possible exposure to arsenic should have a determination of urinary arsenic. If no etiology for such a clinical picture can be ascertained, then arsenic level may uncover an unsuspected diagnosis. Use of a reliable, experienced laboratory is absolutely essential. The normal blood arsenic level is less than seven ug/dl [micrograms per deciliter]; false values are not uncommon. Quantitative twenty-four-hour urine collections are the only reliable laboratory measure of arsenic poisoning."

"What about the autopsy? Would arsenic show up in the body tissues after death?"

" 'Arsenic distributes into the spleen, liver, kidneys, and keratin structures. . . . Arsenic has been demonstrated in the hair and nails within thirty minutes after exposure. . . . It may take ten days for complete elimination after a single dose of arsenic and up to seventy days after repeated administration.' Arsenic is classified as a heavy metal; it doesn't break down too readily. I remember reading somewhere that they found high concentrations of arsenic in a twenty-four-hundred-year-old mummy."

"Morris sure hasn't been buried that long. You're doing great, babe. Let's take a look at the first husband, James Goodyear." Chamberlain read aloud the report from the Orlando naval hospital.

" 'James Edgar Goodyear, a thirty-seven-year-old male USAF technical sergeant, was admitted to the naval hospital in Orlando, Florida, on September thirteenth, 1971, with a two-week history of nausea, vomiting, diarrhea, and abnormal liver function tests. He had returned from South Vietnam three months prior, following a one-year tour of duty. During that time, he took his antimalarials and was not ill. He returned to the United States in June 1971, and since that time had not been feeling well, tending to tire easily, associated with a decrease in appetite and an increased abdominal distention. Two weeks prior to admission, he developed nausea and repeated episodes of vomiting. He had chills and a daily fever of one hundred plus one degree. He developed cramping abdominal pain and diarrhea with no apparent blood or mucus. He had noticed a darkening of his urine, and Mrs. Goodyear stated that she thought his sclera were icteric. He went to McCoy Dispensary and had been seen there at two- to three-day intervals since the onset of nausea and vomiting. He had been treated with various antiemetics without any abatement of his symptoms. In addition, within the past two days he noted tingling and numbness of his fingers and toes as well as diffuse myalgias without any joint pain. Due to the persistence of his symptoms, he was referred to the Orlando naval hospital for further evaluation.

" 'This man has nineteen years of service in the Air Force and is stationed at McCoy Air Force Base, where he worked as a mechanic. He is married with two children and, until the onset of illness, smoked one pack of cigarettes per day. He has no history of excessive alcohol consumption. His wife related that since the onset of illness, he had been disoriented and manifested bizarre behavior and picking at himself. On physical examination, the patient appeared chronically ill and in mild distress. There was evidence of dehydration and guarding of the abdomen without other specific findings. On admission, the differential diagnosis was exhaustive. The leading candidate was some sort of parasitic infestation or inflammatory disease. Laboratory studies showed a relative anemia and changes consistent with hepatic and pancreatic inflammation and behavior consistent with cerebral irritability. He was begun on forced fluids, developing labored respirations and pulmonary edema due to the fluid overload. Despite this, he had very little urinary output. On September sixteenth, he spiked a one-hundred-three-degree temperature and developed labored respiration and an episode of hypertension. He developed respiratory arrest and subsequent cardiac arrest with ventricular fibrillation. Cardiorespiratory resuscitative measures were promptly instituted, but no stable rhythm could be obtained. After sixty minutes, the resuscitation was ended and the patient was pronounced dead at five-fifteen P.M. on September 16, 1971.' "

The clinical diagnosis on James Edgar Goodyear listed septicemia, bronchopneumonia, renal failure, ulceration of the ileocecal valve and ascending colon, cause unknown, and cardiorespiratory arrest, terminal.

"It's all there: vomiting, diarrhea, abdominal pain, numbness in extremities, dehydration, and hepatic abnormalities, followed by renal failure, delirium, cardiac arrhythmia, and arrest. The same clinical profile for Bobby Joe Morris and classic arsenic poisoning," Jerri concluded grimly.

"Except Goodyear didn't put up as much of a fight as Morris. Sounds like he was half dead before he got to the hospital. The poor bastard makes it through a year in Vietnam, and two months after coming home to his wife, he's dead," Chamberlain said bitterly. "You can bet Judi didn't waste any time collecting on his military benefits."

Chamberlain absently fingered the chain bracelet soldered around his right wrist. There had been twelve men in his Special Forces unit in Vietnam. Each one had a chain bracelet, a souvenir made from the tail of a downed helicopter. And each had sworn not to remove it till they all got back and met at a reunion at Port Authority Bus Station in New York City. He was the only one left. He figured the bracelet was never coming off.

9

Her Own Son

"WHO'S LEFT?" Chamberlain turned back to the files in front of them. "The son. Wonder what Judi had in store for him." He reached for the medical files on Michael Buenoano Goodyear.

Private 2nd Class Michael B. Goodyear was admitted to the Walter Reed Army Medical Center on January 23, 1980, with a chief complaint of paresthesias and weakness. This 18-year-old right-handed male developed numbness and tingling of all four extremities distally around November 1979. Within six weeks his weakness had progressed such that the patient could no longer walk or use his hands. In addition, his total body weight decreased from 167 pounds in April 1979 to 123 pounds in January 1980.

According to his mother, the patient has a long history of pica dating to early childhood. He has eaten dirt, licked storage batteries, and eaten a great deal of paint off a wooden house built prior to 1920. The patient was well when he joined the Army in June 1979, performing adequately in basic training. His MOS was that of water purification specialist. A lab course was part of his training from October 1 to 26, 1979. In this laboratory was a one-pint bottle of sodium arsenite from which one-ounce vials were decanted for testing purposes. These vials contained 80 mg of arsenic. On October 16, 1979, the patient was acutely exposed to chlorine fumes and was briefly admitted to Fort Leonard Wood, Missouri, with skin and upper airway irritation. In addition to pica, the patient has suffered from episodic enuresis from childhood to present.

As a child he had frequent upper respiratory infections and questionable history for childhood asthma. In 1975 he suffered a broken nose, with subsequent rhinoplasty. He denies tobacco, alcohol, or medicine usage. Mother states his father was killed in Vietnam with unknown medical history. Mother is alive and well at thirty-six. Two teenage siblings both alive and well.

The patient went through basic training at Fort Leonard Wood, Missouri, from June to October 1979. During his transition to Fort Benning, Georgia, en route to which he visited his mother in Gulf Breeze, Florida, the patient began having symptoms of paresthesias. He reported to Fort Benning on November 6, 1979. Neurological examination on that date was within normal limits except for a slight decrease in distal perception of primary sensory modalities. On November 13, 1979, the patient checked himself into the base hospital with nausea, vomiting, diarrhea, and numbness of extremities. The patient stated he had experienced these symptoms since November 1, 1979. By November 16, 1979, the patient's muscle paresis was clinically apparent, primarily distal and symmetrically involving all four extremities. At that time his weight was 149 pounds and white transverse lines were noted on all fingernails. He was admitted to Martin Army Hospital to rule out a peripheral neuropathy which was initially thought to be of functional etiology. Urine toxic drug screen was normal. By mid-December 1979 the patient had developed leukopenia and mild anemia. Peripheral neuropathy was confirmed by nerve conduction velocity studies with both motor and sensory being significantly impaired. Serum lead level was elevated at 57, normal less than 45, as was urine lead level at 140, normal less than 80. Lead toxicity was also suggested by elevated urine porphyrins. On January 7, 1980, serum arsenic was normal, less than 10, while urine values were elevated at greater than 250, normal range from 0 to 100. The patient was given a course of chelation therapy January 9–17. By January sixteen his weight was decreased to 123 pounds. On January twenty-three 1980 the patient was transferred to the Neurology Service at Walter Reed Army Medical Center. Upon admission, his vital signs were stable. There was generalized muscle wasting and atrophy. Mees's lines were present on all fingernails measuring 10mm from cuticle. Hair arsenic level was seven times normal value. Approximate retrograde dating would place arsenic exposure around mid-October 1979, coincidental with his laboratory course in Water Purification School. Vibration, position, touch, pain, and temperature perception were absent distal to the elbow and distal to the knee. Psychological testing was normal with verbal IQ 92 without evidence of thought disorder or serious intellectual deficits.

The patient was vigorously trained in occupational and physical therapy. The patient intermittently became depressed owing to poor self-imaging and fear of never walking again. He has shown good improvement with the use of leg braces and physical therapy, allowing for an improved outlook toward his future. His concern toward lack of ability to have a penile erection was addressed by psychotherapy. His serum and urine levels of both lead and arsenic failed to rise significantly; however, a second Mees's line did become apparent in subsequent weeks. The patient can feed himself by use of a Robbins hook prosthesis. Dressing and toilet care are not independent. The patient requires a wheelchair. With continued long-term physical therapy, the patient may regain some degree of independent ambulation. His condition is static and not expected to change for better or for worse.

The diagnoses on Michael Goodyear included peripheral neuropathy with motor and sensory components, secondary to lead and arsenic toxicity; lead ingestion, probably chronic, and arsenic ingestion, probable acute, in mid-October 1979, probably secondary to his habit of eating nonfood substances. The medical report concluded that Private Goodyear was unfit for further military duty and recommended "that he be transferred to a VA Spinal Cord Rehabilitation Center, preferably near his mother's home in northern Florida, for further training in physical therapy."

"Bobby Joe Morris worked for the city of Trinidad,

Colorado, as a water purification specialist. Judi must have gotten the kid to opt for the same training in the army. She had to know they worked with arsenic. It figures. She set the army up, then collects on the kid's military benefits too. That's real premeditation," Chamberlain observed.

The medical reports further revealed that in March 1980, Private Michael B. Goodyear was transferred to the VA hospital at Tampa, Florida, pending medical treatment for permanent disability. On May 12, 1980, he was discharged into his mother's care at her home in Gulf Breeze, Florida.

On May 13, 1980, Michael Buenoano Goodyear drowned when his canoe, with his mother and brother aboard, over-turned at approximately three-thirty P.M. on the East River about one-half mile east of the Highway 87 bridge near Milton, Florida. There was an army casualty report.

> At the time of the accident, PV2 Goodyear was wear-ing full leg braces and a device on his right arm which operated a prosthetic hand through cables and braces with the muscles of his right shoulder. His attending physician stated that PV2 Goodyear was completely immobile from the knees and elbows down. He could not walk, even with braces, and had no control with his arms. He further stated it would be impossible for the boy to swim with or without braces, even with a life vest. His mother recovered his brother and swam ¼ mile, where they were picked up by a fellow boater. PV2 Goodyear's body was recovered four to five hours later by Santa Rosa Search and Rescue divers. The assistant medical examiner stated that no alcohol or drugs were involved. Preliminary finding was death by drowning.

The autopsy report on Michael Buenoano Goodyear con-cluded: "The findings are consistent with a severe peripheral neuropathy. Numerous agents are capable of causing this and findings were compatible with the clinical history of exposure to heavy metals. The findings of the remainder of the autopsy were unremarkable, except for the presence of a marked hemorrhagic pulmonary edema typical of drowning.

Final pathological diagnosis: peripheral neuropathy, atrophy of muscles, and congestion and pulmonary edema of lungs caused by drowning."

Chamberlain put down Michael Buenoano Goodyear's files in tense silence.

"What are you thinking, Ted? The others, maybe, but could a mother possibly murder her own son?" Jerri asked incredulously.

"A bitch does it for money, and evil does it for pleasure. This is one evil bitch," Chamberlain answered slowly. "But I'll get her. I'll get her," he repeated with conviction.

Jerri studied her husband's profile, the muscles of his jaw working with the anger that always seemed to lie just below the surface. There was a lot of violence in him, she knew. He needed that rush of adrenaline that only physical danger could provide. He was married to his job first, and there was nothing she could do but accept it. Sometimes she wondered if he hadn't married her as much to have a ready-made family as anything else. Since they'd been together, only twice had she ever felt he truly loved her. Once he had come home late from work, and she had pretended to be asleep. He got into bed beside her and stroked her face gently. "I really do love you," he whispered. But he had never told her to her face. In spite of her desire to help with the case, to share in any part of the work that was so much a part of Ted, Jerri couldn't help feeling a twinge of jealousy at his growing obsession with this Judias woman.

Jerri had met Judi once. Right before the bombing of John Gentry's car, while she and Ted were separated, she had gone to Fingers N Faces. Her girlfriend Vickie, the ex-wife of a Pensacola policeman, had gotten a job there. Jerri never had any nails to speak of, but Vickie had called her down and said she would put fingernails on for free. There were several other women in the small, shiny parlor having their nails done when Judias breezed into the shop carrying a bag of formal clothes for a cruise she was planning to take. She stood there looking down on everyone, hardly speaking at all. Vickie was very impressed with Judias, who claimed to be a doctor. Jerri wondered what a doctor was doing with a fingernail parlor. Judias was very generous to the girls who worked for her. She insisted that they call her "Mother." She gave them each little fourteen-karat gold ornaments for their fingernails. She held special birthday parties for them, presenting them with lavish gifts. Judias had eyed Jerri coolly, with a curt nod. Jerri wasn't one of her "girls."

It occurred to Jerri that she had first seen Ted, three years ago, at the corner of Garden and Baylen, where the bombing of Gentry's car had recently taken place. She had been the dispatching nurse for Life Line, the private helicopter emergency service operating from the roof of Baptist Hospital. It was early in the morning and she was just getting off duty when a call came in for a pedestrian who had been hit by a car. Paula, the nurse coming on duty, had said to her, "Come on, go with me." The pilot had trouble starting the helicopter. The radio was screaming for Life Line. They'd finally lurched into the air and reached the scene of the accident. They had loaded the patient on the gurney and were wheeling him to the hovering helicopter when a uniformed police officer ran up and handed her the injured man's hat. She had shouted at him to keep down from the whirling helicopter blades. He had looked at her as though she were crazy. Looking over the newspaper photos the next day, she had remarked to Paula, "What a good-looking policeman!" A few weeks later she was introduced to Officer Ted Chamberlain at a football game. She promptly fell in love.

Jerri stared at the uneven pile of medical reports spread on the coffee table before her as Ted headed into the kitchen for a beer. She knew from experience that once Ted latched onto a murder case, he wouldn't turn loose until he got his suspect, no matter how long that took. But whatever Ted believed, it would take a lot of evidence to convince her that Judias had plotted and executed the murder of her own son. It was just too unbelievable.

*　*　*

In early October 1983, Ted Chamberlain and Bob Cousson drove the sixty miles back to Brewton, Alabama, to interview the mother of Bobby Joe Morris. Lodell Morris, a forty-five-year resident of Brewton in her mid-sixties, spoke of her dead son with the terse sadness of a woman resigned to life's bitter disappointments.

According to Mrs. Morris, her son started living with Judias in Pensacola sometime in 1973. Bobby Joe had gotten a job in swimming pool construction after graduating from college and moved into a trailer on the outskirts of Pensacola. Johnny Rowell, a lifelong friend, was one of his employees. Mrs. Morris first met Judias at a New Year's Eve party at the White Horse Inn, a club just outside Brewton, in 1972. Judias was there with Johnny Rowell, Bobby Joe, and another girl she introduced as her nanny.

Mrs. Morris used to see her son in Pensacola almost every day. She cooked for him, washed his clothes, took care of him just like he was at home. After he moved in with Judias and her three children, she saw him only occasionally. Bobby Joe and Judias didn't fight much, Lodell Morris said, but there was no real companionship or love—nothing like that. Bobby Joe did like his beer. He would consume six or eight cans a day on weekends.

In 1977, Bobby Joe moved alone to Trinidad, Colorado, where he worked for the city of Trinidad as a water purification specialist. Mrs. Morris believed her son moved to Colorado in order to get away from Judias. Six months later, Judias and her three children followed Bobby Joe to Trinidad. Bobby Joe and Judias bought a small house together. While they were living in Trinidad, Judias attended nursing school. She went by the name of Mrs. Judias Morris.

Lodell Morris visited her son and Judias in Trinidad at Thanksgiving in 1977. As Bobby Joe drove his mother to the Denver airport for her return flight, he told her he would never marry Judias or allow her to take out any life insurance on him. Lodell Morris had told her son that if he ever married Judias, she would disown him. Judias had told Lodell that if she didn't get Bobby Joe, nobody else would. Except for problems with frequent tearing in one eye, Bobby Joe was the picture of health.

The night of January 4, 1978, Lodell Morris received a phone call from Judias telling her that Bobby Joe had come home from work and collapsed at the table during supper. He had been rushed to the hospital in an ambulance. Mrs. Morris assumed her son had suffered an attack of food poisoning. She told Judias she couldn't get a flight out from Brewton and would have to drive to Trinidad in the morning. "Well, you won't make it in time," Judias told her. "He'll be dead by the time you get here." Mrs. Morris left early the next morning and drove eighteen hours straight to San Rafael Hospital in Trinidad. Her daughter, a housewife and mother of three, had arrived just hours before from her home in Minneapolis, Minnesota.

Bobby Joe was unconscious, his legs and arms strapped to the hospital bed, jerking spasmodically. Judias, an LPN working at the hospital, was by his side. Lodell Morris alternated shifts with her daughter at the hospital over the next two weeks until Bobby Joe came out of his bad spell. Judias attended him daily. She brought Hawaiian Punch from large cans she kept at home and administered the juice to Bobby Joe. She said he liked it so well. Judias had to practically pry Bobby Joe's mouth open to get the juice in him, Lodell Morris said.

By January 21 Bobby Joe had improved enough to go to the bathroom by himself. Assured by the doctor that Bobby Joe was out of danger, Mrs. Morris and her daughter returned to their homes. They planned to return to Trinidad the following week for Bobby Joe's release from the hospital.

On the night of January 28, 1978, Mrs. Morris received a telephone call from her daughter. Dr. Raye, the attending physician at San Rafael hospital, had called to inform her that Bobby Joe was dead. He had been away from the hospital the previous weekend, Dr. Raye had explained. The physician on duty had released Bobby Joe into Judias's care on January 21 without Dr. Raye's knowledge. On January 23, Bobby Joe was readmitted to the emergency room in a state of severe shock. His clinical course deteriorated rapidly. Bobby Joe went into cardiac arrest and died early in the morning on January 28, Dr. Raye concluded. He was terribly sorry.

Claiming the body as his wife, Judias tried to have Bobby Joe cremated in Trinidad, but Lodell Morris insisted that her son's body be returned to Brewton for burial. A small funeral service was held in Trinidad. Mrs. Morris's daughter attended. Judias was there, wearing what appeared to be a long black wedding gown purchased for the occasion. A second funeral service was held in Bobby Joe's hometown of Brewton. Johnny Rowell, Bobby Joe's best friend, was a pallbearer. Judias, remaining in Colorado, did not attend. Bobby Joe was buried in Green Acres Cemetery in Brewton, Alabama, next to what will be his mother's grave.

Lodell Morris was relieved that someone was looking into her son's death. She had always known that Judias had done something to Bobby Joe. Back in 1974, Lodell said, a man was found dead in a motel room in Brewton. His hands were bound, his throat was cut, and he had been shot in the chest with a .22. When the news broke in the Brewton paper, Lodell overheard Judias tell Bobby Joe, "The son of a bitch shouldn't have come up here in the first place. He knew if he came up he was gonna die." At the time of his death, the victim was supposed to have been in South Florida laying a pipeline. The murder was never solved. From his hospital bed, Bobby Joe had repeated to his mother and sister in his delirium, "Judi, we should never have done that terrible thing."

"Maybe now Bobby Joe will rest in peace," Lodell Morris sighed.

Taking their cue from Mrs. Morris, Chamberlain and Bob Cousson left her house and headed straight for the Brewton

Police Department. Captain Purnell remembered the 1974 motel murder she had mentioned, but there was little or no evidence to present on the case. No one had taken pictures of the crime scene; no fingerprints were found; no bullets were recovered. There had been an anonymous phone call from a local pay phone. That was it. There was nothing for Chamberlain and Cousson to follow up on.

"You've got to realize, boys, we're a small department here," the captain told them. "We're not equipped too well. We just don't have any big crime-scene unit to go out."

From Brewton, Chamberlain and Cousson drove back to Pensacola in frustrated silence.

"I guess murder's not a major crime in Brewton. If that kind of killing had happened in our jurisdiction, a lot more would have been done," Chamberlain muttered. "We might have had a chance to solve it."

"Are you thinking what I'm thinking?" Cousson queried. "Bobby Joe told that girl we questioned in Pensacola that he was trying to get away from Judias. When she asked him why he didn't just leave her, he told her if he did, he'd be dead in a week. Johnny Rowell wouldn't talk against Judias, even when we threatened to arrest him. You're talking about two men who are probably two hundred fifty pounds apiece, and they're both scared to death of this woman for some reason. One would rather ruin his health and go to jail, and the other died because he was afraid to leave her. There's something Judias had on them that they couldn't get away from. It's only a theory, but I'm wondering if the three of them didn't kill that guy in that motel room in Brewton, each of them participating. A man's not going to do as much for a woman like that as Rowell has done. There's something very strong there that's holding him in check."

"I wouldn't put it past the witch," Chamberlain concurred.

"I reckon we'll find out soon enough just how strong Judias's grip on Rowell really is. The case against him for supplying the explosives in the bombing of Gentry's car

goes before the grand jury next month," Cousson concluded.

"We'll get the bitch." Chamberlain grinned back. "Trust
me."

On December 13, 1983, the case against John Daniel
Rowell was presented to a federal grand jury in the district
court for the Southern Judicial District in Mobile, Alabama.
On December 15, U.S. Attorney Thomas Figures informed
Agent Cousson and Detective Chamberlain that the grand
jury had returned a no-bill on the Rowell case. Apparently,
when the grand jury was empaneled, the members were
told that they were a special group who would only hear
very important cases. During their first sessions they were
presented with a very large narcotics case and a controversial
civil rights–Ku Klux Klan case. In the following sessions,
several lesser cases were presented, including the explosives
possession case against Rowell. All were no-billed. It was
felt that the foreman, a dominant figure in the grand jury,
was flexing his muscles to show the U.S. attorney that he
was displeased with the size of the cases being presented.

Preparations were under way by the U.S. attorney's office
in Mobile, Alabama, to resubmit the Rowell case to another
grand jury. Having been arrested for possession of destructive devices, improper storage of explosives, and failure to
report the theft of explosives materials, John Daniel Rowell
remained free on his own recognizance.

10

Water Mishap

Assistant FLORIDA STATE ATTORNEY Russ Edgar's electric-blue eyes gleamed with special intensity as he pored over the background and medical reports spread over his massive mahogany desk. Chamberlain and Cousson had certainly done their homework on the case against Judias Buenoano. They had established the means of death—poison—and the motive—insurance—in the attempted murder of John Gentry. They were closing in on the bombing case. They had also found indications of poison and the opportunity to use it in the deaths of Bobby Joe Morris and James E. Goodyear. There was enough to seek a subpoena for Judias Buenoano's financial and employment records.

Edgar leaned far back in his reclining leather chair, hands clasped behind his head, feet on his desk, and paused to reflect.

Pensacola wouldn't suffer by comparison with any major Northern city when it comes to the criminal justice system, Edgar told himself. It's not that we have more crime down here. We just catch 'em, and we put 'em away.

Edgar had once put a local murderer in jail for a thousand years. He had put a rapist in jail for 514 years—without possibility of parole. The guy had been out on parole on a prior conviction when he started raping young girls. They had caught Ted Bundy, the serial murderer of young coeds, in the streets of Pensacola in 1976, the year the U.S. Supreme Court ruled the death penalty was not unconstitutional. Bundy was sentenced to death in 1979, the year Florida reinstated the death penalty. His execution had been stayed on appeals ever since. Edgar was a staunch proponent of the death penalty, but not of the endless costly delays of the current appeals process. The Court of Appeals for the Eleventh Circuit in Atlanta, Georgia, was the most liberal bunch of people he'd ever seen. The average wait on death row was getting to be ten years, at a cost of $100,000 per inmate per year. To Edgar, it was a mockery of justice. He'd rather not have the death penalty than tolerate such delay. The man who shot the mayor of Miami in 1937 was caught, tried, convicted, sentenced, appealed, and executed within thirty-one days. That was justice.

The criminals aren't any worse in Pensacola than anywhere else, Edgar thought. Down here they just run into some people who are willing to go toe to toe with 'em. And we win, because we're right.

Edgar believed there was a constant battle going on between good and evil. He saw a bumper sticker once that read, "Who cares?" Well, he did.

Edgar suddenly sat up and reached for the phone on his desk. No sense wasting time, he thought, as he started the process of subpoenaing Judias Buenoano's employment and bank records. The paper chase was on.

On a sunny day in mid-October 1983, Russ Edgar leaned against his third-hand convertible in the unshaded parking lot of the Seville Inn in Pensacola's historic district and waited for the attorney who had prepared the documents on the 1978 purchase of Judias Buenoano's Whisper Bay home. Judias's subpoenaed employment records from the Escambia County Personnel Department revealed that she had worked through 1977 at the Escambia County Nursing Home as a nurse's aide making $3.05 an hour. In the summer of 1978, six months after Bobby Joe Morris's death, Judias had purchased a newly built two-story colonial home in the Whisper Bay subdivision of Gulf Breeze, Florida, through an agent and returned to Pensacola with her three children in a brand-new Lincoln town car. Deed office records showed Judias had no mortgage on her home. How could a licensed practical nurse making the minimum wage afford to pay cash for an expensive new house and car?

Edgar was about to get in his car and leave when the attorney drove into the parking lot, practically running him down. Wearing a sheepish grin, the attorney rushed over and nervously handed Edgar the file that had been requested. He had no idea why the state attorney's office was interested in the closing papers he had prepared on the purchase of Judias Buenoano's home, but he wasn't about to argue the point.

Seated alone in the front seat of his convertible, Edgar reviewed the closing file. Among the papers was a payment reference to a bank draft in the amount of fifty thousand dollars drawn on an account in Trinidad, Colorado. It didn't belong in the file, but there it was. Edgar knew from his experience as a private investigator working his way through law school that a lot of investigation was pure luck. Being there when something fell into place, catching it from a different view, looking at it from the corner of your eye, and seeing things that maybe other people didn't see. . . .

It was close to six when Edgar left the parking lot to meet Ted Chamberlain at O'Riley's neighborhood bar off Ninth Avenue for an afterwork drink. A bond of mutual respect had grown between the two veteran investigators over the Buenoano case. Chamberlain appreciated a prosecutor like Edgar, who would actually come down to the station at three in the morning, help draw up a search warrant, and stay with him through the whole investigation. Edgar had been to every crime scene of every case he'd ever tried. Walking into a crime scene right after a murder, knowing what the defenses could be, he could give his investigators their specific assignments. Chamberlain was the best investigator he'd ever worked with.

Edgar showed Chamberlain the Trinidad, Colorado, bank draft he had discovered in Judias Buenoano's closing file.

"Colorado's a couple of hours behind us. The DA's office is probably still open," Chamberlain suggested. Sliding off his stool, Edgar walked over to the pay phone in a darkened corner and called Colorado State Investigator Lou Girodo at the state attorney's office in Trinidad, Colorado, requesting that they procure the bank records on the numbered account from which the fifty-thousand-dollar bank draft had been drawn. Girodo agreed that the death of Bobby Joe Morris was suspicious enough to warrant an investigation. He would look into Judias Morris Buenoano's financial records in Trinidad and send them along to Edgar.

"You know, Ted," Edgar said, resuming his seat at the bar, "I think we're barking up the wrong tree looking for Thorazine in Morris. We can't determine in a postmortem autopsy how that would have killed him. The medical records kept showing metabolic acidosis. That just doesn't sound right."

"Then it's got to be arsenic. Judias wanted cremation of Morris's body right away. They don't usually do an autopsy on a hospital death. The one they did on Morris was rushed and inconclusive. If we can get an order to exhume Morris's body, we can still test the tissues for arsenic. Same thing with James Goodyear. The navy did an autopsy on Goodyear when he died. They kept tissue samples in paraffin blocks. If we can get the navy to release the blocks, we could have those tissue samples tested for arsenic too."

"If we can prove arsenic poisoning as the cause of death in either victim," Edgar proposed, pausing for a sip of his martini, "we're looking at at least one additional first-degree murder charge against Judias Buenoano."

"We're looking at more than that. Check out the 'accidental drowning' of Michael Goodyear and tell me Judi didn't push her crippled son out of that canoe," Chamberlain rejoined with a final gulp of beer.

The bank records Edgar received from Trinidad, Colorado, revealed the fifty-thousand-dollar bank draft that paid for Judias Buenoano's Whisper Bay home was drawn on a savings account in the names of Bobby Joe Morris or Judias

A. Morris at 1305 Buena Vista, Trinidad, Colorado. Substantial assets had been deposited in the account at one time, within a few months following Bobby Joe Morris's death. Obtaining microfilm copies of the deposit checks, Edgar discovered that the deposits were from different insurance company drafts, complete with insurance claim numbers. Contacting the insurance companies, Edgar obtained the claim files for three different life insurance policies in the name of Bobby Joe Morris, all taken out shortly before Morris's death, all naming Judias Goodyear Morris as the sole beneficiary. Judias had collected over eighty-thousand-dollars in insurance benefits from the death of Bobby Joe Morris.

With mounting conviction, Edgar studied the chronology prepared in the continuing background investigation of Judias Welty Goodyear Morris Buenoano:

4-4-43 Born Judias Anna Lou Welty to Judias Mary Lou Northam (age thirty) and Zia Jesse Otto Welty (age thirty-four) in Quanah, Hardeman County, Texas

1959 Graduates from Foothills High School (a girls' reformatory) in Albuquerque, New Mexico

1960 Moves to Roswell, New Mexico; assumes the name of Ann Schultz; works as nurse's aide at Eastern New Mexico Medical Center

3-30-61 Michael Arthur Schultz born to Ann Lou Welty in Roswell, New Mexico

1-21-62 Ann Schultz marries James E. Goodyear, USAF, in Roswell, New Mexico

1-16-66 James A. Goodyear born to Judy and James E. Goodyear

1967 Goodyears move to Orlando, Florida; Kimberly Goodyear born

1968 Judy and James E. Goodyear open Conway Acres Child Care Center in Orlando, Florida

9-15-71 James E. Goodyear dies at U.S. Naval Hospital in Orlando, Florida

9-20-71 Judy Goodyear surrenders three life insurance policies on James E. Goodyear

1971 Judy Goodyear collects $90,000 in fire insurance from Orlando home that burned

1972 Judy Goodyear moved to Pensacola, Florida

1973 Judy Goodyear lives with Bobby Joe Morris at 6390 Duquesne, Pensacola, Florida

1977 Bobby Joe Morris moves to Trinidad, Colorado

7-77 Judy Goodyear collects fire insurance on house in Pensacola that burned and joins Bobby Joe Morris with her three children in Trinidad, Colorado; Judy Goodyear goes by the name of Judias Morris

1-4-78 Bobby Joe Morris enters San Rafael Hospital in Trinidad, Colorado; no medical reason is found for his illness

1-21-78 Morris is released from hospital into Judias Morris's care

1-23-78 Morris collapses at dinner table and is readmitted to hospital

1-28-78 Bobby Joe Morris dies of cardiac arrest and metabolic acidosis

2-78 Judias Morris surrenders three life insurance policies on Bobby Joe Morris

5-3-78 A change-of-name document is issued by the District Court of Las Animas County, Colorado, changing the names of Judias, James, and Kimberly Morris to Buenoano, a Spanish equivalent of Goodyear

6-78 Judias Buenoano purchases house at 2812 Whisper Pine Drive, Gulf Breeze, Florida and returns to Pensacola with her three children

Edgar returned the background file on Judias to his desk. As the Book says, he thought to himself, "The righteous move bold as a lion, but the wicked flee when no man

pursueth." Edgar placed the three life insurance policies
on Bobby Joe Morris side by side. Item A, he observed,
forged signatures; item B, lies and misrepresentations; item
C, the policies were all taken out at about the same time.
Edgar picked up his phone and called Lou Girodo. An
official investigation by the Colorado State Attorney's
office into the death of Bobby Joe Morris was under way;
preparations for the exhumation of Morris's body had
begun.

On November 22, 1983, Ted Chamberlain contacted Mr.
Vagshaw of the Naval Intelligence Service in Pensacola,
asking him to procure any autopsy records and paraffin
blocks containing tissue samples from the autopsy of James
Edgar Goodyear, deceased September 15, 1971, at the U.S.
Naval Hospital in Orlando, Florida.

That same afternoon, Chamberlain called James E.
Goodyear's sister, Peggy Goeller, at her home in Homossassa, Florida. Peggy Goeller stated that her brother, James,
married Judy, a nurse, while he was stationed with the air
force in Roswell, New Mexico, in 1962. Judy had a baby
boy named Mike, whom James adopted. After they were
married, Judy and James had a son, Jim, and a daughter,
Kim. Later they moved to Orlando, Florida. Her brother
had always been in good health, Peggy stated. James
returned from Vietnam in June 1971 and died in Orlando
in September 1971. In 1972 Judy called and said her house
had burned down. She borrowed a thousand dollars from
James's father. Shortly afterward, Judy moved away from
Orlando and no one could find her. Peggy's husband, Ted
Goeller, found Judy in Colorado through James's military
ID number. They sent a letter to Judy asking her to call.
James's father wanted to know how his grandchildren were.
Judy called, assuring them of the children's welfare. The
next time they heard from Judy, she was living in Pensacola,
Florida. Judy informed Peggy and her family that her son
Michael had died in the service in a "germ-warfare game."
James's father had traveled to Pensacola to visit Michael's

grave site. When asked if she knew if Michael had ever been on any medication, Peggy said that Judy had told her that Michael was overactive and very hyper and had been given medication by a hospital in Miami. She never could believe half the things Judy told her, Peggy Goeller concluded.

Locating Judias Buenoano's father, in Elmore City, Oklahoma, where he was known as Jesse Wayne Welty, Chamberlain requested that a special agent from the Oklahoma City Police interview Mr. Welty. According to the interview report, Anna Lou Welty, aka Judias Buenoano, was born on April 4, 1942, in Quanah, Texas. Mr. Welty said that after the war, around 1946, his wife died, and Ann, being the youngest of their four children, went to live with her grandparents in Texas. Mr. Welty said that when Ann was about ten years old, he got her back from her grandparents, and she lived with him in Roswell, New Mexico. Welty stated that while Ann was living with him, she was never in any trouble, but she told some lies. Welty said Ann stayed with him in Roswell until she married James Goodyear. They dated about three months and were married at Roswell Air Force Base sometime in 1962. They stayed in Roswell until James was transferred to Nebraska in 1963. Mr. Welty did not hear from Ann until sometime in 1978, when she moved from Colorado to Florida. She came through Oklahoma with her three children, Jim, Kimberly, and Mike, and stayed for just a few hours. The last time Mr. Welty heard from Ann was a Christmas card shortly after she moved to Florida.

Mr. Welty's oldest son, Jessie Wayne Welty, Jr., was also interviewed. Jessie said he did not grow up with his sister, Ann, as he was living with his father in Roswell while Ann was at her grandparents'. He went into the army in 1948, returned in 1951, got married, and moved away. Jessie Welty said that when he returned to Roswell in 1961, Ann had an illegitimate child named Mike. Ann worked as a waitress and then as a nurse at the hospital in Roswell. She married James Goodyear and moved sometime later to Nebraska. Jessie Welty received occasional letters from Ann. He heard she moved to Florida and that James Goodyear was in the hospital. Ann did not tell him that James had died. The last Jessie Wayne Welty had heard from Ann was in 1975, when she sent a graduation card to his daughter. She had written that she was married to Bob Morris and living in Pensacola, Florida.

Mr. Welty's younger son, Gerald Welty, was interviewed as well. Gerald stated that he saw his sister, Ann, occasionally in the early fifties, when she was living with her grandparents in Vernon, Texas. He sent Ann money for her graduation from Highland Hills High School in Albuquerque, New Mexico, in 1958, while he was in the armed services. When he returned to Roswell, New Mexico, in 1961, Ann had her son Mike. Gerald stated that Mike was named after his father, Arthur Michael Schultz, who was in the air force. Ann was working as a nurse at the Eastern New Mexico Medical Center in Roswell at the time. In 1962, Ann married James Goodyear. Gerald stayed with Ann and James Goodyear while he was on leave and noticed nothing unusual in Ann's behavior. In 1963, James Goodyear, who was in the air force, was transferred to Nebraska. James and Ann moved back to Roswell in 1965 and lived in a trailer house. Gerald had dinner with them occasionally. In 1966, James and Ann had their first son, Jim, and bought a house in Roswell. In 1967, James and Ann moved to Orlando, Florida. Gerald received a few letters and pictures from them. In early 1971, James Goodyear died. In September 1971, Ann drove to Oklahoma with her son Jim, daughter Kimberly, and a younger female companion she introduced as her secretary. They spent the night with Jessie Wayne Welty, Jr. In 1977, Gerald received a letter from Ann saying she was with a guy named Bobby Morris, who had a ranch in Colorado. The next letter said she was divorced from Bobby Morris. In June 1978, Ann came through Oklahoma with her three children on her way from Trinidad, Colorado, to Pensacola, Florida. They stayed a few hours and left. Gerald Welty received a few letters from Ann after her last visit and a picture of Mike Goodyear in the service. He had not heard from her since.

Pursuing their ongoing investigation into the elusive past of Judias Buenoano—aka Judias Morris, Judy Goodyear, Ann Schultz, and Ann Lou Welty—Ted Chamberlain and Bob Cousson had prepared a report on Judias's firstborn son, Michael Buenoano Goodyear:

Born Michael Arthur Schultz on March 30, 1961, to Ann Lou Welty (age nineteen) in Roswell, New Mexico. According to Chavez County, New Mexico, marriage license, Ann Schultz (Ann Lou Welty) married James E. Goodyear on January 19, 1962, in Roswell, New Mexico. James E. Goodyear adopted Michael Arthur Schultz, changing his name to Goodyear in 1966. On January 16, 1966, Michael's half brother, James Goodyear, was born. In 1967, the Goodyears moved to Orlando, Florida, where Kimberly Goodyear was born. At age six, Michael started school in the Orlando area, where he was diagnosed as a problem student. Michael was evaluated by a psychiatrist at the Orange County Hospital in Orlando and placed in special psychiatric programs. Michael's IQ was evaluated in the dull-to-normal range between 85 and 91, which was too high for him to be placed in a facility for retarded children. Michael spent the next four years in the Montanari Residential Treatment Center for Disturbed Children in Hialeah, Florida, until he no longer qualified for military dependent's benefits. On September 15, 1971, Michael's stepfather, James E. Goodyear, died of mysterious causes. In 1974 Michael was sent to the Florida State Hospital in Chattahoochee, Florida, where he was reevaluated and released to his mother, Judy Goodyear, in Pensacola, Florida. Michael's mother had him reevaluated at the Escambia County Mental Health Center and placed under foster care and continued psychiatric therapy. . . .

A family social worker had made a report on a follow-up visit to Judy Goodyear's home in Pensacola, Florida, on August 28, 1975:

On August 28 this worker met with Mrs. Judy Goodyear in her home in Pensacola. The home is a two-story brick structure in an upper-middle-class neighborhood. It is very stylishly furnished and carpeted, and the home plays a commanding role in Mrs. Goodyear's personal estimation of success. Quite a lengthy discussion centered on Michael's problems and the ensuing grief it has brought the family. Michael's father died as a result of a disease after serving in Vietnam. Michael's mother is a nurse with an MA degree. There are two younger children, James, 9, and Kimberly, 8, living at home. The mother states that these children are "normal" in every way, and she has had no problem disciplining or controlling them. Mrs. Goodyear also shares the house with her brother, Bobby Morris, a building contractor. He briefly chatted with us before continuing his work in the garage. Mr. Morris is a large-frame, "lumberjack"-appearing man. He was friendly and does spend constructive time with Michael. They especially like to fish together. Michael accepts Mr. Morris's authority fairly well, but not as well as her own, states the mother. When Mrs. Goodyear works, often the three-to-eleven shift, Mr. Morris is the adult figure in the home.

The family chose to move from Orlando, where Mr. Goodyear died, to Pensacola, where housing was not so expensive. Mrs. Goodyear was very annoyed that her friends in Orlando had ignored her and the children while her husband was in Vietnam but after his death began to invite her out more. She claims that she does not hold grudges in any situation. She does get mad, but gets over it quickly.

From the time Michael was nine months old, it was apparent that he had many problems. He would not listen to his parents, had very poor eyesight, was uncoordinated, and frequently destroyed things. He had a speech problem that was corrected in a school for the deaf by the use of decibel earmuffs. Michael's hearing was tested as normal. During her pregnancy with Michael, Mrs. Goodyear worked as a nurse and was indirectly exposed to X-rays. She suspected that perhaps this exposure affected her unborn child. Michael's delivery, however, was normal. Michael was enrolled in the Gatewood School in Orlando, Florida, and was later placed in the Montanari Center in Hialeah, Florida, from age eight to almost thirteen. He was then transferred to the state hospital at Chattahoochee. According to Mrs. Goodyear, Michael was very violent before going to Chattahoochee and was also incontinent. Both of these problems have been subdued to a great degree. As Mrs. Goodyear spoke of Michael's escapades, it was generally in terms of how much it had cost her, which shows where her values are at this point. This led this worker to explore just what her childhood was like.

Mrs. Goodyear is an attractive lady of about thirty-two years. She is a fairly tall, large-boned woman, which became more evident as she discussed her Indian heritage. Mrs. Goodyear's parents were full-blooded Mesquite Apache Indians. She is the great-granddaughter to Geronimo. Her mother died of tuberculosis when Judy was only eighteen months old. Judy's two older brothers were placed out for adoption. She went to live with her grandparents because she was too young for the orphanage. At age twelve, she too went to an orphanage. Her father had remarried and took her to live with his new wife and her children. Here, she states, she was treated as an inferior, almost as a servant. She was forced to miss meals. Even though she was denied the meal, she had to sit at the table and watch the rest of the family eat. Finally, a blowup occurred. She threw hot grease on two of the children and got into a fight with her stepmother. For this she was taken to jail to spend sixty days in a locked cell. When asked by the judge whether or not she wanted to return home, she said she didn't. She was placed in a county welfare home for children until she graduated from high school at age sixteen. She had made good grades and received a scholarship in the field of nursing. She married Mr. Goodyear at age eighteen and finished her nursing education while they were stationed in Lincoln, Nebraska.

Mrs. Goodyear talked extensively about the fact that Michael would have to learn to fit into their environment and pattern of living. She would not have his behavior 'ruining' what she had been able to accomplish with her other two children. She sincerely feels that if he cannot fit into their family as it is now, he should be placed in a family where there are no other children to compete with him for attention. In view of her own background of family rejection and extreme poverty, we can see the source of her bitterness and hostility as well as her overcompensation with material goods.

Mrs. Goodyear does not know how to control Michael. She does far-out things in retaliation to his actions. For example, once Michael was pawing through the kitchen cabinets. She asked him to stop, and when he didn't, she flew into a rage and threw all the contents of the kitchen cabinets into the trash compactor. She says she has caught Michael in homosexual acts, and has come down on him very hard for that. She does let him know what is expected and what behavior will not be tolerated but does not effectively deal with his defiance of her wishes. She states that Michael has never been afraid of anything and doesn't have good sense when it comes to his own safety. She seems unable to be positive in her approach to Michael, although she is constantly setting limits. She needs, I feel, to set them in love, and not out of fear or anger. We did not talk about rejection per se, but indeed it is there. Her own self-image is not strong. . . . She is not facing reality much of the time. She could benefit by learning constructive responses to acts [such] as Michael's frequently losing or breaking his eyeglasses. This first meeting was used to establish rapport and determine the problems. Only a minimum of treatment goals were set.

In 1977, Michael moved with his family to Trinidad, Colorado, where they lived with Bobby Joe Morris until Morris's death in January 1978. Michael continued psychiatric treatment in Trinidad. In May 1978, Michael's family name was legally changed to Buenoano, and the family returned to Pensacola, Florida, purchasing a home in Gulf Breeze.

Michael attended Gulf Breeze High School but dropped out after the tenth grade. In June 1979, he joined the U.S.

Army, requesting that he work in the water purification field. In July 1979, Michael received treatment at an army hospital for numbness of toes and was returned to duty. After basic training, Michael attended water purification school at Fort Leonard Wood, Missouri, from October 1 to October 26, 1979. While at the school, Michael inhaled chlorine gas, was treated at the base hospital, and was returned to duty the following day. The school included forty hours of instruction on the handling of arsenic compounds.

At the completion of his training, Michael appeared to be in good health. He was assigned to permanent duty at Fort Benning, Georgia, on November 6, 1979. He is believed to have visited his mother in Gulf Breeze, Florida, en route to Fort Benning. Michael reported to Fort Benning on November 6, 1979, already suffering from classic symptoms of metal-base poisoning, which normally show within seventy-two hours of their administration. The symptoms had begun, Michael said, on November 1.

Within six weeks of entering the hospital, Michael's lower legs and arm muscles had atrophied to the point that he could neither walk nor use his hands. Doctors at Walter Reed Hospital discovered that Michael's body contained seven times the normal arsenic levels. His condition would not get any better or any worse. The leg braces and prosthetic hand device Michael wore weighed altogether over sixty pounds. Michael could not have swum with or without these devices.

Acting on Chamberlain's and Cousson's strong suspicions, Assistant State Attorney Russ Edgar officially reopened the 1980 drowning case of Michael Buenoano Goodyear. The deaths of Bobby Joe Morris and James E. Goodyear may have been outside Edgar's jurisdiction, but Michael's drowning had occurred in Santa Rosa County's East River on the outskirts of Milton, Florida, right in Edgar's own backyard.

An article in the *Pensacola News Journal* on May 14, 1980, headlined "Water Mishap," described the accident.

A paraplegic died in a boating accident on the East River near Highway 87 bridge Tuesday afternoon. Dead is Michael Buenoano, 19, a military veteran of 2812 Whispering Pines Drive, Gulf Breeze. A brother of the victim, James Buenoano, 14, was injured in the mishap, but was treated and released from West Florida Hospital.

According to Santa Rosa County Sheriff's Lt. Ron Boswell, the Buenoano brothers, along with their mother, Dr. Judias Buenoano, had been on a canoe expedition on the East River when the boat apparently struck a submerged object and overturned. The accident occurred about three P.M.

Dr. Buenoano and James managed to swim to a passing boat and were rescued, but the older youth disappeared under the water. It was at first feared James Buenoano had suffered severe back injuries, but this proved untrue.

Boswell said nineteen-year-old Michael wore braces on both legs and on one arm. His body was found at seven P.M. by members of the Santa Rosa search and rescue team about three-quarters of a mile upstream.

Dr. Buenoano is a clinical physician at the alcoholic rehabilitation center at Fort Walton Beach.

Edgar put the *Journal* article aside. Presumably, Michael Buenoano Goodyear had received a military burial in Barrancas National Cemetery at the U.S. Naval Air Station in Pensacola. No obituary had been published.

Edgar turned his attention to the latest files on his desk. Through court orders releasing military personnel and medical records, he had obtained the complete army casualty report investigating the facts and circumstances surrounding the death of PV2 Michael B. Goodyear.

Appointed investigating officer by the assistant adjutant general of the army headquarters at Fort Rucker, Alabama, on May 21, 1980, Capt. Paul D. Carmichael had begun his official investigation into the drowning of Private Michael B. Goodyear on the morning of May 27, 1980, with a telephone call to Michael's mother, Mrs. Judias Buenoano, at her home in Gulf Breeze, Florida.

Asked to describe the circumstances of her son's drowning, Judias Buenoano had replied that they were fishing on the East River on May 13, 1980, at about three-thirty P.M. in a sixteen-foot canoe. There were three people in the canoe—herself, Michael's younger brother, James, fourteen, and Michael, nineteen. They all had on life jackets, Judias stated. When asked how the craft overturned, Judias replied that the tide was going out; the canoe struck a submerged log and tipped over. James's seventh cervical vertebra was fractured in two places, Judias added.

"Were there any rocks or rapids in the river?" Carmichael asked. "No," she replied. Michael was in leg braces for "weak ankles and knees" from a chemical explosion in Fort Leonard Wood, Missouri, Judias explained, but he could walk with crutches.

After the craft turned over, Judias said, she came up and found James facedown in the weeds, recovered him, and looked for Michael, with no results. They could not go ashore there, she stated, because of the marsh, so she swam with James for one mile, where the two were recovered by a boater. Judias further stated that Santa Rosa Search and Rescue divers first found life jackets, followed by Michael's glasses, then three-quarters of a mile down the river, Michael's body.

Asked if she could swim against the river's current, Judias answered, "No, it was too strong," so she swam downstream. They had been fishing for six hours up and down the river, also visiting friends. No one expects such a thing to happen, Judias said.

"Are you certain about the life jackets?" Carmichael reiterated. "Yes, they were white," Judias insisted. She made an identification of Michael's body that evening. She was bruised all over, Judias added, not from having hit anything in the water but from the rescue by the boater who picked them up.

"Mother very calm, no outward emotion," Captain Carmichael had noted on his report. He proceeded to call Lt. Ron Boswell of the Santa Rosa Sheriff's Department in Milton, Florida.

"Are you investigating the death of Michael Goodyear?" Carmichael began.

"Yes," Boswell replied.

"Was it a drowning at fifteen-thirty hours on May thirteen on East River?"

"Apparently."

"How many on board?"

"Three. Michael Goodyear, his mother, and younger brother, James Buenoano."

"Did they have belts?"

"The mother and younger brother had on water-ski belts, but the victim had no belt."

"Wasn't a belt found by Santa Rosa Search and Rescue?"

"No."

"Who did the on-site investigation?"

"Deputy Billy Jenkins and Lieutenant Aiken."

Lieutenant Boswell stated that the victim had full leg braces and a prosthesis which connected the right arm to the left so the muscles of the left arm controlled the right hand. The victim was wearing shorts, no shirt, and black military shoes, no socks. The body was received by Assistant Medical Examiner Dr. Nicholson. His preliminary finding was death by drowning.

"Do you think the boy could have possibly been able to swim?" Carmichael asked.

"Absolutely not," Lieutenant Boswell answered. "This was very reckless. The worst I've seen. I do not see how his mother could have done this. She has a Ph.D. in counseling and works at the Rehabilitation Center in Fort Walton Beach."

"Was the brother, James, injured?"

"Yes, allegedly so, but examined and released."

"Who picked up Mrs. Buenoano and James?"

"Ricky Hicks, number two Woodlawn, no phone." It was rumored that there was bad blood between mother and son, he went on, but not confirmed. He would send his report and a copy of the autopsy ASAP. Because of the circumstances, Dr. Nicholson was going to perform a full autopsy.

"Helpful, could not believe circumstances," Carmichael noted, and called Lieutenant Aiken of the Santa Rosa sheriff's department.

Aiken had investigated the circumstances of the accident. "They were casting, and the lines got hung on a tree on the bank. Someone stood up to retrieve the line and the craft tipped over," he explained.

When told Mrs. Buenoano's explanation that the craft struck a submerged object, Aiken became very defensive. He knew that his version was correct, he said, as the body was found right where the fishing float was found in the tree.

"Did the victim have a life jacket?" Carmichael continued.

"Yes, but it came off and was found by Santa Rosa Search and Rescue," Aiken replied.

"Are you sure that belt was found?" Carmichael pressed.

"No," Aiken admitted.

"Did you question Mrs. Buenoano?"

"Yes."

"Did you question James Buenoano?"

"No, there was no need. There is no misconduct."

Carmichael explained to Aiken that he was not concerned with any criminal misconduct. He was simply gathering the facts to determine whether Michael Goodyear was negligent in riding in a canoe. Whether he was or was not wearing a safety belt could be important. Lieutenant Aiken agreed to question James Buenoano and the Santa Rosa Search and Rescue team to confirm the fact.

"Very defensive. Lt. Aiken obviously feels that his investigation was poor at least," Carmichael concluded in his report.

Next day, May 28, 1980, Captain Carmichael spoke with Specialist Fourth Class Cooper of the Walter Reed Army Medical Center. Cooper confirmed that Michael Goodyear had been transferred to the VA Hospital in Tampa, Florida, pending medical discharge. PV2 Goodyear left the hospital in a wheelchair with a prosthetic device connected to his arms. Michael Goodyear told Cooper that he had been poisoned several times with arsenic, resulting in his injuries.

Dr. Nicholson, the assistant medical examiner at Sacred Heart Hospital in Pensacola, stated that his autopsy on Michael Goodyear was not complete; however, the results so far indicated the cause of death as drowning. No alcohol or drugs were found. The victim showed severe muscular atrophy of hands, feet, and lower legs and arms and could not possibly swim.

On May 29, 1980, Captain Carmichael again spoke with Lieutenant Aiken.

"Did the Santa Rosa Search and Rescue divers find the life preservers?" Carmichael asked again.

"Two were found," Aiken replied. "One was opened and one was closed. Mrs. Buenoano confirms that one was on Michael when the craft overturned."

"Did you interview James Buenoano?"

"Yes. He says that Michael was wearing a preserver also," Aiken stated.

That afternoon, Carmichael spoke with Joe Diamond, a local diver working with the Santa Rosa Search and Rescue Unit.

"Did you recover Michael Goodyear's body?" Carmichael asked Diamond.

"Yes, myself and two other divers. I was the first to locate him."

"Was the victim wearing braces?"

"Yes, he had braces on both legs and a brace on one of his arms, I can't remember which one."

"Did the victim have a life preserver on?"

"No, but they said he was wearing a ski-belt type of preserver when the craft overturned. They found one ski belt down the river."

"How did the craft overturn?"

"I heard that it happened when a snake entered the boat, or when they were struck by a tree limb."

"Do you think that the victim could swim?"

"Absolutely not. He only weighed one-hundred-twenty-five pounds and was wearing a lot of weight in braces. Even the ski belt could not have kept him afloat. He went straight to the bottom. The others who pulled him into the boat even commented on the excessive weight," said Diamond.

Carmichael called Judias Buenoano a second time.

"Are you sure that Michael was wearing a ski belt?" he asked her.

"Yes, I put it on him myself," Judias answered.

"Did you see the belt come off during the time the craft was overturning?"

"No."

"How did the craft overturn?"

"It hit a submerged object."

"Did you see this object?"

"No, not until I returned with the sheriff. It was like a limb."

"Was that Lieutenant Aiken?"

"I can't remember. There were a lot of people there."

"Was there a fishing line hung in the tree there?"

"Yes."

"Was that your line?"

"Yes. We lost it just before we overturned."

"Were you hesitant about taking your son out in a canoe in his condition?"

"No. If I showed him any fear, it would discourage him, and he could do almost anything."

"Didn't he also have a brace on his arm as well as both legs?"

"Yes, but he could even paddle the canoe with it."

"Did you think he could float with just a ski belt on?"

"Yes, there was no reason why he should not have stayed afloat."

"How is James?"

"Okay. He has to wear a temporary neck brace part of the time," Judias concluded.

Carmichael then spoke with Dr. Waters, Michael Goodyear's examining physician at Walter Reed Army Medical Center. Dr. Waters recalled Michael Goodyear's severe muscular atrophy. Even his head and neck muscles were weak; he had poor head control. He had no significant mental difficulties. Asked how a chemical explosion had caused Michael's injuries, as his mother had stated, Dr. Waters explained that Michael had been assigned as a water purification specialist at Fort Leonard Wood, Missouri, to attend school. While cleaning out a water storage tank, he had inhaled chlorine fumes and been treated for about a week for respiratory difficulties. This episode had nothing to do with his partial paralysis. When Michael was assigned to Fort Benning, Georgia, he complained of tingling sensations in his hands. Due to apparent instability, Michael was admitted to a psychiatric ward. He remained there for a couple of months before he was finally referred to neurology and it was discovered that he had a "real" muscular problem. When he was referred to Walter Reed Army Medical Center, white markings on his fingernails indicative of arsenic poisoning were discovered. It was also noticed that Michael suffered from "pica syndrome" and unconsciously put things in his mouth. The criminal investigation division was contacted at Fort Leonard Wood, Missouri. Their investigation revealed that during his training in water purification school, Michael did daily lab work using samples of sodium arsenite, a colorless, tasteless liquid. Each of the pint bottles used in the lab contained enough arsenic to kill 250 people. The CID found no evidence of intentional poisoning by other persons and stated that Michael had probably ingested enough arsenic during his two weeks of school, either by sampling the solution or unconsciously putting his unclean hands into his mouth, to cause the arsenic poisoning. The time frame that Michael was at water purification school agrees with the time established by medical examination of his fingernails. His mother knew Michael could not swim; she also knew that his condition was not due to a chemical accident, Dr. Waters stated.

That afternoon, Captain Carmichael received a telephone call from Dr. Michael Barry, Michael Goodyear's attending intern at Walter Reed.

"I called you as I heard you were doing the death investigation of Michael Goodyear," Dr. Barry began. "I was Michael's assigned intern and I talked with the boy's mother on at least three occasions. I always felt she was rather cold and indifferent. For example, she told me that she was having over forty thousand dollars' worth of renovations done to her house to include a sunken pool, new bathroom with a sunken bath, et cetera, for Michael. She also said that she was independently wealthy and would quit working when Michael came home. She said the renovations would be completed no later than May 1, 1980. Even with all her supposed money, I never could get her to come out and see Michael, even when he lost hope and was dying from refusing to eat. Why didn't she come? She should be investigated for at least criminal neglect for putting him in that boat. She knew better and had no right to do so. I would say that if you visited her home, you would find that none of the renovations she talked about were ever done to the house. I think she might have planned the accident."

On May 30, 1980, Judias Buenoano Goodyear submitted a sworn handwritten statement to the army investigating officer:

> I, Judias Buenoano Goodyear, want to make the following statement under oath: Michael Buenoano Goodyear had been canoeing and fishing since age two. His whole life has been spent in water sports. He has canoed every river in Florida; traveled the Mississippi on a trip for 90 days from St. Paul, Minnesota, to New Orleans; traveled the Colorado River; skied, surfed, scuba dived. All he could talk about was coming home and going out in his canoe fishing. It was his whole life, one of the only things left he could enjoy. He was no longer able to play football, basketball, ski, surf, scuba dive or ride his motorcycle. But canoe, fish and swim he was sure he could do, and was going to do if I didn't take him. He said, "Some of my high

school friends will." He called me at work many times. My aides and other staff nurses talked to him and heard me talking to him, assuring him I would take him fishing and out in his canoe as soon as he came home. His calls were always about some wild fishing trip he was planning when he came home. Mike had a ski belt when the accident happened. He has always refused to wear any other type of life preserver, stating that they hurt him. None of our family ever wear anything but ski belts. And I honestly didn't know that they were not Coast Guard approved until the Santa Rosa Sheriff's Department on May 27th informed me that the labels were misleading. The accident happened about 3:25 P.M. on May 13, 1980. We had been fishing for about six hours. After Mike got his line hung up in a tree, I pulled it off, restrung the line. He fished another treetop that he hung it on, and we started for the dock. I heard a thump, and the canoe started turning. It happened so fast, throwing us out of the canoe. When I surfaced, I looked around for the boys. I finally spotted James lying upside down in the water. I turned him over and cleared his airway, got him to breathing, hung him on a limb, and looked for Mike. I could see nothing, the water was so dark. I got Jim and started swimming down stream. A boat came from nowhere. He helped Jim and I in and took us to the dock, where he called for help. James was taken to the hospital, treated for hairline fractures of the 7 C.V. and released. In summing it up, all I can say is, I thought the ski belts were safe. I really do not know why we capsized, maybe there was more weight on one side, so when we hit the log it turned. All I can say is I will carry this great burden of guilt that, unknowing, I caused his death out of a misleading label on life saving equipment. We loved him very much and it is a great loss to our family.

On May 31, 1980, James Buenoano Goodyear submitted a hand-printed sworn statement:

My big brother and I have canoed, fished, skied, surfed, rode motorcycles and hunted together ever since I can remember. When my brother was in the hospital, he called us every day. All he could think about was going canoeing, fishing, and me riding him on the motorcycle, or him modifying his motorcycle so he could ride it. On May 13, we were fishing in the East River in Mike's canoe when we hit a log. Most of our own weight was on the one side, causing us to turn over. The canoe struck me in the neck. Next thing I can recall was the ambulance taking me to the hospital, where I was treated for hairline fractures of the 7th C. vertebrae and released c̄ a soft neck brace.

On June 3, 1980, Sergeant Forbie Hiram Privette of the Santa Rosa County Sheriff's Department submitted a sworn statement in which he noted that Hicks "had heard the mother calling for help and had taken his bass boat up the river and pulled the mother and younger brother on board and took them ashore." Searching the area with Hicks, Privette had recovered an overturned canoe, two ski jackets, and a shower clog floating in the water. One ski belt was open, the other fastened into a circle. He saw no other safety devices.

The canoe was a two-man type, and a folding lawn chair had been fastened to the center brace with a small rope to serve as a third seat. "Drowning was termed accidental by the Sheriff's Department," Privette concluded.

The Santa Rosa County Sheriff's Department Investigating Officer's Report submitted by Lt. Ronald Boswell read in full:

Subjects were in a small canoe on East River, ¾ mile east of Hwy. 87 when the canoe overturned. The victim had braces on both legs and when the canoe turned over, the ski belt he was wearing came off and, according to the mother and brother, he sank immediately. Mother and brother continued on westward in the water until they were picked up by Ricky Hicks (2 Woodlawn Dr., Mary Esther, Fla.) who heard them screaming for help. Santa

Rosa Rescue was called to the scene. They searched for the victim and at 18:52 found the victim at the bottom of the river. Body was transported to Santa Rosa Hospital, Milton, Florida by Medical II per instructions of Lt. Boswell who met them at the hospital. Details: Accidental drowning in East River after canoe in which deceased was riding struck a submerged log and turned over.

On June 9, 1980, Captain Paul Carmichael submitted his final investigation of death report on Private Michael B. Goodyear. The report concluded:

Inspection of the accident site on the river along with the deputy who recovered the canoe reveals a calm section with little or no current. The canoe was a two-man variety with one seat at each end and a center cross brace. A short-legged lawn chair was found tied to the center brace and his mother confirms that PV2 Goodyear was sitting in this chair. Both the mother and deputy who handled the case were interviewed. . . . I have reason to doubt the creditability of his mother's statements based on my interview with her. The interview revealed that none of the proposed house modifications she had indicated would be done to Dr. Barry has even been started. Also, judging from the slow moving current in that area of the river, I believe it would be most difficult to turn the canoe over by striking a submerged object. It is more probable that she allowed someone to stand or stood herself to remove a fishing line from the trees and upset the canoe. Additionally, she first stated that they had life jackets on and it later appears to be ski belts. PV2 Goodyear's apparently came off as he sank to the bottom with the weight of his braces and the immobility of either arms or legs.

PV2 Goodyear's decision to go canoeing in his physical condition may evidence a reckless disregard of the possible consequences, but his mother's decision to put him in that canoe with only a ski belt may be considered neglectful, if not bordering on criminal neglect.

Shaking his head slowly, Russ Edgar put down the army casualty report on Michael Buenoano Goodyear. It was a near-perfect case of circumstantial evidence. Circumstantial evidence has to be presented through witnesses; the circumstances have to be presented beyond a reasonable doubt; any circumstance has to be consistent with guilt and inconsistent with innocence. There were enough potential witnesses and circumstantial evidence before him to build a strong case against Judias Buenoano for at least negligent homicide.

Now if he only had the motive. . . .

11

"Take Judias Buenoano..."

"MA'AM, IF I HAD the claim number, I wouldn't be asking you, I'd just be subpoenaing it," Edgar politely told the lady behind the insurance company counter and turned away with a sigh of resignation.

Personal insurance policies were indexed only by claim number, not by name. If Judias had privately insured the life of her son Michael as she had her other victims, he'd have to find out the hard way.

Obtaining the claim file on Michael B. Goodyear's military life insurance had been a simpler matter. Edgar had issued a grand jury subpoena duces tecum to the custodian of records of the Office of Serviceman's Group Life Insurance in Washington, D.C.: "You are hereby commanded to be and appear before the Honorable Russell G. Edgar, Jr., Assistant State Attorney in and for Escambia County, Florida, at First Floor Judicial Complex, Government and Spring Streets, on January 3, 1984, to testify, and the truth to speak, in a certain matter pending and under investigation."

According to the OSGLI claim file, on June 4, 1980, Judias Buenoano had received a letter from Winfred S. Gideon III, director of OSGLI, extending his deepest sympathy for the loss of her son, Michael Buenoano Goodyear, and informing her that a review of his military records certified that at the time of his death, her son was insured for twenty thousand dollars under the Serviceman's Group Life Insurance Program. She was to complete the attached claim form and return it to the OSGLI in the enclosed postage-paid envelope, along with the insured's birth certificate and advisement of the relationship of Ann Lou Welty to the insured.

On June 18, 1980, Judias received acknowledgment of her claim form from the OSGLI director. He assured her that the matter was receiving attention. Accompanying Judias's claim form was a handwritten note stating: "Sirs, Judias Anna Lou Welty Goodyear was [crossed out] is Mike's mother. Now my name is Judias Anna Lou Welty Buenoano. See enclosed birth certificate."

The Certificate of Live Birth from the State of New Mexico, Chaves County, Roswell, that Judias enclosed was apparently forged, for it listed the child's name as Michael Arthur Goodyear, date of birth March 30, 1961; father of child: James E. Goodyear, age twenty-seven, USAF; mother of child: Ann Lou Welty, age nineteen; informants: Parents, Roswell, New Mexico.

As OSGLI departmental memo dated July 28, 1980, stated: "The Department of Army indicated that 'there may be foul play' in the death of the insured on the part of the next of kin. They also indicated that there may be an illegitimate child. The information about an illegitimate child has not been confirmed."

A second memo that same day stated: "It appears that death was ruled as 'accidental.' However, to confirm, please write to the sheriff's office and inquire if any criminal charges have been filed. Also, gather usual proof of paternity of illegitimate child."

An additional memo dated July 29, 1980, stated: "The investigative services known as Equifax is also investigating the death. There appear to have been private insurance companies involved."

On July 31, 1980, the OSGLI director sent Judias a third letter stating that their records indicated that the proceeds of Michael's insurance program were to be paid in the order of precedence as set forth "by law": (1) wife, if none to (2) children, if none to (3) parents or survivors of them, if none to (4) insured's estate. Information reviewed by the office indicated that the insured may have been survived by a child. The office requested Judias's cooperation in providing any evidence available regarding said child.

Judias promptly returned the OSGLI letter, having scrawled at the bottom: "Mike was only nineteen; he had no children or was never married."

On August 4, 1980, Judias called the OSGLI regarding their letter of July 31. According to an office memorandum, Judias "stated that her son, Michael, had never married and never had a steady girlfriend; therefore, she knew of no children. She was very upset and contended that other insurance companies had already paid off. She might see her Congressman."

On August 11, 1980, the director of the OSGLI received a statement from Lieutenant Boswell, of the Sheriff's Department of Santa Rosa County, Milton, Florida, confirming that Michael Goodyear's death was accidental: "There is no indication of criminal negligence in this matter."

On September 12, 1980, the OSGLI issued a check in the name of Judias Anna Lou Buenoano in the amount of $20,451.20 in full payment of insurance benefits plus accumulated interest in the death of Michael Buenoano Goodyear.

Convinced from the OSGLI reports that Judias had insured Michael through additional private insurance policies, Edgar proceeded to subpoena every bank account in every bank in Escambia and Santa Rosa Counties—about eighteen banks in Escambia and another half dozen in Santa Rosa. Obtaining all of the banks' signature cards, Edgar identified accounts belonging to Judi Buenoano and subpoenaed all of the bank statements for them. Then he subpoenaed the draft copy of the microfilm of every check over twenty-five-thousand-dollars deposited in those accounts over the past ten years. In the end, Edgar found two insurance company drafts in the amounts of forty-thousand-dollars and thirty-thousand-dollars paid to the order of Judias W. Buenoano. They had been deposited in Judias's local bank account in July and August 1980. Apparently, Judias had collected over ninety-thousand-dollars in insurance benefits through the death of her son.

When he had finally obtained the policy claim numbers from the encashed insurance checks—the process took several weeks—Edgar sent photocopies of the checks along with a letter to the insurance companies explaining that he was investigating a possible insurance fraud case. After that, to say that he received cooperation would be an understatement.

Edgar studied the application for insurance that he received from Prudential Insurance Company of America with growing excitement. Michael Buenoano, the proposed insured, had been approved for a modified 25–10 life insurance policy in the initial amount of twenty thousand dollars and an accidental death coverage of twenty thousand dollars, with an option to purchase additional coverage in the amount of twenty thousand to understate the matter. The applicant and beneficiary was designated Judias W. Buenoano, mother, age thirty-five. The application, made in Pensacola, Florida, and dated October 8, 1979, was signed by the proposed insured, Michael Buenoano, and by the applicant, Judias Buenoano, and was witnessed by the insurance agent, Donald J. Fournier.

Two things immediately leaped out at Edgar: The date of the application made in Pensacola fell within the dates when Michael Buenoano Goodyear was attending water purification school in Fort Leonard Wood, Missouri, from October 1 to October 26, 1979. In addition, Michael's signature was *not* misspelled.

Edgar compared the signatures on Michael Buenoano Goodyear's military records with that of the insurance application. Every military form was signed either Michaele B. Goodyear or Michaele Buenoano Goodyear. A statement of name for official military records form dated March 3, 1979, stated that Michael Arthur Goodyear, without having changed his name through any legal procedure, preferred to use the name of Michaele Buenoano Goodyear.

Michael Buenoano's signature on his insurance application had obviously been forged.

Edgar allowed himself a cat-who-ate-the-canary smile. Since he had first opened the drowning case, the other attorneys in the DA's office had discouraged him. Even the judge to whom he had presented the search warrants and affidavits didn't think he had much of a case. Maybe negligent homicide. Edgar knew now that he was looking at the best circumstantial murder case he'd ever had.

On January 6, 1984, Detective Ted Chamberlain spoke with Don Johnson, the instructor at the Water Purification Specialist School in Fort Leonard Wood. According to Johnson, Michael B. Goodyear graduated from the school on October 26, 1979. Students in the school were subjected to sodium arsenite for a total of forty hours of their four weeks' training. They were well supervised and at no time in contact with more than one fluid ounce of the substance. Johnson insisted Goodyear left his school in good health.

Chamberlain also called Michael Goodyear's company commander in Ford Benning, Georgia. "You've restored my faith in justice," the officer told Chamberlain. "I always knew the mother did something to that boy."

Chamberlain spoke with Michael's former coach at Gulf Breeze High School. The coach advised Chamberlain that throughout his enrollment in the tenth grade, Michael had been physically uncoordinated and exhibited no athletic ability or desire to participate in sports of any kind, including water sports.

On January 10, 1984, Russ Edgar issued a subpoena duces tecum to the custodian of records at West Florida Hospital for the medical records of James Buenoano on May 13, 1980.

The ambulance report stated that James Buenoano had been transported to West Florida Hospital in answer to a trauma-to-spinal-cord emergency call and critical fracture-to-neck injury. The victim was dazed and complained of neck pain because he had been hit in the back of the neck when his canoe allegedly ran into another boat and capsized. The victim was immobilized and placed on full backboard in prone position.

The radiology report said: "Lateral swimmer's view shows lower cervical and upper thoracic vertebral bodies to be well aligned with no significant compression, subluxation, or other abnormality. Conclusion: Normal cervical spine. Patient was fitted with a soft cervical collar and released at seven-fifty P.M."

There was no record of a hairline fracture of James Buenoano's seventh cervical vertebra.

Circumstantial evidence notwithstanding, Edgar knew that in order to get a grand jury to indict Judias Buenoano for the first-degree murder of her first-born son, he'd need some critical testimony. He also knew that if he issued the standard grand jury subpoenas to James and Kimberly Buenoano several days in advance, they would consult with their attorney and get their stories together, and he would probably have to give them immunity.

Just before closing in the court clerk's office on January 10, 1984, the day before the grand jury was to be seated at the Santa Rosa County Courthouse in Milton, Edgar issued grand jury subpoenas for James and Kimberly Buenoano. The subpoenas were prevalidated and did not show the court record.

At eight the next morning, after Judias had left her Whisper Bay home for work, James Buenoano was gotten out of bed by a Santa Rosa County police unit. Shortly afterward, Kimberly Buenoano was taken from class at Gulf Breeze High School and escorted with her brother in a marked police car to the Milton courthouse to appear before the grand jury.

James and Kimberly managed to call their attorney, James Johnston, who met them at the courthouse and demanded to speak with his clients. Edgar gave Johnston a few minutes to talk to James and Kimberly, just enough time to tell them to say, "I don't remember."

After Edgar presented the grand jury with documentary evidence of the circumstances of the drowning of Michael Buenoano Goodyear, and the forged insurance policies and supported it with the testimony of Detective Ted Chamberlain, James Buenoano was called into the courtroom.

Edgar showed James the sworn statement he had written to the army investigating office during its inquiry into the death of his brother, Michael, and asked him to read the statement to the grand jury. James stumbled through the handwritten document. He had difficulty pronouncing many of the words. He did not know what some of the words meant. He did not know if the handwriting was his or his mother's. He could not remember any of the circumstances of the drowning. He could not account for anything that had happened on the afternoon of May 13, 1980. James could barely remember his own name.

Kimberly Buenoano was called into the courtroom. Kimberly nervously testified that on May 13, 1980, at the age of twelve, she had sat alone on a secluded dock in the middle of the woods in the middle of the day for five or six hours while her mother and brothers fished on East River.

Meanwhile attorney James Johnston had informed Judias of the grand jury proceedings. She had driven directly from her Fingers N Faces salon to the Milton courthouse. She paced back and forth in the hallway, outside the closed courtroom doors as her children gave their testimony within.

By five o'clock the jury had returned an indictment against Judias A. Buenoano. The Florida First Judicial Circuit Court of Santa Rosa County immediately issued a capias to arrest Judias Buenoano for First Degree Murder and Grand Theft over twenty-thousand-dollars: " . . . These are to command you to take Judias Buenoano, and do safely keep, so that you have her body before the Judge of our Circuit Court, when arrested to answer an Indictment found and now pending. . . ."

By six o'clock, Detective Ted Chamberlain, accompanied

by Special Agent Bob Cousson and Capt. R. E. Cotton of the Santa Rosa County police, was at the front door of 2812 Whisper Pine Drive with a warrant for the arrest of Judias.

Judias appeared in the doorway wearing a blue silk robe, a cigarette holder poised in her perfectly manicured fingertips.

"Judi, you're under arrest," Chamberlain informed her. "Give me a moment to get dressed," Judias replied calmly.

Fifteen minutes later, Judias reappeared in the same white blouse, black skirt, and short mouton jacket she had worn at the Milton courthouse earlier that day. Handcuffed beside Ted Chamberlain in the back of the patrol car, Judias rode in tense silence down the long, straight stretch of County Highway 87 on her way for the second time to the courthouse, which also housed the Santa Rosa County Jail.

Halfway into the forty-five-minute drive to Milton, they crossed the East River Bridge. A quarter of a mile upstream, three and a half years before, Michael Buenoano Goodyear had sunk helplessly to his death. Judias stared straight ahead, avoiding Chamberlain's penetrating glare.

Twenty minutes later, the patrol car pulled to within one hundred yards of the sally port of the squat, unpretentious Santa Rosa County Jail beneath the courthouse in the middle of downtown Milton.

Suddenly Judias broke into a wild convulsion. Her whole body began jerking spasmodically in what appeared to be some sort of seizure. Pulling her from the back of the patrol car, Chamberlain wrestled with Judias's fitful contortions, forcing her face down on the driveway. Straddled over Judias's prone, struggling, sweat-drenched body, Chamberlain was overwhelmed by the powerful odor of animal fear she exuded.

"Look, woman," Chamberlain panted, "there's nothing wrong with you. You're going to jail if I have to strap you to a backboard and carry you in."

At seven P.M. Judias was strapped to a hospital trolley and transported by ambulance to the Santa Rosa Hospital Emergency Room. Special Agent Bob Cousson and Officer Nancy Cabannis of the Pensacola Police rode in the ambulance with Judias. Detective Ted Chamberlain followed in an unmarked police car.

"Oh, Nancy," Judias sobbed, clutching onto Officer Cabannis's arm, "how can they do this to me? I would never do anything to harm them; I love my children. . . ."

Officer Cabannis murmured vague reassurances, attempting to calm the hysterical prisoner. It had been over a year since she had first met "Dr." Judias Buenoano in the summer of 1982 under very different circumstances. . . .

Susan Williams, an employee at Judias's Finger N Faces salon, had suggested that Nancy and a mutual friend join them on a bargain-rate Caribbean cruise. Judias was generously paying Susan's fare, and they needed two more people to share a cabin. Due for a vacation, Nancy and her fellow officer, Barbara, agreed to go along.

Judias and her entourage arrived at the airport for the preliminary flight to Miami with champagne for everyone. Judias was with her two children, James, fifteen, and Kimberly, fourteen, and her boyfriend, John Gentry. Gentry had seemed overwhelmed by Judias. At her beck and call, he remained largely in the background throughout the cruise. James and Kimberly were allowed to run wild, smoking cigarettes and roaming over the ship. James, Nancy noticed, exhibited a remarkable assurance with older women on the cruise. He knew just when to laugh, and seemed experienced beyond his years. Obviously Judias's favorite, James was well on his way to becoming an accomplished young con-artist. Susan Williams dutifully played the devoted groupie.

Possessing a master's degree in counseling and human development, Nancy had observed Judias's control-oriented behavior from the start. Surrounding herself with the gullible and naive, Judias shamelessly manipulated her close circle of admirers, buying their loyalty and affection with flattery and gifts. Judias had to be in charge, and women police officers did not meet the requirements of her mutual admiration society. As tablemates on the cruise, Nancy had asked Judias about her purported doctorate in pathology. An experienced crime-scene officer, Nancy had studied pathology and frequently attended autopsies.

Judias told Nancy that the government frequently contracted her to do pathology work. She was paid the same handsome fee whether it took her three weeks or three months to complete the job. Certainly, she had attended autopsies. Perhaps they could get together and discuss their mutual experiences, Nancy suggested. After that, Judias actively avoided Nancy, excusing herself to go to the gambling tables whenever the two of them were alone. Nancy felt there was something wrong with Judias's story at the time, that she was into something illegal, perhaps selling or transporting drugs. But then police officers are naturally suspicious.

Nancy Cabannis searched Judias's contorted, tear-streaked face as she lay strapped on the ambulance stretcher, looking for some clue to her true identity. At the beginning of her seizure, Nancy had lifted Judias's limp arm, letting it drop onto her face to test her degree of control. A person having a real seizure would not consciously stop her hand from hitting her face. Judias had halted her arm in midair. Nancy knew Judias was a very good con-artist. She knew she wouldn't trust Judias or her children as far as she could throw them. If Judias were also a sociopath, then killing someone she had held in her arms would be like squashing a bug.

Upon arrival at the emergency room, Judias was treated and given a full medical examination by Dr. James Estuold. His report stated in part:

Apparently, no history of previous seizure disorder. Reported episodic "shaking" of torso and extremities. Also reports a heaviness in her chest. Patient appears in nervous anxiety disorder. Initially, patient did not communicate, but later verbalized without difficulty. . . . Alert and oriented; central nervous system intact; EKG— sinus tachycardia with some arrhythmia. Impression: Probable hysterical conversion reaction. Patient given 50 mg Vistaril PO and released to SRC Sheriff's officers.

Stating that she was unable to sign her name, Judias gave Captain Cotton permission to sign her medical release form.

Waiting outside the emergency room, Ted Chamberlain called Russ Edgar at the DA's office from the lobby pay phone.

"Hey Russ, Judi pulled one of her 'can't move' routines on the way to jail. She tried to escape and I shot her," Chamberlain joked matter-of-factly.

"Did you kill her?" Edgar asked in alarm, half-believing his hotheaded investigator.

At approximately nine-thirty P.M. Judias was transported back to the Santa Rosa County Jail by Special Agent Charles Griffith, Officer Cabannis, and Captain Cotton and booked on the charge of first-degree murder.

At ten-thirty P.M., Judias was transported in an unmarked police vehicle by Detective Ted Chamberlain and Officer Nancy Cabannis to the Escambia Count Jail in Pensacola to be held without bond until arraignment. There were no permanent facilities for female prisoners at the Santa Rosa County Jail. Five minutes after midnight, a grimly silent Chamberlain remanded a subdued Judias into the custody of the Escambia County Sheriff's officers.

From the second-floor window of the Escambia County Jail, Judias looked down at Ted Chamberlain dragging on a cigarette in the parking lot below.

"There he is," Judias said bitterly, "that Chamberlain. He's after me."

Judias paused for a moment and then resolved, "I'll see him ten feet under with the worms crawling through his eyes." The prison matron led her away to her cell.

On January 25, 1984, written permission was obtained from Lodell Morris and a permit received from the State of Alabama to exhume the remains of Bobby Joe Morris. The district attorney's office in Trinidad, Colorado, having found evidence that Bobby Joe Morris's signature had been forged on two life insurance applications made by Judias A. Morris in 1977, had issued an order to compel.

At seven-thirty on the morning of January 26, 1984, Captain George Underwood of the Pensacola Police Department and Officer Nancy Cabannis, along with detectives Rick Steele and Ted Chamberlain, left the Pensacola Police Department parking lot headed for Brewton, Alabama.

"I thought I told you to put a lid on this case weeks ago, Geronimo," Captain Underwood growled.

"Yes, sir, you did. But we keep finding more victims," Chamberlain replied.

"You'll have us digging up bodies from here to Alaska. It's costing the department a bundle. From now on, stay in your own jurisdiction, Geronimo. That's an order," Underwood concluded.

At the cemetery Steven Bolyard of the district attorney's office in Pensacola and Investigator Louis P. Girodo of the state attorney's office in Trinidad, Colorado, waited with five workmen of the Harvey Vault Service beneath a large metal scaffold erected over the bronze headsetting inscribed "Morris." A single black vase of red plastic roses graced the barren grave site.

Thick gray clouds hung low in the Alabama winter sky, casting a dismal reflection over the flat brown fields and widely spaced grave markers of Green Acres Memorial Park. An even grimmer cast was lent to the somber face of the small party gathered uneasily around Garden 2, Lot 270, Space 2, where the remains of Bobby Joe Morris had lain for six years. They were about to be exhumed.

It wasn't a cold day, only about fifty-five degrees, but a heavy damp hung in the still morning air. Those without shovels instinctively shoved their hands into their pockets and hunched deeper into their windbreakers.

At nine-fifteen the digging began.

Fifteen minutes of uncomfortable silence passed, punctuated by the uneven thuds of the shovels, before the top of the metal vault was exposed. The workers halted as Girodo, who in his orange baseball cap, khaki jumpsuit, and running shoes bore a striking resemblance to Ted Chamberlain, began carefully taking samples of dirt from the top, head, rear, and sides of the vault.

By ten A.M. the rusting vault, groaning in protest, was slowly wrenched on heavy chains from the open pit of red clay. Girodo jumped into the empty grave to take additional soil samples from beneath the vault. It would be necessary to eliminate the possibility that any arsenic in the surrounding earth had seeped into and contaminated the grave site.

At ten-ten the massive lid was lifted off the vault, and the olive-green metal coffin was removed from its protective shell and set on the ground. The five workers, wanting no part of the next step, promptly disappeared.

Girodo took more samples of the rancid black liquid that had seeped from the coffin into the bottom of the emptied vault. Then, at ten-twenty, the coffin lid was pried open.

Chamberlain stared at what was left of Bobby Joe Morris's face. The features were barely visible beneath the white mold that covered the huge head. Morris had been a big fellow. His six-foot-four frame was tucked tightly into the rotting satin that lined the coffin. The enormous frowning corpse reminded Chamberlain of a melting waxwork of Frankenstein's monster.

"So that's what you look like when you've been dead for six years," Chamberlain thought, and gave an involuntary shudder.

The Brewton chief of police had attended the exhumation to identify Bobby Joe Morris's body, but the only recognizable effect was a white handkerchief in the right jacked pocket bearing the initials B. J. M.

At eleven A.M. the closed coffin was transported from the Brewton cemetery to the US Army Medical Center in Mobile, Alabama. Dr. Reddick conducted the autopsy.

Chamberlain forced himself to watch as Dr. Reddick and his assistants removed the corroded satin pillow from under Bobby Joe Morris's massive head, still covered with a thick crop of black hair, and carefully turned the heavy body over on its side to remove it from the coffin. The skin of the exposed back was like leather. The legs, wrapped in plastic from when the body had been shipped to Brewton for burial, still had meat on the bones.

The body was placed on a stainless steel table and wheeled into X-ray. Comparison with past X-ray records of previous leg fractures would be needed for positive identification of Bobby Joe Morris's body. After removing the clothes from the partially decomposed body, Dr. Reddick took samples of the hair and fingernails and removed the toenails. Opening the body cavity, Dr. Reddick took samples of the liver and kidneys and collected fluids. The lungs had shriveled into three-inch black prunes. Samples of brain tissue were taken from the cranium. The teeth were removed from the detached lower jaw.

At two forty-five P.M., the body was put back into the coffin and the lid resealed. The hair, nail, tissue, and soil samples were delivered to the Alabama and Colorado Toxicological Laboratories to be tested for arsenic content.

Chamberlain drove the sixty miles back to Pensacola with a deeper sense of his own mortality.

On February 1, 1984, the Pensacola Police Department received a phone call from an anonymous woman in Pensacola, stating that she had known Judias Buenoano in 1971 and 1972 and that Buenoano had told her that she used arsenic and lead to poison her husband, James Goodyear. Buenoano had told her she used arsenic and lead because the doctors would not be able to find them in the body. Buenoano had also revealed that she had a friend named Connie who knew about the death of Goodyear, and that Connie was blackmailing her and she was thinking of killing Connie too. The anonymous caller stated that she would come forward and testify, but she was afraid of Judias Buenoano.

Connie was identified as the former Connie Gilmore, whose ex-husband had had an affair with Judias Buenoano in Orlando before James Goodyear's death. George Gilmore had moved to Pensacola soon after Judias had relocated to the city from Orlando. His three-year-old son had died under suspicious circumstances in Pensacola, and Gilmore had relocated to a small suburb in Texas. Connie was living in Dover, Delaware. Plans were made to interview both Gilmores.

On February 11, 1984, Judias Buenoano was arraigned before Judge George E. Lowrey of the First Judicial Circuit on charges of the first-degree murder of Michael B. Goodyear and grand theft over twenty thousand dollars.

Prosecutor Russ Edgar was familiar with Judge Lowrey from his early days with the Pensacola DA's office. In the summer of 1978, he'd gone over to the Milton courthouse to file a complicated complaint, and he'd asked the clerk how they picked the judges there, by computer? The clerk had looked at him and said, "Uh? We only have one judge."

Edgar knew that Judge Lowrey looked askance at granting bond in first-degree murder cases after what had happened just a few months before. In November 1983, four men— two brothers, a father, and a cousin—had been brought before Judge Lowrey on an attempted murder charge. They were ne'er-do-well farmers growing dope instead of soybeans, and they'd caught a local boy stealing their marijuana. They kidnapped the boy at gunpoint, took him to Alabama, wrapped him like a mummy in duct tape, locked him the trunk of his car, and pushed the car into the river. Miraculously, the boy managed to escape. The four men were arrested for kidnapping and attempted murder. Judge

Lowrey reduced their bonds and the men were released on bail.

Three weeks later, the boy, his father, and a friend were ambushed by the clan of four and shot down with a barrage from mini-fourteen assault rifles and 9mm pistols. The father and son were killed; their friend survived to report the murders.

After that, Judge Lowrey wasn't likely to grant bond to anybody in a murder case.

Judias entered a plea of not guilty to the charge of murdering her son.

"No bond," Judge Lowrey ruled.

Without bond, Judias's attorney, James Johnston, demanded a speedy trial.

He had no idea what he was going up against.

By mid-February 1984, verbal confirmation was received from the Alabama Toxicological Laboratory that tissue samples taken from the body of Bobby Joe Morris contained high levels of arsenic, enough to kill eleven men. On February 18, the El Paso County coroner confirmed that lethal amounts of arsenic were found in Morris's liver, brain, and kidneys.

John Barclay, the district attorney in Trinidad, Colorado, announced that he would prepare an indictment against Judias Buenoano for the first-degree murder of Bobby Joe Morris and grand theft insurance fraud.

By the end of February 1984 the paraffin block tissue samples of James E. Goodyear, seized as evidence from the naval hospital in Orlando, Florida, on December 1, 1983, and forwarded to the Naval Intelligence Services (NISRA) in Pensacola, were found to contain traces of arsenic and lead.

Notified by the state attorney's office in Pensacola, Felony Investigator Dusty Rhodes of the ninth Judicial Circuit state attorney's office in Orlando, Florida, opened an investigation into the circumstances of James E. Goodyear's death.

State Attorney Robert Eagan of Orange County, Orlando,

Florida, petitioned the circuit court for an order of exhumation of James E. Goodyear's body. On March 14, 1984, the Orlando authorities exhumed the remains of James Edgar Goodyear, buried twelve and a half years before. The results of the autopsy were pending.

12

"The Taking of a Life"

By TEN O'CLOCK ON THE MILD Thursday morning of March 22, 1984, close to half of the 126 hard wooden seats in the Santa Rosa County Courthouse were filled. A curious mixture of housewives, retirees, and students and a panoply of working press buzzed collectively within the lime-green walls and polished wooden panels of the Milton courthouse.

Intrigued by the real-life melodrama of the mysterious dark-haired, dark-eyed woman with the strange name on trial for her life, dozens of Milton's seventy-two-hundred-plus citizens had forsaken their daytime soaps to witness firsthand the trial of Judias Buenoano for the drowning murder of her nineteen-year-old son, Michael, and the grand theft of over $100,000 in insurance monies collected after his death.

Assistant State Attorney Russell Edgar, Jr., and defense Attorney James A. Johnston had waded through forty prospective jurors when the trial began the day before. By the time court recessed at six-thirty P.M., ten jurors had been seated. Another forty prospects waited to be considered.

Pretrial publicity was the first question. Barely a third of the prospective jurors said they had not heard or read about Judias Buenoano and the trail of suspicious deaths that followed her. Only days before, Donald Dossett of Chassahowizka, Florida, had asked Okaloosa County officials to investigate the death of his brother, Gerald Dossett, a forty-eight-year-old man from Mary Ester, Florida who had dated Judias Buenoano for a year prior to his sudden demise in 1980. Authorities planned to exhume Dossett's body, buried in Fort Walton, Florida.

The second question was the possibility of applying the death penalty. The only two possible sentences for premeditated murder in the State of Florida were life in prison without any possibility of parole for twenty-five years or death in the electric chair. Not one venireman had said he or she was opposed to the death penalty.

The town of Milton had been a lively trading center for lumber and shipbuilding in the days of "wooden ships and iron men," long before the sawmill industry was replaced by the Whiting Field Naval Air Training facility in the early days of World War II. Miltonians boasted a colorful history of vigilantism when it came to rendering local persons and property secure from the vicious and depraved. Local folklore has it that during the Spanish-American War of 1898, cavalry troops from Teddy Roosevelt's regiment of Rough Riders on their way by train from San Antonio, Texas, to Tampa, Florida, had raised no end of trouble in drunken revelry in every town unfortunate enough to lie along the route. After passing through Galt City, the desperate conductor had announced in each car: "The next town is Milton. The men there are proud of their town and their women. They actively resent any real or implied insult to either. I myself have seen men hanged to the cross arms of telegraph poles and riddled with shot. I have had them take a train from me to search for one man. They would have no qualms about burning your horse cars and contents. Please, for your own sake, go quietly."

The Milton courthouse, an unadorned postwar blond brick and jalousie-windowed institution with a narrow sidewalk leading to three cement steps and double glass doors, sat in the middle of Milton's historic courthouse square. The old courthouse, dedicated in 1887, had stood on the northeast corner of the square, having replaced the original wooden courthouse and jail that were destroyed by a fire of "peculiar and undetermined origin" in 1875, along with most of the county's records. Flanked on the east by the grim, red-brick, one-hundred-year-old Exchange Hotel, the Santa Rosa county seat squatted opposite its contemporary, the Milton Opera House, across the main highway, which was empty at midday save when an occasional semi roared through the sleepy town.

Inside the crowded Milton courtroom, Jerri Chamberlain sat on the edge of her wooden chair, her clear blue eyes reflecting the intense scene around her. Ted Chamberlain, having been subpoenaed as a witness for the prosecution, could not be present in the courtroom during the testimony of other witnesses. Jerri was to be her husband's eyes and ears throughout the trial.

Behind the plain wooden railing separating the spectators' gallery from the judge, jury, prosecution, and defense, Prosecutor Russ Edgar, dark-suited, bespectacled, and mustached, sat with his back to the audience at the table closest to the jury, his head bent studiously over court notes. Edgar's young girlfriend, perched behind him in the front row of the gallery beside the church-going Mrs. Bob Cousson, attempted vainly to pull her short skirt down over her long crossed legs under the disapproving stares of Milton's moral matrons.

Presiding from the raised bench at the center of the courtroom was Judge George E. Lowrey, dwarfed by the massive trappings of official justice. Judge Lowrey, his double chins resting on his chest, his hands folded patiently over his black robes, his expression masked by a short, bushy black mustache, peered at the courtroom from behind a large pair of horn-rimmed glasses.

To the judge's left, the panel of prospective jurors fidgeted in the jury box, waiting to be questioned by the counsel for prosecution and defense.

Across the room from the jurors, James Johnston conferred at the defense table with his wife and co-counsel, Rebecca Johnston, an attractive Mississippi blonde in a sophisticated gray suit. At the end of the table, defendant Judias Buenoano sat slumped in a white ruffled blouse and blue pin-striped suit, her chin resting on her hand. A uniformed jail matron sat a few feet away, guarding the defendant. Ignoring the crowd behind her, Judias raised her dark eyes from the jury box to the judge, and back to the table. Doffing her suit coat, she turned to her children, James and Kimberly, seated in the gallery behind her, and formed a kiss to them with her mouth.

The stifling one-room setting seemed straight from the pages of *Inherit the Wind*.

By the middle of the afternoon a jury panel of eight men and four women had been chosen. In response to a request by defense counsel, Judge Lowrey had decided to sequester the jury for the duration of the trial, prohibiting the jurors from discussing the case among themselves or with anyone else or being exposed to any newspaper, radio, or television accounts of the trial. The jurors would be housed at the local motel for the duration of the proceedings.

Following Judge Lowrey's lengthy instructions to the jurors concerning their trial duties, prosecuting attorney Russ Edgar stepped up to the microphone at the wooden podium before the prosecution table. In a carefully modulated voice heavy with the gravity of the crime, Edgar delivered his opening statement to the jury:

"May it please the court, counsel, ladies and gentlemen of the jury. . . . The case of the death of Michael Goodyear, or Michael Buenoano, is the most bizarre circumstantial murder case one could possibly conceive of, the taking of a life of one's own child. The death itself is more than suspicious by its circumstances. The motives of the defendant to take the life of her own son—"

"Now, Your Honor," defense attorney James Johnston interposed, "I'm going to object to him arguing the case to the jury. If he wants to state the evidence is going to show that, that's one thing, but he's making a closing argument."

"The objection will be sustained," Judge Lowrey ruled.

"Nineteen-year-old Michael Goodyear," Edgar resumed, "was taken by his mother on a canoe trip in which he was placed in a canoe, sat in a lawn chair while he was wearing full leg braces, an arm brace, and a wrist support, suffering from paralysis of his arms and his legs.

"Michael Goodyear could not swim; he could not walk; he could not dress himself; he could not use the toilet by himself; he was a hundred percent disabled and totally dependent upon others.

"He was found at the bottom of the river without a life preserver."

The prosecutor then recited the findings of the Santa Rosa Sheriff's Department. He told of how Ricky Hicks, while fishing on the East River, had seen the defendant and her son, James, in the river near an overturned canoe and had heard their screams for help. He related how Hicks pulled them aboard his boat and was told that the defendant's other son, Michael, had fallen overboard and drowned, but that the defendant did not want to rush back and find him. She just wanted to be taken ashore, where she sat drinking a cold beer before the ambulance and the police were even called. He told of how the ambulance personnel finally arrived to attend to her and James and how the rescue personnel then turned up and were guided by the defendant to the scene of the drowning, where divers recovered Michael's body in the middle of the river.

"The drowning allegedly occurred at approximately three-thirty; the body was found at approximately six-thirty," prosecuting attorney Russ Edgar pointed out. "The diver will testify that the bottom of the river is flat and sandy, and that the current on that particular day was very, very silent. The diver will also testify that the body of Michael Goodyear was rather difficult and heavy to manage; he had full leg braces on and prosthetic devices, and this struck him as peculiar inasmuch as he discovered from his examination that the deceased was not wearing any lifesaving device whatsoever. In fact, the only lifesaving devices that were found were two ski belts floating in the water near the canoe.

Point by point, the prosecutor laid out the peculiar circumstances of Michael Goodyear's life and death. He noted that the United States Army had declared Michael one hundred percent disabled: before his death by drowning, the deceased had suffered peripheral neuropathy—paralysis—and was virtually unable to move his arms or legs. True, the drowning had been deemed accidental by the Santa Rosa County Sheriff's Department. "What the Santa Rosa Sheriff's Department did not know," Edgar continued, "was that the deceased had a fear, a deathly fear of water. They did not know that the deceased had just the day before, within twenty-four hours, been checked out of a VA hospital where he was undergoing training to learn how possibly to feed himself, to learn how possibly to use a wheelchair, to learn how to pick things up. They did not really know what the military had experienced with Michael Goodyear."

Reviewing Michael's military career, the prosecutor noted that the boy had spent a ten-day leave at home in Gulf Breeze before reporting to his first duty assignment at Fort Benning, Georgia, in November 1979. "It was there that he began to experience such severe medical problems that he had to be hospitalized. . . ." The medical authorities "concluded that he was suffering from peripheral neuropathy due to toxic exposure. But the process of paralysis had already set in. It had been discovered too late."

Neither the Santa Rosa Sheriff's Department nor the military knew that Michael was heavily insured, Edgar went on, yet "after Michael's death, his mother collected over a hundred thousand dollars' insurance. And within a year of his death, she had spent approximately the same amount, buying a new boat, a new Corvette, a business—she quit the job she had that only paid three seventy an hour—furniture, trips, and other lavishments, including accounts and certificates of deposit for her children, loans to her friends."

The evidence would show, the prosecutor contended, that "the signatures on the policies taken out while Michael was in the army and while he was in the hospital were not signed by Michael. . . . They are forgeries."

The evidence would reveal Judias Buenoano to be a liar who had had a "peculiar relationship" with her son since his birth, "a relationship of neglect, shame, embarrassment, hatred."

Michael "was a stranger to his own family. From the time he was eight years old until he was sixteen, he perhaps spent only weekends and a few selected short vacations at home, because his mother put him in various schools for the emotionally disturbed."

Michael was of low intelligence, perhaps, but not retarded. Neglected and emotionally disturbed, "Michael wasn't like the other children. . . . Michael was always losing things, breaking things; he was hyperactive. He had a deviated septum—his nose ran all the time. He had a speech impediment. He was slow in school. He just couldn't remember things; he couldn't follow instructions. . . . His mother didn't want him around the other children, didn't want him around her male friends. She did not want him in that house. And she put him from one school to the other. . . . The kids made fun of him; he was a joke. He was awkward; he was uncoordinated; he was unloved.

"The evidence will show that this peculiar relationship of mother and son was a compelling motive for murder. And although the State does not have to prove any evidence of motive, that motive is the premeditation in this case.

"The evidence will show that the defendant's thought was to finally get rid of Michael and to collect the insurance so that she could lead the life-style that she'd become accustomed to. . . .

"In short, the State will prove that the defendant deliberately, with calculation, planned the death of her own son, and diabolically executed him by drowning him on May thirteenth, 1980."

Rising to his impressive six-foot-two height, defense attorney James Johnston strode to the center of the room to make his opening statement. He faced the jury with the casual confidence of a native-born politician addressing his local constituency. Johnston's white linen double-vented suit, pastel shirt and tie, and thick, wavy blond hair presented a sharp contrast to the prosecutor's darker, conservative profile. Standing with his thumbs hooked beneath his lapels, Johnston projected an image reminiscent of evangelist Billy Graham in his prime.

In a few words he dismissed Edgar's description of events as a mere "horror movie" far removed from the truth. "Let me tell you what the purpose of this opening statement is. It's not for me to argue the case, but to give you a road map. To let you know what we expect the evidence to be. There will be witnesses put on the stand. That is evidence. Nothing that I say to you or nothing that the State says is evidence. We're not under oath. . . ."

Johnston walked measuredly toward the defense table. "It is true that Michael may not have been a normal child. But the evidence will also show that his mother loved this boy like she loved and still loves the other two children." Johnston's gaze rested briefly on James and Kimberly Buenoano.

"I think the evidence will show that the boy did have some problems. For one, he wet his bed right up until the time that he went into the army and even after he got into the army. The boy, over the period of his life, did go to some facilities to assist him. The evidence will not show that his mother shoved him in there to get rid of him. It was for his own good that he went there."

Johnston walked back toward the jury. "At any rate, the boy was normal enough to be accepted into the United States Army, and he enlisted, I think, in June of 1979. Then, around the first of November 1979, the boy came home. The evidence will show that when he arrived home, he was not in the best of condition. . . . The mother was so concerned with her son that she and her other two children drove in the dead of night to take this boy to a hospital to see that he did get the proper care and treatment. And the records will show that at two A.M. in the morning, this mother took that boy to an army hospital. There the boy stayed. Ultimately, he was transferred to Walter Reed Hospital, approximately a thousand miles or so from Gulf Breeze.

"The records will show that the mother and the brother and sister did, in fact, communicate. She didn't whisk him off and slam him in a clothes closet and forget him. The VA hospital said the boy was looking forward to coming home, and the records will show that the boy said, 'My mother is concerned about my condition; can you help me?'

"And when he was discharged from the hospital, the VA personnel thought that he was of sufficient ability that all he needed was tender loving care and rehabilitation. He wasn't paralyzed to the extent that the State says he was. The evidence will show that the boy did, in fact, have braces, but the boy could, in fact, walk. He could in fact feed himself. He was not defenseless, as you have been told he was.

"The defense will disagree with Michael's fear of the water. The boy had a boat before he went into the army, and the testimony will be that he and his brother went boating. And after being cooped up in the hospital, the evidence will show that the one thing this boy wanted to do was the same thing that he did before he got crippled."

Johnston strode back to the defense table. "The evidence will show that my client, the mother, drove to Tampa with her two children and picked this boy up. Even though the government was obligated to pay for his way, she herself went down there and got the boy and brought him back home."

Johnston gestured toward Judias. "And this lady who the State has charged with premeditation, malice aforethought, first-degree murder, kept her other two children home from school the day the accident happened to go canoeing as a welcome-home present for Michael.

"They loaded up their vehicle, packed a lunch, and went to the place they normally went. And the boy could use his hands to fish. The canoe had a capacity to accommodate at least four persons. There were four persons there, but they did not want to take the daughter because she has a problem with her skin. . . . So they loaded up the boat, the mother on one end, and the other brother, James, on the other end. They had a chair so the boy could sit in the chair in the middle of the boat. They had the chair tied down so it wouldn't come loose and there wouldn't be any shaking. And off they go canoeing, picnicking, fishing."

Johnston paced back toward the jury box. "The evidence will show that at one point the line did get caught in one of the trees on the banks of the East River. And in the process of trying to free the line, a portion of the limb came down, and there was a small snake that fell in the boat.

"The evidence will not show that that's what caused the boat to overturn. The boat apparently hit some submerged limb or log, and you will hear an expert on the river say that that's not uncommon to happen. And when it hit the log, the boat capsized.

"The testimony of the defense will be that every occupant in the boat had a lifesaving device on. . . .

"What the boat turned over, it apparently stunned or temporarily knocked out of commission her other son, James. And here this mother is, in a dangerous river, the boat overturned, the one son she cannot find, the other son lying in the water unconscious. And she grabs the boy and starts swimming. She can't go ashore because there's nowhere to lay the boy. And Mr. Hicks comes along and sees this mother, almost exhausted, paddling and swimming and saving the other boy, and rescues them.

"The military investigated it; the Santa Rosa Sheriff's Office investigated it and ruled that this was an accident, pure and simple."

Johnston paused before the prosecutor's table. "Mr. Edgar makes a big to-do of the finances, and he suggests to you that the motive was she needed money. I don't think by any stretch of the imagination that you will be convinced from the evidence that this lady was in any dire financial need. She was not the destitute desperado that he would have you make her out to be."

Turning to face the jury, defense counsel continued. "The only insurance policy that was taken out that could be remotely connected with a motive by this lady was in October of 1979. The other policies, one was taken out in 1978, and I believe the others were taken out when the child was a youngster. The evidence will not show that she goes out here and loads up on insurance. The evidence will show that she never called anybody in October to sell her any insurance. That was an afterthought.

"Basically, these are the facts that the defense will prove. That it was an accident in 1980, and it's still an accident today. Unfortunate, but nevertheless an accident."

The next morning the State called its first witness, Ricky Hicks. The sandy-haired, medium-built Oklahoma truck driver shuffled shyly into the courtroom from an upstage door and ascended the witness stand. Having been duly sworn, he sank nervously into the chair as Edgar stepped forward.

"Mr. Hicks, sir, on May 13, 1980, did you take your boat and go fishing on East River?" Edgar began.

"Yes."

"Could you tell me approximately what time you went to the river to go fishing that day?"

"It was between two and two-thirty."

"Two and two-thirty. And where did you put in the river?"

"The dock right beside the bridge, East River bridge."

"I would like to show you a State exhibit, which purports to be two aerial photographs of East River. . . ."

Walking over to a display of two enlarged aerial photographs of East River, Edgar asked Hicks to indicate the site. Ricky Hicks stepped down from the witness stand and crossed over to the exhibit.

"Right here is the bridge," Hicks pointed. "And right here is the dock."

"And that would be on the west side of the bridge?"

"Yes, sir."

"And after you put in, where did you travel?"

"I came on out here to East Bay and I cast out a couple of times and there wasn't much luck there, so I came back and went up East River."

"After coming back toward the bridge, what, if anything, unusual occurred?"

"Okay, when I came back to the bridge and everything, you know, approximately right here in this area where I see Judi and the boy."

"Would you look around the courtroom and see if you can identify the person that you picked up?"

"Yes, sir. That lady sitting over there in that green blouse."

"Let the record reflect the witness pointed at the defendant. Now, what were they doing, this woman and boy when you saw them?"

"Judi was swimming and holding on to the boy, and she was holding up her hand, calling for help."

"What, if anything, else did you observe?"

"I noticed that the canoe was upside down, and the ice chest, and a flip-flop, and a bread sack that had a lunch in it were floating in the water."

"And where was that in relation to the defendant and the boy?"

"Real close. Twenty or thirty feet. Everything was right, you know, right together."

Having marked the spot on the photograph as requested, Hicks returned to the witness box.

"Now, when you saw the defendant and the boy waving their arms, what did you do?" Edgar resumed.

"Well, right there in that area is a rope swing, and when I first seen them, I thought they was playing, and then that's when I spotted the canoe and everything. I went and picked them up and I helped her get the boy in the boat. Then I brought them back to shore. She at that time told me that she lost another boy."

"Did she say how she lost the other boy?"

"She said the canoe tipped over and he went under."

"Did she say how the canoe tipped over?"

"She said a snake fell in the boat and she was holding it down with a paddle, and uh, tipped it over."

"Did you offer to go back and look for the boy?"

"Yes, sir."

"What did she say to that?"

"She said there's no use going back because the boy was already gone."

"Did she indicate to you how much time had gone by since he had gone under?"

"No, sir, she didn't mention no time."

"How long had you been fishing, from the time you put in until the time you saw her?"

"Approximately an hour, a little less than an hour."

"At the time you put in, did you see any other persons there?"

"No, sir, I was the only one there."

"Did you see any vehicles there?"

"No, sir."

"When you brought the defendant and the boy to shore, did you see anybody then?"

"Yes, sir. It was her daughter. She was sitting on the bank right beside the boat dock."

"And when they came to shore, did anyone explain to the daughter what had happened?"

"The most talk that was going about was the other boy was hurt—hurt his back."

"Was there any conversation about a brother named Michael that had drowned?"

"Objection, leading the witness, Your Honor," James Johnston interjected.

"Objection will be overruled," Judge Lowrey responded.

"Answer the question," Edgar directed.

"No," Hicks replied.

"What, if anything, did the defendant indicate to this girl about the drowning?" Edgar continued.

"Right at the time, well, really nothing."

"Now, did you sit with the defendant and the boy for a while?"

"Well, as soon as I got back and put my boat up on the bank, that's when I got in the defendant's car and drove and called the Santa Rosa rescue squad."

"Was the defendant's car present at the time you put in?"

"At the time I put in the boat, no."

"And when you returned to the scene, what occurred?"

"The sheriff showed up, and that is when the sheriff and I went out looking for the body."

"Where was the canoe after you made these phone calls and the sheriff arrived?"

"Approximately right in the same area I picked up Judi."

"It hadn't moved much?"

"No, not much at all."

"Now, you and the sheriff went looking for the boy that had drowned. Did you find anything?"

"As far as a body, no. We just picked up debris and threw it in the boat. And we just drug the canoe in and put it up on the bank."

"Did you see any life jackets?"

"Yes, sir. There was a couple of ski belts."

"When you picked up the defendant and the boy, were they wearing any lifesaving devices?"

"Not as I recall."

"Did you remain until the body was recovered from the river?"

"Yes, sir."

"And at the time the body was recovered, was the defendant present?"

"She was gone."

"Now, once you had reached the shore with the defendant and the boy, did you share any food or drink with them?"

"She asked if I would mind if she had one of my beers, and I said no."

"And did she drink a beer while you all sat there?"

"She was drinking, yes."

"Now, you say that you had fished that river before and you'd fished that river that day. Do you recall if the current was strong that day?"

"No, it wasn't too strong at all that day."

"Have you ever seen any snakes in any trees there at East River?"

"I haven't, no."

"When you were trying to find the body with the deputy sheriff, did you have any trouble with any debris in the water such as stumps or logs?"

"No, sir."

"Mr. Hicks, what time did you commence fishing?" James Johnston began his cross-examination.

"I put in the water between two and two-thirty. At that time, my uncle and brother brought me out. Just let me off."

"And what did you have, a boat that you were pulling by a trailer?"

"Yes. And they took the car. We dropped the trailer and went on back, and they was coming back later that day to pick me up."

"And you were prepared to go fishing. What were you fishing for?"

"Went out there down by the power lines just to be fishing, and I came back up the river to catfish."

"How long were you down here fishing by the power lines?"

"I probably stayed there approximately ten minutes or so."

"How long would it take you from where you put in to get down to the power lines?"

"Approximately ten minutes."

"And ten minutes to come back. So you were gone about thirty minutes?"

"Right."

"When you put in at the bridge, you say you didn't notice a car?"

"There was no other vehicles there."

"Are there other places that you can put in on this river?"

"You'd have to go through a lot of brush, lot of trees."

"Are you saying that this is the logical place that somebody would put in a canoe?"

"Yes."

"How wide is the river where you found Judi carrying her son?"

"I was trying to think. I ain't too good on measurements. I'd say anywhere from—"

"Excuse me, Your Honor. There is a scale on the map. If the witness cannot answer without approximation, counsel could refer to an actual scale," Edgar interrupted.

"Well, I'm going to let him approximate what he thinks the river is," Johnston interposed.

"Forty to fifty feet wide right there," Hicks answered.

"All right. Did you tell my wife yesterday that you thought that was about a half a football field?"

"Right."

"And half a football field, now, Mr. Hicks, would be fifty yards, not fifty feet. Would that help you better if you could describe it as half a football field wide?"

"Yeah, probably, that's about right."

"All right, sir, and how deep is it there in the middle of the river?"

"Right there, if I recall, we're looking at probably about thirty foot of water there. Because on my boat, you know, I had a depth finder."

"And you have the canoe how far from the bridge?"

"Okay, talking about football fields again, probably about a football field and a half."

"So that would be approximately one hundred fifty yards."

"I said a football field and a half, so that would be approximately, what, four hundred."

"Four hundred yards. And how far, then, was Judi and her son from the canoe if the canoe was four hundred yards from the bridge?"

"Twenty to thirty feet. Everything was, you know, right there within twenty feet, thirty feet."

"Have you lived in that area? Because there was a lot of Hicks in Holley Navarre."

"Uh, I have never lived in that area until that month before that with my uncle. I came down to help him with construction."

"And you had been in this area, then, only a month before you witnessed this particular accident?"

"Yes, every day."

"When you talked to the sheriff—I have the report right here—did you tell the sheriff, 'Picked up by Ricky Hicks, Two Woodbine Drive, Mary Ester, Florida'—Is that where you were living at the time?"

"At the time, yes."

"Who heard them screaming for help? Did you tell the sheriff's office you heard them screaming for help?"

"I might have, but—"

"Either you don't know, you might have, or you didn't?"

"Well, at the time, yes, she was yelling for help."

"Was she in the middle of the river?"

"Not quite the middle. She was closer to the bank on this side."

"Certainly deep enough, water over her head?"

"Yes."

"And did she have her other son under her arm?"

"She was holding on to her other son, swimming, yes."

"You said also that you did not remember or were not sure whether or not she was wearing a life preserver or a life belt when you picked them up?"

"I can't remember if she had the belt on or not. It was belts, what they had."

"How did the son appear? Did he appear to be unconscious?"

"Well, like I was telling your wife yesterday, he just

moaned a couple times; he just didn't do very much moving at all."

"Did the ambulance come and pick the boy up?"

"Yes."

"Do you recall the mother going with the boy to the hospital? And I understand, this was 1980 and if you don't remember . . ."

"I remember she left. I don't recall if it was in the ambulance."

"When you rescued Judi, was her blouse tore off?"

"No, it wasn't tore off. What do you want to know about her clothing?"

"Tell the jury what kind of clothing she had on."

"What I'd call it—I don't know if it's right—it's called a kind of sunsuit, or like that. And I remember it being white."

"Do you recall what the boy had on, James?"

"If I remember it, I think just swimming trunks."

"Are you sure? I don't want you guessing if you're not sure."

"I'm almost positive; yes, I am."

"Were you drinking before you got there?"

"Oh, no."

"Did you have some beer?"

"Yes. When I went out there, see, I filled the boat and bought a twelve-pack of beer."

"All right, sir, did you have anything to drink while you were in the boat before you rescued Judi and her son?"

"I had a couple beers."

"A couple beers. . . . What time, approximately, was the body recovered?"

"It was getting late. I'd say around six or seven o'clock."

"Do you recall if Judi was there when the body was recovered?"

"No, I don't remember Judi being there at that time."

"You just do not remember?"

"That's right."

"Thank you," Johnston murmured and returned to his seat.

"Any redirect?" Judge Lowrey addressed Edgar.

"Just a few questions," Edgar said, rising.

"Now, counsel asked you some questions about how far it was from the bridge that you saw Judi and the canoe. The distance, you would say, was a football field and a half from the bridge?"

"Yes."

"That would be a hundred yards plus fifty yards, that would be four hundred fifty feet, wouldn't it?"

"Right."

"When you said four hundred yards before, did you mean four hundred feet or four hundred yards?"

"Four hundred feet."

"Okay. Are you a little nervous?"

"Kind of." Hicks laughed.

"Have you ever testified before?"

"No, sir. This is my first time in the courtroom."

"Now, concerning the fishing you were doing, did you see Judi Buenoano, the defendant, or her son with any fishing equipment?"

"Judi or the boy, no, sir."

"Did you see any fishing poles or dead fish floating in the water?"

"No, sir."

"Did you see any fishing tackle other than your own on anyone that day?"

"Yes, sir. The girl was sitting on the bank, the daughter, she was fishing there at the bank."

"From the time that you put in, which was either two or two-thirty, how long went by before the sheriff arrived?"

"About an hour and fifteen minutes."

"That would mean either three-fifteen or, at the most, four o'clock?"

"Yes."

"Thank you. No further questions. . . . Oh, one last question. Were you intoxicated that day?"

"Oh, no, sir."

"You just had a couple of beers?"

"Right."

"A lot of people say they just had a couple beers."

"Well, that's all I had."

Edgar returned to the prosecution table satisfied that despite Johnston's attempt to discredit his testimony, the jury had believed Ricky Hicks.

"The State calls Forbie Privette."

Edgar's second witness took the stand, the heavy leather belt and holster of his police sergeant's uniform slung below his protruding gut. Under questioning Privette confirmed that his marked patrol unit had been called to the scene of the drowning at about four o'clock.

"The ambulance was already on the scene," Privette recalled, "and they were treating two subjects inside the ambulance, and Mr. Hicks was present. He stated to me that he had picked up two people from the overturned canoe to the east of 87 up the river. And he said there was a third party with them, and that one was missing."

"Did you interview anyone at that time other than Mr. Hicks?"

"Not at that time. As I said, they were in the ambulance being treated."

"What did you do at that point?"

"Mr. Hicks and I got in his boat, and he took me up to where he had picked the people up. We were trying to pinpoint the location, so that when the divers and rescue arrived, they would be able to locate the area."

Referring to the aerial photograph, Sergeant Privette corroborated Ricky Hicks's account of how they recovered the overturned canoe and floating debris. "We went up the river just out of sight of the bridge, approximately a quarter of a mile or less, where we came upon an overturned canoe, two ski belts, and a shower clog."

"And can you tell me how close to the canoe the two ski belts and shower clog were?"

"Well, if I remember correctly, they were all right there together."

"Sergeant Privette," Johnston cross-examined. "Did you have any indication that a line had got hung in a tree?"

"Yes sir, later I did."

"Who gave you that information?"

"I was with a boat, and we saw the line hanging in the tree."

"And where was the line in reference to where you found the canoe?"

"Quite some distance up the river from where we found the canoe. Probably twice the distance from the bridge as where the canoe was. . . ."

"Were you specifically looking for a fishing line?"

"No, sir. We were looking for any further debris or anything to indicate where the canoe had actually tipped over."

"You found at the canoe two ski belts?"

"Yes, sir. One was fastened in a circular position and the other one was open."

"Did you learn or have any information in your investigation that the reason the canoe overturned was that a line got hung in a tree?"

"Not until we returned later did I hear this—and we said, well, that might be the line."

"And is that why you went back and checked the tree to see if you could find the line?"

"No, sir. As I say, we were going up the river looking for any further debris or anything to indicate what had caused the accident or where it might have happened, and we just happened to see the line hanging in the tree."

"Is that the approximate point where the divers located the body?"

"From what I understand, yes, sir. I was not present when the body was located."

"Do you want to come down, then, and give us—"

"Your Honor," Edgar interjected, "I object. The witness can't indicate where he doesn't know the body was located."

"The objection will be sustained," Judge Lowrey ruled.

Johnston paused before continuing. "In your official report with the sheriff's office, did you not write or put in where the line and cork were found in the tree is the approximate place where the body was located?"

"Yes, sir, I did. My report was written after the body was found."

"Thank you," Johnston murmured and retreated to his seat.

"But you don't know where the body was found?" Edgar redirected.

"No, sir."

"Do you fish these freshwater rivers?"

"I have fished that river on a couple of occasions, yes, sir."

"Is it a very unusual thing to find a fishing line in a tree?"

"No, sir."

"How far up the river did you go?"

"I went all the way as far as you could go in a small boat."

"Did you find anything else among the debris?"

"No, sir."

"I believe in your report you mentioned there was an aluminum chair tied to the canoe."

"Yes, sir. It was tied on the middle brace of the canoe. It was a two-seat type canoe—"

"I object to that, Your Honor," Johnston intervened. "In all respect to Sergeant Privette, he's not an expert on canoes and the capacity of the canoe. I ask that the Court instruct the jury to disregard that comment. It's purely an opinion."

"The objection will be overruled," Lowrey droned.

"How many seats did the canoe have?" Edgar reiterated.

"It had one on each end, sir," Privette replied.

* * *

As Sergeant Privette left the courtroom, Edgar called his next witness, Tom Roche. The trim, suntanned Search and Rescue officer testified that on May 13, 1980, he had received a call concerning a possible drowning in East River. Arriving on the scene, he met a woman, who identified herself as the mother of the drowned boy. "If you saw that woman again, would you be able to identify her?" Edgar directed.

"Possibly. I'm not quite sure because it's been four years. I believe it's that lady there at the end."

"Let the record reflect the witness has identified the defendant. . . ."

"When you arrived," Edgar asked, "did you have a conversation with her?"

"Yes, sir. At the time, we wanted to find out where the accident occurred, so we took this lady with us in the boat back up the river to locate the site of the accident."

"Did she indicate to you where the canoe overturned?"

"Yes, sir. It was up the river after a couple of bends, at one of the bends in the river close to the bank."

Roche testified that to the best of his knowledge, the prosecutor's pin on the aerial photograph indicated the spot where Judias Buenoano had told him the canoe overturned. "The only way I could really pinpoint that location would be to be on the river itself and locate it. . . ."

"Do you believe that you could be certain if you went to the river during lunch?"

"Pretty certain."

"Maybe we can make some arrangements. . . . How long was it before the body was discovered?"

"According to searches, it wasn't a very long time. Approximately an hour."

"And who discovered the body?"

"The diver, Joe Diamond."

"Mr. Roche," Johnston crossed, "if you can't really remember what the lady looked like that you talked to in May of

1980, how can you go out there and remember where she told you the boat overturned?"

"Well, sir, I live just behind the river, and I've probably been on that river a hundred times. I was more familiar with the river than I was with the lady."

"And someone who's not familiar with the river, is it unusual to get lost?" Johnston asked.

"Not on that particular river because in that area there's no tributaries going off on either side. Although it curves around, it's a straight river that comes right on to the bridge."

"Is there any distinguishing feature from this bend as opposed to that bend?"

"No, sir, except one curves to the south and one curves to the north."

"And what about this bend, where the second red marker is. How far is that from the bridge?"

"Approximately half a mile."

"You can't see the bridge from there, can you?"

"No, you can't see the bridge, but you can see the trailers that are on the south side of the river, and the boat docks."

"What time did you get there, sir?"

"I can't remember the approximate time."

"Did you make any notes or reports?"

"Yes, sir. But they're unable to find them in the county office."

"And whose boat did you go up the river in with Judi?"

"The Santa Rosa County rescue boat."

"Was anyone else with you besides her?"

"Yes, sir, my son, John, and one other search and rescue helper."

"For the record, would you state your name and occupation, please, sir?" Edgar asked his fourth witness.

"My name is Joseph E. Diamond. I was and still am the head diver for Santa Rosa County Search and Rescue," the rugged, muscular scuba diver replied.

"Now, on the thirteenth of May 1980, were you summoned to East River to search for a possible drowning victim?"

"Yes, sir, I was."

"When you arrived at the river, what were you briefed on?"

"There was a boy that was in the water, supposedly had braces on both legs, a possible brace on one arm. There were three people in a canoe, and it turned over. Somebody told me about a snake. Supposedly there was a snake in a tree; a fishing line was caught; the canoe was turned over. They took me up river, showed me the spot where it happened, and I started getting things together for the searching operation."

"Now, the area where you began your search, did you find the body in that area?"

"Where we started our search was where they told us the canoe was placed. There was a fishing line on an overhanging limb, and that's where I was told that the canoe went ashore and supposedly the body had fallen out of the canoe. From there we started our search. There were three of us searching. We worked our way out, made a search across the river to the other side, turned around and came back, and this is where we found some sunglasses on the bottom, about fifteen feet down river. . . ."

"Where were the sunglasses in relation to the sides of the river?"

"They were toward the middle. Almost in the middle of the river."

"What else, if anything, did you find?"

"Okay. From that point we started making a circle search pattern. One person stays in the middle with the rope, and we pivot around him, just like a compass. One person at the end moving the rope about five feet each time, moving over, a third person running between the both of us each time, so we can cover the bottom well. As soon as I got about due south of the pivot point, I stretched the line out and I felt something bump me in the back. I reached back and I felt some braces and shoes. I turned around, and there was the boy down there."

"Now, the river runs in which direction?"

"East to west."

"Where was the fishing line?"

"The north side of the shore."

"Where were the glasses found?"

"Toward the middle, fifteen feet down."

"Where was the body found?"

"Exactly twenty-five feet down from there."

"In the middle of the river?"

"Yes, sir."

"Would you look at this aerial photograph and, if you can, locate in relation to the curves in the river where you found the body?"

Diamond left the witness stand and strode over to the aerial photograph display. He pointed his finger to a spot in the middle of the second bend of the river, just below the point Santa Rosa Rescue Officer Tom Roche had testified the defendant had told him the canoe overturned.

"Where that red pin is?"

"Yes, sir."

"Could you tell us what the conditions of the river were?"

"You could see maybe four feet to the bottom. There were no obstructions on the bottom that we found. It was a sandy bottom. Right in that area where we found the boy, it was flat."

"What was the depth of the river where you found the body?"

"Twelve to fifteen feet."

"When you found the body, did you notice anything on the body, or how it was dressed?"

"He was facedown in the river. I say 'facedown' because of the way his toes were pointing. I did not look at the face or upper extremities. He had braces on both his legs at the time. I attached a rope to one of the braces, took the rope upstairs to one of the spotter boats, and they brought him on board. From there, I had nothing else to do with it."

"By leg braces, what do you mean?"

"Well, there were shoes on the gentleman, but then, braces all the way up the full length of the legs."

"Do you recall what the approximate weight of the body was?"

"I really don't know. I didn't see the whole body, just from the waist down. His ankles appeared to be very thin."

"What was the strength of the current in the river that day?"

"It was very, very slow. Maybe one or two miles per hour. It was very weak."

"Would it impede an average person from swimming upstream?"

"No, sir, it wouldn't."

"Where were the glasses in relation to the body?"

"Straight due east of the body."

"Which way was the current flowing?"

"It was flowing west."

"From the glasses toward the body?"

"Yes, sir."

"Mr. Diamond," Johnston began when he took over, "how long did it take you to locate the body?"

"From the time I went into the river to the time we found him was approximately an hour."

"Do you know when the boat overturned?"

"From the time span I know of, it was maybe an hour and forty-five minutes to two hours before I went in the water."

"How far is the spot where you located the body from the bridge?"

"Approximately three-quarters to a half a mile."

"Who went with you to point out where the canoe overturned?"

"That I don't remember. We had about three or four people with us at the time. I don't know if it was Mr. Roche who showed me or not. There was a float hanging in a tree, was the object that we went with."

"Now, Mr. Diamond, as I understand your testimony you found the sunglasses first."

"Yes, sir. About fifteen feet from the fishing line, pretty close to the middle of the river."

"Fifteen feet back towards the bridge?"

"West, yes, sir."

"And where did you find the body?"

"From the sunglasses, twenty-five feet back."

"Twenty-five feet towards the bridge?"

"Yes, sir. West again."

"The river flows west, doesn't it?"

"Yes, sir. There's always a current running towards the bay. . . ."

Ted Chamberlain glanced at his waterproof wristwatch as he shoved the two-man aluminum canoe off the shallow clay bank with his paddle and headed upstream against the lazy current of East River. It was a few minutes past three o'clock on the partly cloudy afternoon of March 24, 1984. A light breeze rippled across the amber water, gently rustling through the thickly wooded shoreline that shaded the meandering river in alternate patches of dappled sunlight. Except for a slightly cooler temperature, the weather and current conditions were very similar to what they had been the afternoon of May 13, 1980, when paraplegic Michael Goodyear, perched precariously in a lawn chair between his mother and brother, had taken his last canoe ride.

Chamberlain took mental inventory of the canoe's contents as he rounded the first sharp bend in the winding river: one metal cooler containing a six-pack of Coke; four sandwiches packed inside an empty bread wrapper; two cane fishing poles; two ski belts, one opened, one closed; a pair of flip-flops; a short-legged aluminum lawn chair tied to the center brace. Everything was exactly as Judias Buenoano had described it the day of the drowning.

Within fifteen minutes, Chamberlain had passed the trailers and fishing docks of Turkey Bluff and rounded the second bend of the narrowing river, beyond the sight of anyone on shore. The dense foliage and underbrush hugged the river closer as it snaked its way eastward, increasing the stifling sense of solitude. Breaking the rhythm of his paddling only to smack a hungry mosquito, Chamberlain continued his silent expedition.

A few hundred yards further, Chamberlain came upon the spot in the middle of the thirty-foot-wide stream where diver Joe Diamond had discovered Michael Goodyear's body. Forty feet upstream was the fishing line caught in the overhanging tree limb on the north shore where Judias had told Santa Rosa rescue officer Tom Roche the canoe had overturned. Having confirmed the spot on the river earlier in the afternoon, Roche had returned to the Milton courthouse to continue his testimony.

Chamberlain halted the canoe opposite the fishing line marker. He sat still for a few moments, listening to the sporadic calls of hidden birds in the tranquil, lonely setting, the smooth surface of the sluggish river disturbed only by the leap of an occasional catfish. Then, throwing his weight to one side, he dumped the canoe and its contents over into the water.

Coming up for air, Chamberlain bobbed up and down in the river, treading water in one spot as the overturned canoe and its contents floated slowly downstream. From the middle of the river, he was about fifteen feet at most from either shore. Even in a panic, almost anyone would be able to make it to one side and grab hold of an overhanging branch. Anyone, Chamberlain thought grimly, who wasn't paralyzed and carrying without a life preserver the extra weight of braces.

Fifteen feet downstream and twelve feet under, equidistant from the shores, they had found Michael's glasses. Twenty-five feet downstream from there, Michael's struggling body had come to rest face down in the flat, sandy bottom of the apparently harmless river. Chamberlain tried to picture the expression on the youth's face as he sank helplessly beneath the water's murky surface, knowing—hoping—his mother and brother would save him.

Chamberlain watched the still-floating canoe and its dispersed contents. Within a few minutes, the upside-down canoe, the lawn chair still attached to the center brace, had caught on some protruding branches against the south shore of the twisting river, not more than thirty feet downstream. The two life preservers, the flip-flops, and the cane fishing poles had gotten hung up on the same shore several feet beyond the canoe. The cooler with its six-pack of Coke and the sandwiches in the bread wrapper had filled with water and sunk almost immediately.

Ricky Hicks had testified that when he first came upon Judias and James in the water near the overturned canoe, just around the first bend from the bridge, he had seen sandwiches in a bread wrapper floating among the other debris in the immediate vicinity. According to his own reenactment of the event, Chamberlain told himself, there was no way that the paraphernalia could have floated downstream along with the canoe for at least half a mile to where Hicks had discovered them in the water.

If Judias had swum the half mile downstream with James as she claimed she had, how could the canoe and paraphernalia have floated intact down the twisting river bends along with her? And how did the cooler and sandwiches manage to stay afloat the fifteen to twenty minutes it had to have taken Judias to swim with James the half mile downstream to their rescue?

Chamberlain swam over to the capsized canoe, righted it, and hauled himself aboard. He retrieved the ski belts and fishing poles from the shoreline and headed back. Paddling briskly downstream to the bridge landing, he knew what he had suspected all along.

He believed that Judias, with James as her assistant, had tossed her paralyzed son out of the canoe three-quarters of a mile up East River, within forty-five minutes of their arrival at the bridge landing. Judias and James had then paddled their canoe back down river toward the dock where Kimberly waited. As they came around the last bend in the river, just out of sight of the bridge, they were alerted by the sound of Ricky Hicks's approaching boat motor. Judias had immediately overturned the canoe just before Ricky Hicks rounded the bend and discovered them thrashing in the water. Thinking quickly, Judias had made up the story about the snake falling from a tree into the canoe and the canoe capsizing, and her having swum the half mile downstream with an unconscious James. For his part, James had moaned and swooned and pretended to have a neck injury, an injury for which no medical record was found. Later, the conveniently placed fishing line discovered by the Santa Rosa police in an overhanging tree limb, along with an elusive submerged log, became Judias's explanation for the "accident."

It was the only conclusion that fit all the facts of the physical evidence. Chamberlain could hardly wait to present the results of his investigation to Russ Edgar.

13

Lapse of Memory

THE STATE'S PRESENTATION PLODDED relentlessly on into the late Friday afternoon of March 23, 1984, with the testimony of the corpulent, bejowled Capt. Ronald Lewis Boswell, former lieutenant of the Santa Rosa Sheriff's Department in charge of crime-scene investigation.

On May 13, 1980, Boswell had been called to the Santa Rosa Hospital to handle the inventory and personal effects and to prepare for the autopsy of the body of one Michael Buenoano Goodyear.

"Did you examine the body?" Edgar questioned the witness.

"If I might refer to my report. . . . 'The shirt was trimmed in blue. There were blue shorts, black shoes, no socks, no belt. And white shorts. There was a brown wrist support on the left wrist, and the subject had braces on both legs and a prosthesis device on his right arm. He had a gold watch on his left arm, and the time was three thirty-four, the time it stopped. He had a gold chain with an oval disk with a star-type emblem.' "

"What did you do after you inventoried the personal effects?"

"Dr. Cole, a physician with the Santa Rosa Hospital, pronounced him dead. I then notified the medical examiner's office and arranged for the body to be transferred to Sacred Heart Hospital for Dr. Nicholson to perform the autopsy."

"Who was the investigator assigned to this case?"

"Lieutenant John Aikin."

"And John Aikin is deceased?"

"Yes, sir."

"There's a letter dated August eleventh to a Winfred Gideon. It expresses an opinion on your part concerning this case for the purposes of payment of life insurance. When you made that opinion, what knowledge did you have of this case?"

"The case reports and conversation with Lieutenant Aiken. The information I had available to me at the time."

"What information did you have at the time you wrote the letter concerning the amount of insurance upon the deceased?"

"I had none, sir."

"What information did you have at the time you wrote the letter concerning the medical condition of the deceased?"

"Only what we obtained posthumously. And the fact that he had braces on."

"Did you know if he was paralyzed or not?"

"No, sir, I did not know it."

"What information did you have concerning the deceased's athletic abilities?"

"I had none. I was only in the technical end of this case."

"Were you not asked for a conclusion concerning the status of this case?"

"Yes, sir."

"And the status of the case at that time was that it was not a homicide?"

"That is correct."

"Thank you," Edgar concluded.

"If it was not a homicide, Mr. Boswell, what was it?" Johnston asked on cross-examination.

"Objection to opinion," Edgar inserted.

"The objection will be overruled. He can explain what he means by the term 'homicide,' " Lowrey rejoined.

"A homicide is the willful criminal killing of another human being. That's my understanding of it," Boswell answered.

"And it was not a homicide?" Johnston repeated.

"It was a death investigation."

"And there was no criminal negligence either?"

"At that point in the investigation, there was no indication of criminal negligence," Boswell testified.

"Thank you." Johnston rested as Edgar stood to redirect.

"Captain Boswell," Edgar addressed the witness, "if you had to report this case over again, knowing what you know now, would you draw the same conclusion concerning the status of this case, that it was not a homicide?"

Boswell's sagging jowls shook emphatically from side to side before Johnston could object to the question.

"No, no, no, sir," he answered.

"The court calls James Buenoano," the bailiff announced.

The slightly built, polo-shirted seventeen-year-old sauntered toward the witness stand, a James Dean half-smile on his sullen young face. The only other witness besides the defendant to the drowning of his brother, James had been called as a court witness to be cross-examined by the state due to his persistent lack of cooperation and animosity toward the prosecution.

"Good afternoon," Edgar greeted the hostile witness from behind the shield of his podium. "For the record, would you state your name and address?"

"James Buenoano. Twenty-eight twelve Whisper Pine Drive, Gulf Breeze, Florida," James mumbled.

"Whose house is that?"

"My mother's."

"And who do you live there with?"

"My mother, Judi."

"And who else?"

"My sister."

"The deceased, Michael Goodyear Buenoano, was your brother?"

"Yes, sir."

"How old was your brother when he died?"

"Nineteen."

"Where did he die?"

"In East River."

"How did he die?"

"He drowned."

"How did he drown?"

"The canoe capsized, and he drowned."

"What canoe was that?"

"The canoe we were fishing in."

"You were fishing in a canoe?"

"Yes, sir, I was."

"What was the date?"

"The thirteenth of May?"

"What year?"

"Eighty. Seventy-nine, excuse me. No, it was 1980." James vacillated.

Over the next tedious hour and a half, Edgar continued painstakingly to extract testimony from James, who delivered his brief answers in a low monotone.

James testified that on May 13, 1980, his family had arrived at the fishing site at approximately ten-thirty or eleven A.M. with the canoe tied to the top of the family Ford Granada. There were no other cars parked in the area. They had not taken James's truck, as he had previously testified to the grand jury. They had not arrived at two-thirty or three P.M. as James had previously stated.

James testified that although Michael had worn leg braces and a hook device on his arm that worked with cables, he had walked to the car without his wheelchair. Michael had crawled into the canoe by himself; then they had strapped him into a beach chair positioned in the center of the canoe. All three family members riding in the canoe, James, Michael, and their mother, were wearing ski belts as a safety precaution.

James also testified that in the canoe they carried two cane fishing poles, a tackle box, and some bait. Kimberly remained on the dock with a third fishing pole. James and his mother each had a paddle. Michael tried to paddle the canoe using his hook device. They caught a few fish—bream—and put them in the ice chest. They had been fishing a little more than an hour before the canoe tipped over.

"Do you remember being asked by the grand jury, 'How long had you been fishing?' and do you remember your answer?" Edgar pressed.

"I couldn't remember how long we had been. I didn't keep track of time. I was under a lot of pressure. My sister had been picked up from school with seven police cars, and I'd been snatched. . . ." James mumbled.

"Wasn't your answer to the question, 'What time did you get there?' 'In the afternoon'?" Edgar interjected.

James paused before answering.

"I really couldn't remember."

"You do remember now?"

"Yes, sir, I've had an opportunity to think about it."

James continued to testify that they headed east upriver in the canoe for about a mile, fishing along the edges of the bank. Michael had trouble getting his line back into the boat when he caught a fish. Once his line caught a branch on the bank. The canoe turned over about six to eight feet from the north shore when a water moccasin fell into the boat causing confusion, and something hit the front of the canoe, possibly a submerged log.

"Do you recall writing a statement to the United States Army concerning what happened that day?" Edgar queried.

"Yes, sir."

"Would you look at the second page? Can you identify your signature?"

"Yes, sir, it is my signature."

"The state will move into the evidence state exhibit one-B," Edgar announced.

"Your Honor, the best evidence is what he has said, and therefore there's no relevance for that statement going in," Johnston objected.

"Objection will be overruled," the Court directed.

"Will you review that statement, please?" Edgar addressed James, handing him the handwritten account of the drowning incident submitted to the army investigator. James complied.

"Is there any reference to a snake in that statement?" Edgar asked James.

"No, sir."

"Why didn't you put it in there?"

"I really couldn't tell you."

"Where was that statement written?"

"In my home."

"Did your mother also write a statement that day?"

"Yes, sir. I believe so."

"Let me show you state exhibit one-A. Can you identify your mother's handwriting?"

"Yes, sir."

"When the canoe turned over, what happened to you?"

"I was hit in the back of the neck by the canoe. It knocked me unconscious."

"You don't recall anything from the time the canoe turned over until you were in the ambulance?"

"No, sir."

"What injuries did you suffer?"

"From what I was told, I received a fracture of the seventh vertebra."

"Who told you that?"

"The doctor. The one that saw me at West Florida Hospital."

"In your statement to the army—you have it there before you—did you not make the statement, the last sentence, 'All I can recall is the ambulance taking me to the hospital where I was released with a hairline fracture of the seventh cervical vertebra'? Do you see that?"

"Yes, sir."

"Read the rest of that."

" 'And released to a soft neck brace.' "

"That *to*, that's not written very well, is it? Actually, it's written more like a zero with a bar across the top, isn't it?"

"Well, it looks like a *c* with a bar across it."

"And that's what you mean, *t-o?*"

"Yes, sir."

"Are you familiar with the fact that a *c* with a bar across the top medically means 'with'?"

"No, sir."

"You don't remember your mother swimming downstream with you?"

"No, sir."

"Did you talk to her about what happened after the canoe turned over?"

"Well, I didn't talk to her until that night. She really didn't go into detail on that."

"Did she say she saved your life?"

"She said she turned me over. I was facedown in the water, and I had almost drowned."

"Did you have your life belt on?"

"Yes, sir."

"Did it remain on?"

"Yes, sir."

"Did you have it on when you were rescued?"

"I don't believe so. . . . I don't remember. . . . I don't remember what happened between the time the accident happened and I got to the ambulance. I didn't have any clothes on when I got to the hospital."

"Do you remember where the canoe tipped over on the river?"

"Not the exact spot."

"Did your brother scream out? Did you hear your brother say anything when it tipped over?"

"Uh . . . I couldn't . . . I don't remember. I don't believe so. I believe he said something, but I don't remember exactly what it was."

"Michael couldn't swim very good, could he?"

"Yes, sir. He had swam with us all his life."

James proceeded to testify to Michael's extensive athletic abilities over the years. Michael played football, basketball, and baseball. James could provide school yearbooks with team pictures of Michael suited up in sports uniforms. James verified his statement to the army that "my brother and I had canoed, fished and skied and surfed and rode motorcycles and hunted together ever since I can remember." Michael had gone canoeing with the family eight or nine times before he went into the army. They had gone fishing together many, many times. They went hunting in the neighborhood woods with BB guns and a .22. They had surfed on Pensacola Beach.

But James didn't really know where his brother Michael had lived during the years from 1966 to 1970. He believed Michael spent the years from 1970 to 1976 in the Chattahoochee State Hospital. From 1976 to 1978 Michael lived at Camp Emachamee. James could not name a single year that Michael had spent at home before the family moved to Colorado in May 1977. The longest period James could remember Michael spending at home before 1977 was two or three weeks. James had understood that his brother had spent those years in mental hospitals because Michael had been in a car accident when James was two years old. The accident had messed Michael's mind up a little bit. Michael liked to pretend to people that he was awkward and uncoordinated in order to get attention. Michael had always been an attention-getter, James said.

"Do you recall what month and year your brother went into the army?" Edgar continued.

"Seventy-nine. I believe it was June tenth," James mumbled.

"And where did he go for his first assignment?"

"Fort Leonard Wood, Missouri. He went all the way through basic training, and then he went to water treatment school."

"Did he want to be a water treatment expert like your stepfather, Bobby Joe Morris?"

"I don't know if that was the reason he went."

"Did he want to be in the service like your real father, James Goodyear?"

"I couldn't say that was the reason he went in."

"When is the first time Michael came home on leave?"

"After he got through with school. I don't remember the exact date."

"How long was he home on leave?"

"Less than a week."

"Then, after he was home on leave, where did he go for his first assignment?"

"Fort Benning, Georgia."

"How long was he there?"

"He stayed there. He was . . . he started . . . they tried to tell him—and he got sick and all, was in the hospital."

"Did he take any leave between the time that he went to Fort Benning and the time he came home?"

"No, sir, I don't believe so."

"Where was he right before he came home?"

"Tampa, Florida."

"Did you go down with your mother and pick Michael up on May twelfth, the day before he drowned, and drive straight back here?"

"Yes, sir."

"Do you recall being asked by the grand jury how long Michael had been home before the drowning and making the statement that he had been living at home?"

James paused before answering. "No, sir."

"When he came home on leave, where did Michael stay in the house?"

"I believe he slept in his room."

"Where is his room?"

"Where mine is now."

"How many bedrooms are in the house?"

"Three."

"And your sister had one?"

"Yes, sir."

"And you had one."

"Yes, sir."

"And your mother had one."

"Yes, sir."

"So, where did you sleep when Michael came home?"

"I believe I slept with my mother."

Edgar did a double take. He had watched James, during the previous break, stroll over to Judias seated at the defense table and kiss her hard on the mouth. It was not the sort of kiss a son normally gives his mother.

"Do you recall being asked . . . where Michael slept before the grand jury?" Edgar resumed.

"Yes, sir."

"What was your answer?"

"Downstairs. It was a roll-away bed."

"Is that because he couldn't climb the stairs?"

"No, sir."

"There wasn't anything wrong with Michael when he came home on leave?"

"No."

"Wasn't your answer to the question for the grand jury, you don't remember where your brother slept? You remember now?"

"Yes, sir."

"How long did you testify before the grand jury?"

"I believe it was about an hour and a half."

"You don't remember what you told the grand jury?"

"No, sir, not all of it."

"Do you recall me telling you that you may be possibly prejudicing your mother by failing to remember details?"

"No, sir."

"Do you recall me asking you, 'Please try to remember what happened that day'?"

"No, sir."

"Do you know David Lackey?"

"Yes, sir. He was my sister's boyfriend."

"Was? Not anymore?"

"No, sir."

"What did you tell David Lackey about how your brother drowned?"

Over defense counsel's objection, the judge allowed the witness to answer. "I really couldn't tell you," James said slowly.

"You can't remember that either?"

"No, sir, I try not to. I try not to discuss it. It was a very emotional thing for me."

"Well, you hardly knew your brother, did you?"

"No, sir, I loved my brother. You don't have to know somebody very well to love them. He was my brother."

"The day after your brother died, is it not true that you had a bunch of teenagers over at the house and you all were playing rock-and-roll music and partying?"

"No, sir."

"Do you know Dr. Nye, a neighbor?"

"Yes, sir."

"Do you know why he would make up such a thing as that?"

"I could imagine. We've never gotten along with him. His children egg our cars, shoot our house with BB guns."

"Do they have any reason to be hostile to you and your family?"

"No, sir. I don't believe so."

"So there are neighbors that dislike you in the neighborhood for no reason?"

"Yes, sir."

"But you did not throw a party the day after your brother died?"

"No, sir."

"What happened to the canoe?"

"After the accident?"

"Yes."

"We didn't want to have anything to do with it because it reminded us of what happened. Mr. Hill came and got it from the scene of the accident and took it and put it in storage."

"What about the motorboat?"

"There at the house."

"You skied with that boat that your mother bought for you, didn't you?"

"Yes, sir."

"And that was the boat you had available to you when your brother drowned?"

"Yes, sir."

"Well, why didn't you take the motorboat instead of the canoe?"

"Because he wanted to go canoeing."

"It was Michael's request?"

"Yes, sir."

"And Michael wasn't afraid of the water, because he was an athlete?"

"Yes, sir."

"Your brother lost a lot of weigh when he came home?"

"He lost a pretty good amount. Maybe twenty, twenty-five pounds."

"So how much did he weigh approximately when he died?"

"I really couldn't tell you."

"How tall was Michael?"

"I believe he was six foot."

"Do you recall the next question that I asked you before the grand jury, 'And you remembered that he was dying'?"

"Yes, sir."

"So the grand jury testimony was correct in one respect. You do remember your brother was dying when he went canoeing?"

"I was under the impression— I knew that to myself."

"Well, now that we have reached a point where you testified correctly, let me ask you: How did you get the impression that your brother was dying?"

"He was losing a lot of weight, and that's just the impression I got from him."

"He told you he was dying?"

"No, sir, he never told me. He just looked like he was dying."

"Did your mother tell you he was dying?"

"No, sir."

"Did the doctors tell you he was dying?"

"No, sir."

"Nobody in the world told you Michael was dying, but you thought he was."

"In my own mind, yes."

"So when you went canoeing, you figured that he might die any day now, so we better take him canoeing. Sort of a last wish?"

"No, sir. It was just something he wanted to do. See, he had been in the hospital cooped up for a long, long time."

"So, knowing that your brother was going to die, did you also understand that there was some insurance on his life?"

"No, sir, I never thought about that."

"You never really knew that your mother had collected over a hundred thousand dollars' insurance? . . . Do you have personal knowledge of great wealth your family came into after your brother's death?"

"No, sir, not until this happened."

"Is it not true that after your brother died, your mother bought a new Corvette?"

"I believe it was several months after."

"Did your mother also buy a business?"

"About a couple years after, I believe."

"Did your mother also quit work?"

"A long time after that happened."

"Did your mother also buy a mobile home?"

"Yes, sir."

"Did your mother also buy a new powerboat?"

"Yes, sir."

"Did you all take a trip on a cruise ship?"

"A couple of summers after."

"Is it not true that your mother opened a savings account in your name after your brother's death?"

"I believe they're in all our names."

"Is it not true that your mother purchased fifty-thousand dollars in certificates of deposit in your name after your brother's death?"

"I couldn't tell you. I don't keep up with her bank business."

"You don't remember going to the bank and signing the accounts?"

"Yes, sir. All I did was sign a card, though. It was used as a safeguard in case she— there was an accident and she couldn't get to the money, that we could."

"And there were accounts between you and Bob Hill, and your mother?"

"Yes, sir."

"Do you have any knowledge of your mother loaning Bob Hill any money?"

"Yes, sir."

"What relation is Bob Hill to you?"

"He's a friend."

"Now, since you have been testifying, is there anything that you recall that you would like to correct?"

"No, sir, I don't believe so."

"Do you still stand by your statement to the army?"

"Yes, sir."

"And lastly, would you tell the ladies and gentlemen of the jury, please, did I not give you an opportunity to read that statement to the grand jury?"

"No, sir, you handed it to me and let me look at it, and snatched it back."

"Did I ask you to review your signature?"

"Yes, sir, you did ask me to review my signature."

"Isn't it true that you said that you didn't know if that was your signature?"

"Yes, sir."

"But now you do recall that it is your signature?"

"Yes, sir, by seeing this. I didn't remember writing this at the time."

"You agree that I gave you an opportunity to write each and every word of that statement before the grand jury?"

"Yes, sir."

"And you didn't remember any of it, did you? Didn't even recognize your own signature on the statement, did you?"

"No, sir, but I was real nervous, and I had been—"

"You're not nervous at all today, are you?" Edgar interjected.

"Yes, sir."

"How come if you're so nervous now, and you were so nervous then, that your memory is so much better now?"

"Because I've had a lot of time to think about it and—"

"It wouldn't have anything to do with the fact that your mother's on trial, would it?" Edgar interposed.

"Yes, sir."

"The time you were summoned before the grand jury, you were under a John Doe subpoena. You were not told why you were going to the grand jury, were you?"

"No, sir, I was snatched up and put in a trailer out back."

"You didn't have an opportunity to discuss your testimony with anyone, did you?"

"Well, I didn't know what was going on, and I got in there, and you made all kinds of accusations towards me, accused me of things that I knew nothing about."

"And the grand jury was allowed to ask you questions?"

"Well, the way I took it, you already had them believing what they wanted to believe before I even got in there."

"So, you think the grand jury was unfair?"

"I believe you were unfair, sir," James retaliated with a resentful glare.

As Judge Lowrey declared a thirty-minute recess, James slunk back to the witness room with a backward glance at his mother. Judias, a twisted tissue clutched between her hands, blew her son a kiss from across the room.

Following the prosecution's grueling confrontation, Johnston's cross-examination of James was mercifully brief. The blunt edge of his hostility softened by a note of indignant self-pity, James gazed up at his lawyer, earnest and doe-eyed.

"Now, James," Johnston asked confidently, "did your mother murder your brother?"

"No, sir, she did not. She loved my brother dearly. So did I," James protested as Judias dabbed at her eyes with a tissue.

"If you thought your mother murdered your brother, would you say so?"

"Yes, sir."

"Did your mother show any partiality among her children?"

"No, sir. We were all treated alike."

"Did she at any time express to you being ashamed of Michael?"

"No, sir, never."

"Did she provide for Michael the same things she provided for you and your sister?"

"Yes, sir."

"Did she buy him a motorcycle?"

"Yes, sir."

"Did she agonize and worry over his hospitalization?"

"Yes, sir. Day and night. That's all she thought about."

"Approximately when did Michael come home from Fort Leonard Wood, Missouri?"

"Around November first. 'Cause it was Halloween, and I know Michael wasn't there during Halloween."

"And you say that he lost about twenty pounds?"

"Yes, sir. When he got off the plane, he was real flushed in the face and looked like he'd been sunburned. And I remember my mother making the statement that she didn't understand how he could be sunburned in the middle of winter in Missouri."

"And how long was he able to stay home on his leave?"

"I believe he stayed home a couple of days, and then he got sick and we took him to the hospital. He never even got to finish his leave."

"Who took him to the hospital?"

"My mother. And just me and my sister. We left a couple of days before his leave was ended and took him back to Fort Benning, Georgia, to the hospital there."

"And did you arrive at Fort Benning around two o'clock in the morning?"

"Yes, sir. We stayed there several days."

"And then they finally admitted him to the hospital?"

"Yes, sir, and then we went right back home after that."

"Do you know whether your mother had suggested to Michael to seek medical help?"

"I don't believe so. I believe she wanted him to see a doctor 'cause he didn't look right, his face and all. And then when he got sick, you know, that was when she, uh—"

"Took him?"

"Yes, sir."

"Where did you spend Christmas 1979?"

"We went to spend Christmas with my brother in the hospital. You had to wear plastic gloves and a mask to go in to see him."

"How did that affect your mother?"

"It upset her real bad. She couldn't understand what happened—why he was like this."

"And where did Michael go after he left the hospital at Fort Benning, Georgia?"

"He went to several hospitals in that area."

"Did your mother contact him by phone?"

"Yes, sir. He called almost every night."

"Did you really keep up with your brother's condition?"

"I didn't really want to know what was going on. I was afraid, and it would upset me and my sister. So we sort of tried to stay out of the picture."

"Is it true, then, that you didn't see Michael from Christmas until he was discharged from the VA hospital on May twelfth, 1980?"

"Yes, sir."

"What was his condition when he came home?"

"He could walk with his crutches and his braces. He could maneuver up the stairs. He got in and out of the bathtub by himself."

"And the day that you decided to go canoeing, was Michael able to walk to the car?"

"Yes, sir, I figured he could do anything that he could've done before, but it was with greater difficulty."

"Do you know whether your mother had talked about making any special preparations for Michael?"

"Yes, sir, she was going to have a room built on the house where she could take better care of him. She was going to have a bathroom built with bars and all, so he could maneuver in and out a lot easier. She was going to put ramps on all the house stairs and doors so he could get in and out when he couldn't walk or was in his wheelchair. You know, just in general."

"Does your mother drink?"

"No, sir, she does not. I've seen people hand her drinks and seen her standing there and hold them just to keep from hurting their feelings, and not drink it. Find a place to set it down or pour it out."

Johnston paused before continuing. "I want to refer you now to state's exhibit 1-B, which is your statement. Are you saying to this court and this jury that without a doubt you wrote that statement?"

"No, sir, I'm not—I don't really—I couldn't honestly tell you that I did," James stammered.

"Did you not say on direct examination that you wrote it?"

"Yes, sir."

"Why did you say that?"

"I don't really know. After looking at it, and thinking back, I really couldn't say that I wrote it. It was handed to me, I looked at it, and it was taken back. And all I saw was my signature."

"The signature on page two and the initial on page one, is that your signature and initial?"

"I really couldn't tell you. They look like mine."

"Is it your best judgment, then, that it is your signature?"

"Yes, sir."

"Is everything on this statement exactly true and correct?"

"Yes, sir," James stonewalled.

It was after five P.M. when Edgar began to refute James's testimony with a parade of medical experts.

Dr. Michael Dupuis, the physician who had treated James in the West Florida Hospital emergency room the day of the drowning, testified that James had told him that he had never lost consciousness from the time the canoe capsized. At no time had Dr. Dupuis informed James or his mother that James had a hairline fracture of the seventh cervical vertebra.

Dr. David Nicholson of Sacred Heart Hospital, who had performed the autopsy on Michael Goodyear's body, stated that the cause of death was drowning. Dr. Nicholson believed the cause of Michael's nervous disorder and paralysis was heavy metal poisoning due to ingestion of arsenic and lead. On cross-examination, Johnston succeeded in raising the point that such poisoning could have been the result of Michael's condition of pica, in which he would compulsively put objects into his mouth such as pencils, dirt, and paint.

Following a brief recess, Edgar called Dr. Michael Barry to the stand as the beleaguered jury returned to its box at six P.M.

The young Walter Reed Army Medical Center physician had treated Michael Goodyear on a daily basis from January to April 1980. His testimony painted a very different picture of Michael's limited capabilities from what James had described.

At the time he first met Michael in January 1980, Dr. Barry testified, the patient was suffering from severe peripheral neuropathy to the extent that he had no neural or muscular function from his knees or his elbows down.

Dr. Barry demonstrated the limp angle at which Michael's wrists and ankles had uselessly hung. Essentially paralyzed from the elbows to fingertips, and knees to toes, Barry stated, Michael suffered from both physiological and emotional stress. Severely depressed, Michael had expressed concern to Dr. Barry over his inability to walk or have an erection. The last time Dr. Barry saw Michael, in April 1980, his condition had improved only slightly. There was some movement in his fingers and wrists, but there was not enough strength in his muscle group to move the joints. Michael could not write. Before he was hooked up to his Robbins' Hook device, Michael would circle his choice of food on the hospital menus by holding a pencil in his mouth, Dr. Barry explained.

As plaintiff's exhibit, Edgar produced a Robbins' Hook device similar to the one worn by Michael on his right arm. Dr. Barry obliged by strapping the ungainly metal pincher to his wrist and connecting the attached cord to a device on his shoulder fixed in two places in the back. Barry demonstrated to the jury how the pincher was opened by shrugging his shoulder forward, or closed to form a grip by relaxing his shoulder back. The strength of the grip depended on the tightness of the band holding the pinchers together. In Dr. Barry's opinion, Michael could not possibly have paddled a canoe or cast a fishing line using the Robbins' Hook device.

Edgar next produced plaintiff's exhibit ten, holding aloft a long pair of stainless steel braces with heavy black orthopedic shoes attached. Dr. Barry identified the Watson leg braces worn by Michael. Barry explained how the braces locked the legs in full extension with a locking bale brace behind the knees. By using his hips and thigh muscles, Michael could manage to walk peg-leg without using the distal part of his legs. The last time Dr. Barry had seen Michael, he was able, with assistance, to walk at most fifteen feet in his leg braces with the use of platform crutches. The predominant motion Dr. Barry had witnessed Michael do on his own was scooting backward and forward along the floor. Dr. Barry's medical opinion was that Michael's condition was permanent.

Judias's pallid face remained an immobile mask as the doctor's devastating testimony continued.

On at least one occasion, Dr. Barry said, Michael had mentioned the possibility of a boat ride. Dr. Barry had told Michael that, if the craft turned over, he would never be able to swim and would probably drown unless he was protected by an adequate life preserver. Michael had made no mention of a canoe to Dr. Barry.

Edgar's direct examination further revealed that in telephone conversations with Dr. Barry, Judias had stated that Michael started to do poorly in school in the tenth grade, and that while in school he had eaten everything, including lead paint from a house built in 1909. On March 28, 1980, Judias told Dr. Barry that she was planning to spend forty thousand dollars on renovations to her house in preparation for Michael's return home. Judias told Dr. Barry that she was a Ph.D. and worked at a drug and alcohol rehabilitation center. Judias had indicated that she was independently wealthy and, if needed, would be willing to quit work to take care of Michael. She was willing to do anything for Michael except visit him in the hospital, Dr. Barry said.

At the time Michael was released from Walter Reed in April 1980, his prognosis was very poor, in that he had reached a static equilibrium with his muscle and nerve function. The best he could ever hope for was to be able to wash, toilet, and feed himself, Dr. Barry concluded.

It had already been a very long day when Johnston rose to cross-examine. "Doctor, the warm sunshine and fresh air of Florida can do a lot of therapy, can't it?"

"I guess so, sir," Dr. Barry replied.

"A lot of willpower, particularly for a nineteen-year-old, will go a long way in accomplishing rehabilitation?"

"I would think so, sir, but it doesn't cure dead nerves," Barry insisted.

"What is your medical specialty, Doctor?"

"I'm in internal medicine."

"Isn't that really a matter for the neurologist to determine?"

"A point well taken, sir," Barry conceded.

14

Friends and Forgery

On SATURDAY, MARCH 24, EDGAR continued his assault on James Buenoano's testimony, enhancing the pathetic portrait of Michael Goodyear with the personal testimony of neighbors and friends of the Buenoano family.

Dr. John David Nye, a nattily attired Baptist Hospital surgeon, lived about two hundred feet from the Buenoano home. Pointing out the defendant, Dr. Nye said that he had known Judias Buenoano casually since she first moved into the neighborhood a few years before. Dr. Nye's four children would play ball in the neighborhood with James. Michael, who appeared physically uncoordinated, did not participate in the neighborhood games, Dr. Nye stated. Michael seemed lonely and a little slow, and he often came into the kitchen and sat and talked to Dr. Nye and his wife about nothing in particular.

Dr. Nye remembered introducing himself to Judias at her front door shortly after she moved in. The previous owner, a contractor, had told Dr. Nye excitedly that he had sold the house for cash to another doctor. Dr. Nye had thought it would be nice to have a colleague in the neighborhood he could talk with. When Dr. Nye said he understood she was a doctor, Judias had said she was. She had indicated that she was a psychologist in Fort Walton. Judias had also indicated that Michael was not her son but a stepson from a second marriage. Michael had been in an accident with his father, who was killed. Michael was seriously injured and that was why he was slow, Judias had explained.

Shortly after the drowning, Dr. Nye testified, he had

Judias Buenoano on trial for the murder of her husband,
James F. Goodyear. *(Pensacola News Journal)*

In happier days, on a holiday cruise. Judias with her younger son, James, and her fiancé, John W. Gentry.

With son James, daughter Kimberly and fiancé John W. Gentry.

Judias's older son,
Michael Buenoano,
in army uniform.

East River Bridge over Highway 87 in Santa Rosa County,
Florida, the scene of the drowning of Michael Buenoano.

John W. Gentry's bombed automobile, from which he miraculously escaped alive though badly injured. *(Pensacola News Journal)*

Detective Ted "Geronimo" Chamberlain, who painstakingly followed the clues which led to Judias's arrest.

Russell Edgar, Florida Assistant State Attorney, who successfully prosecuted Judias.

Special Agent Robert Cousson, representing the Federal Bureau of Alcohol, Tobacco and Firearms (ATF).

A television clip of Judias with Ted Chamberlain, whom she considered her implacable enemy.

Judias with Rebecca Johnston, who worked with her husband, James Johnston, as co-counsel for the defense.

DEATH WARRANT
STATE OF FLORIDA

WHEREAS, Judias Buenoano did on the 16th day of September, 1971, murder James E. Goodyear; and

WHEREAS, Judias Buenoano was found guilty of murder in the first degree and was sentenced to death on the 26th day of November, 1985; and

WHEREAS, on the 23rd day of June, 1988, the Florida Supreme Court upheld the sentence of death imposed upon Judias Buenoano, and

WHEREAS, it has been determined that Executive Clemency, as authorized by Article IV, Section 8(a), Florida Constitution, is not appropriate; and

WHEREAS, attached hereto is a copy of the record pursuant to Section 922.09, Florida Statutes;

NOW THEREFORE, I, BOB MARTINEZ, as Governor of the State of Florida and pursuant to the authority and responsibility vested by the Constitution and Laws of Florida do hereby issue this warrant directing the Superintendent of the Florida State Prison to cause the sentence of death to be executed upon Judias Buenoano on some day of the week beginning noon, Wednesday, the 24th day of January, 1990, and ending noon, Wednesday, the 31st day of January, 1990, in accord with the provisions of the laws of the State of Florida.

IN TESTIMONY WHEREOF, I have hereunto set my hand and caused the Great Seal of the State of Florida to be affixed at Tallahassee, the Capitol, this November 9, 1989.

_____
GOVERNOR

ATTEST:

_____
SECRETARY OF STATE

G-739 (New 7/77)

Judias's death warrant, signed by then Governor Bob Martinez on November 9, 1989.

Judias during a tense trial moment. *(Pensacola News Journal)*

offered his condolences to James for his brother's death. Asked how the accident happened, James had told Dr. Nye that Michael and his mother were in one canoe and he was in another canoe with his sister. A snake had dropped into Michael's canoe, and the canoe overturned. James had tried to save his brother, he said, but he couldn't.

Upon cross-examination, Johnston brought out the point that Dr. Nye had called the police on James some fifteen times for speeding and driving before he had a license. Dr. Nye explained that he had had several conversations with Judias concerning her inability to control James's language and his smoking marijuana, at age thirteen, in front of the Nye children.

"Your kids are angels and James is a devil?" Johnston charged.

"Don't talk that way to me, sir!" Dr. Nye fired back. "James got into trouble and did a lot juvenile-delinquency-type activities."

"Your kids egged his house, and that's not juvenile trouble?" Johnston argued.

"Our cat was killed by one of James's friends leaving the Buenoano house. My youngest, a ten-year-old, threw one egg that landed in their driveway, and the police were called. I took my son over the next day and had him apologize to them," Dr. Nye explained testily.

"Doctor, if I talked aggressively, I do want to apologize," Johnston retreated.

"You did, and it was uncalled for," Dr. Nye replied.

Edgar's impeachment of James Buenoano's testimony continued with the depositions of Michael Goodyear's high school counselor and teachers.

Conrad Owens, a counselor at Gulf Breeze High School for over twelve years, testified about Michael's school records. In 1976–77 Michael had attended J. Lee Pickens School in Pensacola in the educationally handicapped program. The following year Michael attended Trinidad Catholic High School in Trinidad, Colorado. Notations on Michael's transcripts indicated that he did not attend the full school year in Trinidad. Michael's grades were in the C and D+ range, including a quarter credit in physical education. Michael's grades during his attendance at Gulf Breeze High School in 1978–79 were all below passing with the exception of physical education for which he was basically required merely to wear a gym uniform each day. Michael completed one out of six credits that he took in the eleventh grade. Where seventy was passing, Michael's final grade in general science was fifty-nine; in record keeping, fifty-seven; in general business, twenty; in basic composition, forty-six; in American literature, twenty-five; and in physical education, eighty-nine.

A psychological examination made on Michael in February 1979 indicated his IQ was in the vicinity of ninety-one. Though below average, Michael did not have a specified learning disability, Owens stated.

Michael's complete school transcripts had been sent to the educational division at Fort Benning, Georgia, on November 19, 1979, seven months after Michael was inducted into the United States Army.

Jerry Henderson, a coach and trainer at Gulf Breeze High School since 1967, testified that Michael Goodyear had been his manager for the girls' basketball team, in charge of taking care of the equipment for practice and road games. Michael had not played basketball, football, or baseball, Coach Henderson said. He did not participate in track, wrestling, boxing, swimming, water skiing, or scuba diving, or any other sports program offered at the high school. Michael was a very poor athlete, in Coach Henderson's opinion.

Henderson had taken time with Michael. He felt Michael was often treated cruelly by the other students. After Michael left school and joined the army, he would call Coach Henderson at his home in the evenings, just to talk.

Johnston objected to the relation of any conversation between Henderson and Michael on the basis of hearsay; Judge Lowrey sustained.

In response to Edgar's questioning, Henderson related that in a conversation with Judias Buenoano, she had revealed that she was not Michael's mother, that his real mother had been killed in an automobile accident with Michael and that just about every bone in Michael's body had been broken. Johnston moved to strike the statement, but Judge Lowrey overruled.

Coach Henderson's last telephone conversation with Michael was just before he came home for leave in late October 1979. He did not see or hear from Michael again.

"The state calls Mrs. Constance Lang," Edgar pronounced.

The woman known to Pensacola police as the former Connie Gilmore, a friend of Judias Buenoano in Orlando whose ex-husband purportedly had an affair with Judias before the death of her husband James Goodyear, stoically approached the witness stand.

Pointing out the defendant as Judi Goodyear, Constance Lang tightened her long upper lip into a thin line. Her square jaw firmly set and her dark-circled eyes hidden behind thick lenses, Mrs. Constance Lang said that she had known the defendant since they were neighbors in Orlando in 1969. She had moved with Judias to Pensacola in 1972. Lang had moved in with Judias in Orlando shortly after her first husband, James Goodyear, died. Judias started having seizures at the funeral, and she had asked Lang to stay with her and help her out with the children. In return, Judias would pay her living expenses and twenty or thirty dollars a week, Lang explained.

Lang first met Michael Goodyear in Orlando while he was home for a visit from his special school in Miami. Lang remembered Michael living at the Miami school from 1969 to 1972. She recalled James Goodyear being home on Michael's occasional visits with the family.

"Judi and James didn't have a very good relationship, but a lot of people don't," Lang said.

Michael's relationship with his father was pretty good, but Judias was very distant with Michael. She was ashamed of him, Lang said. Particularly in Pensacola, whenever anybody would come to visit, Judias would tell Lang, her live-in baby-sitter, to put ten-year-old Michael in the car and drive around with him until the visitors had left. Lang had to take Michael out six or eight times in the two weeks he was home for the Christmas holidays.

"There was something wrong with Michael," Lang said. "He wasn't bad as in misbehaving. He just didn't behave the way a normal child would. He was messy. He slobbered a lot and was hyper, waving his arms and that kind of thing. He had trouble with coordination."

There was almost no interaction between Judias and Michael, Lang continued.

"As long as he wasn't making a ruckus, he was pretty much left on his own. She was really good with Kim and Jimmy, but not with Michael."

Judias never admitted to Lang that there was anything wrong with Michael, saying that he was at a school for children with special talents. Judias had not discussed Michael's parentage, but Lang knew Michael did not belong to James Goodyear. She had assumed Michael's father was from a previous marriage or relationship.

On cross-examination, Johnston brought out the fact that Constance Lang had given up her own two children, Lisa and George, into her husband's custody.

"I couldn't afford to keep them," Lang replied bluntly. "They were doing without because my husband wouldn't pay child support. I had my choice of letting them go hungry or letting him take care of them. I chose the one I thought was best for them."

"What occupation did the defendant have when you knew her in Orlando?" Edgar redirected.

"She opened a child care center. She ran it all day. But she couldn't have given Michael any specialized help," Lang volunteered.

"You were and are the defendant's friend?"

"Yes."

"You bear no malice toward her?"

"No, Judi was probably the best friend I've ever had," Constance Lang attested.

Next a lanky young uniformed air force sergeant stumbled up to the witness stand. Having been duly sworn, Sgt. Kenneth Barnes nervously stated that he was a line mechanic on the F-16, that he had graduated from Gulf Breeze High School in May 1979, and that he had known the Buenoanos since they had moved into the neighborhood three houses down from his own family's home at 2803 Whisper Pine Drive. Then he asked for a glass of water.

"Let me ask you this, Sergeant Barnes," Edgar gently directed. "Were you a friend of Michael Buenoano?"

"Yes, very much. From the day I met him," Barnes gulped.

"Was there anything different about Michael from the other kids in the neighborhood?"

"Mike was slow. Mike had a whining or a nasal type of tone in his voice, like he talked halfway through his nose. Mike was severely scarred on his face and parts of his body. Mike was not very coordinated."

"Was Michael ridiculed in the neighborhood by any of the other children?"

"Yes."

"Did you ever engage in ridiculing Mike?"

"Yes, I have. But we were real close friends in the neighborhood. I was protective of him, in a way. He was a year under me in school."

"What were some of the activities that Michael and you engaged in? What did you all do together?"

"We rode his motorcycle together."

"Did Mike like surfing?"

"No. Mike never surfed that I know of."

"Did he ever like to go water skiing?"

"Not that I know of."

"Did you ever go canoeing with him?"

"No, never."

"Did you ever go swimming with him?"

"No, never that I can remember. I took my dog swimming down to East Bay—not even half a mile, really. We would walk down there numerous times, and Mike would usually stay up on the beach, writing in the sand or throwing stuff in the water."

"Are you one of the fortunate ones whose family has a swimming pool?"

"Yes, I am."

"Was Mike invited to come use the swimming pool?"

"Mike would come over and he'd usually sit on the end of the brick wall there and talk with people when they'd come out of the water."

"What was your opinion of Mike's athletic abilities?"

"Very poor."

"Were Michael and James friends?"

Sergeant Barnes paused, unable to answer directly.

"Did it appear that James liked Michael?" Edgar reiterated.

"James and Michael didn't really get along." Sergeant Barnes paused again. "I cannot say there was hatred there, but there wasn't a brotherly-love bond between them."

"Did they do anything together?"

"Not that I can remember, no."

"Did they ever play sports together?"

"To the best of my knowledge, no."

"Did Mrs. Buenoano, from what you observed, give much attention to Michael?"

"While all three were together, there was no doubt in my mind that James was Mrs. Buenoano's boy. That's how I'll put it. You could definitely tell the difference between Mike and James. There was a true, hard bond between James and Mrs. Buenoano, whereas with Mike, the bond wasn't there. Mike tried. Mike's heart was all in it. But the feedback he got from her wasn't the same as it was with the other children."

"Do you think that Michael loved his mother?"

"Yes, very much."

"Did you ever observe Mrs. Buenoano disciplining Michael? Did you hear her call him any names?"

"She called him 'stupid.' She called him 'idiot.' She called him 'dumb.' "

"Had Michael done something to warrant such treatment?"

"No. The way I was raised, parents don't call their children 'stupid,' 'idiots,' 'dumb.' "

"Do you recall the last time you saw Michael before his death?"

"It was shortly before he died. He was in bed downstairs in the living room. He was awake. He was in a reclined position with his legs stretched out on the bed. He was a paraplegic at that time. I talked to him around fifteen minutes."

"Did you have the opportunity to talk with Mrs. Buenoano?"

"Yes, I did. Mrs. Buenoano and myself were standing at her front door. She said that Michael was not doing very well, and that they—I assume she meant the doctors—said he would not live another six weeks. She said that Michael was a dead man. There were no emotions in her face. It was like a normal conversation."

Spying James Johnston standing alone in the courthouse hallway during a recess in the Saturday afternoon proceedings, Edgar marched smartly up to his courtroom adversary.

" 'Flog the prisoner!' said Captain Bligh," Edgar quoted without ceremony. " 'But Captain, the prisoner's dead.'

" 'Flog him anyway!' " Edgar quipped, and turning on his heels, walked away from the bewildered Johnston.

The prosecution of Judias Buenoano pressed relentlessly on through Monday, March 26, as a parade of insurance agents, former employers, and bank custodians set the stage for Edgar's planned introduction of similar-fact evidence to establish a common motive of insurance fraud in the deaths of Michael Goodyear, Bobby Joe Morris, and James Goodyear.

First, Edgar laid out the insurance payoffs on Michael Goodyear before the increasingly strained jury. Walter Davis, Jr., of Newark, New Jersey, an attorney for the Prudential Insurance Company, testified that Goodyear's OSGLI military insurance paid $20,451.20 on June 6, 1980, to Judias W. Buenoano.

On cross-examination, Johnston made the point that Michael had listed the beneficiary on his military insurance policy as "by law," though he could have specifically listed his mother, a friend, or even a charity. In the absence of any living father, spouse, or children, Michael's insurance benefits went to his mother, Judias Welty Buenoano.

John W. Burgess of Metropolitan Life Insurance Company's Tampa office testified that his company paid Judias Buenoano $2,071.85 and $1,750.31 on two policies purchased in 1962 and 1964. On April 5, 1980, five weeks before Michael's death, Metropolitan received a written request to reissue copies of the policies because the originals had been lost. The request was signed by both Judias Buenoano and Michael Goodyear.

Stanley Ball of Prudential's Jacksonville office testified that Prudential paid claims to Judias Buenoano on two other policies taken out on Michael Goodyear. One payment was on a $15,000 policy purchased in 1978 with a double indemnity clause that paid $45,000. The other was $40,493.97 paid on a $20,000 policy with a single indemnity accident rider purchased seven months before Goodyear's death.

Roy Black, a retired Prudential investigator from Birmingham, Alabama, who checked out Goodyear's death for the insurance company, said that Judias Buenoano had given him an impressive account of her medical training.

"She went on to explain that she had a doctor's degree in nursing and a degree in anatomy, and at the time she was preparing to get an M.D.," the investigator testified.

Edgar next called Donald J. Fournier to the stand,

the Pensacola Prudential agent who had sold Judias the last twenty-thousand-dollar policy purchased on Michael Goodyear in October 1979. He presented the slow-talking veteran insurance agent with state exhibit nineteen—the insurance application dated October 8, 1979, signed by Fournier, Judias Buenoano, and the proposed insured, Michael Buenoano.

"With respect to her son, Michael, did the defendant indicate to you that she already had previous insurance?" Edgar asked.

"I believe, as far as I know, she had a fifteen-thousand-dollar policy with us taken out years before," Fournier drawled.

"Did she indicate whether there was current insurance, in addition, on the insured?"

"She said her son was in the army, and all army people have SGLI insurance. On the form here, it says, 'SGLI, twenty-thousand-dollar 1979 group insurance.' "

"What previous health problems, if any, or hospitalization did you make note of when you talked to Mrs. Buenoano about insuring her son?"

"On the application it says the last time he went to a doctor was April 1979 for a US Army enlistment physical." Fournier read the document.

"Who told you that?" Edgar asked.

"Mrs. Buenoano."

"Did she say when he was last hospitalized?"

"Yes, she said he was hospitalized in September of 1975 for one day for a broken nose from a football injury."

"Did she indicate any other hospitalization or inpatient treatment?" Edgar queried.

"No, sir, not according to this," Fournier stated, referring to the application in his hands.

"Was there any information in there about a Montanari School or hospital in Miami?"

"No, sir."

"Was there any information in there about Camp Emachamee, Eckerd's Boys' Camp, or Orange Memorial

Hospital in Orlando, Florida?" Edgar persisted.

"No, sir," Fournier replied meekly.

"Does the application have the signature of the insured?"

"Yes, it does."

"And did he sign that application in your presence on October 8, 1979?"

"No, sir. I didn't really talk to him."

"Did you ever meet or shake hands with Michael?"

"No, sir."

"Do you normally sit down and go over detailed background information or get a physical on a child with a policy of this small size?"

"No, sir. We usually trust the parents' judgment."

"Now tell me," Edgar continued, "did the defendant in this case get insurance on her own life at this time?"

"Yes, she did, fifty-thousand dollars."

"Did she maintain the premiums on her son Michael's policy?"

"Yes, she did."

"Did she maintain the premiums on the policy on her own life?"

"She made one or two payments on the policy, then it lapsed. Then, of course, we chased her down two or three times and the policy renewed again."

"Tell me, why did you chase her down?" Edgar asked.

"Well, any policy that is in a lapsed condition in the first two years gets charged back to the company from the agent all the way up the line to the vice president of the corporation. With a policy like hers, we get fifty thousand dollars writing credit in the district for trophy points. So by reinstating it, we get credit. It's part of the business," Fournier explained.

"Did you give the defendant a form to fill out for the claim for benefits after Michael's death?"

"Oh, yes."

"Where was that signed, sir?"

"It says in Gulf Breeze, Florida, on May 21, 1980," Fournier read from the form.

Edgar resumed his seat, leaving his point unspoken. Judias had barely waited a week after her son's death to stake her insurance claim.

Johnston strolled up to the witness stand to cross-examine.

"Mr. Fournier, your best recollection is that Mrs. Buenoano did not call Prudential requesting a new insurance policy to be written?"

"Yes. She called and talked to my manager, and my manager gave it to me to go out there and service this good client from Colorado," Fournier volunteered.

"And the call was made to get necessary forms to change her mailing address?" Johnston prompted.

"That would be one reason, yes, sir. You would want your billing to be in the right location—"

"And you thought that this might be a good prospect for you, so you did what a good insurance man would do and you called on her?" Johnston interposed.

"Oh, yes, we have to service our clients," Fournier responded.

"And was it through your power of persuasion, or salesmanship, that she finally decided to buy something?"

"I would like to think that, sir," the agent deadpanned, prompting general laughter in the tense courtroom.

"Just a routine call, a new policy holder, let me go out here and see if I can sell her some insurance?" Johnston continued.

"Yes, I didn't see nothing unusual about this case, sir," Fournier insisted.

"Is it unusual for a parent to take out insurance on a child that's in the service?"

"No, definitely not."

"In fact, you wrote not only a policy on Michael, you wrote one on her and all the other children," Johnston remarked, producing defendant's exhibit two. "Mr. Fournier, is that the copy of the other policy you wrote on Mrs. Buenoano?"

"Yeah, it looks like— Yes, sir, I would say it is a copy

of the policy," Fournier confirmed, examining the document Johnston handed him. "I sold her an economatic term policy to sixty-eight. That's a level term policy that expires when she is sixty-eight years of age. The policy was fifty-thousand dollars with double indemnity for accidental death."

"And it's dated the same day?"

"No, this is dated April third, 1980," Fournier read from the document.

"Okay, I believe that was when it was reinstated," Johnston quickly interjected. "Who were the beneficiaries on Mrs. Buenoano's policy?"

"It states here on the policy that the first beneficiary was Michael Buenoano, James Buenoano, and Kimberly Buenoano, children of the insured, provided for each beneficiary alike," Fournier read. "In the death of Mrs. Buenoano, the money would be given to a Robert E. Hill, a friend, trustee for any children under the age of twenty-one. Any child over the age twenty-one would get his proportionate share, with the balance to the trustee."

"Now, turning to your salesmanship on the date of October eighth, 1979, who was it that suggested to Mrs. Buenoano that she take out fifty-thousand dollars' worth of insurance on herself?"

"Well, the insured wanted to insure the children. . . . On a child, an insurance company will not insure more than half what the parent is carrying. At the time, Mrs. Buenoano wanted term insurance, and we couldn't put the three children on because Michael was too old to be put on a child's rider. I believe at the time, 1979, the maximum on children was twenty thousand dollars," Fournier explained.

"In the case of Michael, though, his was not a rider. It was a regular policy. She could've gotten a hundred thousand, two hundred thousand?" Johnston proposed.

Fournier hesitated.

"Fifty thousand?" Johnston pressed.

"With their life-style, yes, sir. Anybody who lives in Gulf Breeze—Gulf Breeze is not a questionable community with the Prudential. I would consider Gulf Breeze residents as class people, sir."

"That would include my client?" Johnston asked, with a sweeping gesture toward the expressionless defendant.

"Yes, sir," Fournier agreed.

On redirect, Edgar asked the agent when the defendant arrived in Gulf Breeze. "Wasn't it August 1978? The policy is dated October 1979. You didn't know the defendant had already been in town fourteen months when she called your agency?"

"No—No, I did not, no, sir. I personally did not know," the witness protested.

"Now, you said a person with her kind of life-style. What type of employment did she have?" Edgar quietly persisted, cross-examining his own witness.

"I was told she was an RN; she was going for a doctor's degree in Birmingham. That's all I knew at the time," Fournier insisted.

"Did you know she was making three dollars and seventy cents an hour?" Edgar rejoined.

"I was not aware of that," Fournier vowed, shaking his head slowly.

Pressing on, Edgar next called representatives of Judias Buenoano's former employers, effectively demonstrating that her income could not have supported her classy Gulf Breeze life-style and disproving once and for all her repeated claims to advanced degrees.

John McCullen of University Hospital in Pensacola testified that the defendant had worked there as a nurse's aide in 1975 and 1976, starting at $2.56 an hour and ending at $2.64 an hour. Judias's employment application had listed her education as completion of high school and attendance at a university for study of general subjects. Edgar supplied Judias's job application as state's evidence for the jury's perusal. Attached to the application was a snapshot Judias had submitted of herself in 1975 slouched cross-legged in an armchair wearing a miniskirt and a braless tank top. The jury was not favorably impressed.

Shirley Hoggard of the Escambia County Nursing Home testified that Judias had worked there as a nurse's aide from November 1976 to January 1977 making $457.60 a month. Judias had listed her education as completion of high school with a course in nurse's aide training, and no college.

Greg Kelly of the Okaloosa Guidance Clinic testified that Judias Buenoano had worked there as a licensed practical nurse from December 1978 until September 1980 making $3.70 an hour. She listed her education as two years of junior college in Colorado and attendance at the University of South Alabama in Mobile.

Edgar completed his carefully constructed presentation of the defendant's educational and financial background with testimony on Judias's bank records.

Dorothy Balsley of Barnett Bank in Pensacola attested that between June 1979 and July 1980, Judias had twenty-four checks totaling $1,129.34 returned for insufficient funds. Her account balance dropped below zero thirteen different times. (On cross-examination, however, Balsley said that such a record was about average for any account holder.) Balsley also testified that beginning in July 1980, Judias began depositing insurance checks into her account, nearly forty thousand dollars that month and more than twenty thousand dollars two months later.

Kathleen Smith of Pensacola Home and Savings testified that in July and September 1980, Judias purchased fifty-six thousand dollars in certificates of deposit in her and her surviving children's names. Much of the money came directly from insurance checks; more came from the Barnett Bank checking account, Smith stated.

From financial background, the prosecution proceeded to more personal testimony. The defendant's sister-in-law, a tall, gaunt, horse-faced woman, took the witness stand with an erect bearing and a dour expression.

Having identified the defendant as the former Ann Goodyear, married to her brother, James Goodyear, who died in 1971, Margaret "Peggy" Goeller of Homossassa Springs, Florida, proceeded to testify in the short, restrained tones of long-suppressed anger.

"What relation were you to Michael Goodyear?" Edgar directed.

"My nephew."

"And James Allen and Kimberly Goodyear?"

"My nephew and my niece."

"Was Michael Goodyear your brother's natural son?"

"No."

"Was he Ann or Judi Goodyear's natural son?"

"I thought he was . . . I don't know. She had him before they were married."

"After your brother died, did you have any contact with your niece or nephews?"

"From 1971, the next and last time I saw them was Christmas Day 1980. They came to my house for Christmas dinner."

"Was your father, their grandfather, there?"

"Yes."

"And did you have much correspondence with the defendant and her children between 1971 and 1980?"

"I had one letter from my sister-in-law. We didn't know where to find her after she left Pensacola. My husband worked for the government and he got in touch with the VA to find out where she was. My father was concerned about the grandchildren. The VA said if we wrote her a letter, they would forward it to her. Consequently, I got a letter back from her."

"Do you have that letter with you?"

"Yes, I do," Mrs. Goeller replied, presenting four handwritten pages and an envelope postmarked February 11, 1978, to the prosecutor. Edgar moved the letter into evidence as state exhibit twenty-seven to serve as a standard for handwriting analysis.

"Did you have any telephone conversations with the defendant between 1971 and 1980?" Edgar resumed his direct examination.

"Yes, I did. Two in one day. If I could explain?" Peggy Goeller asked.

"Please," Edgar invited.

"My father took quite ill in March 1980. He was in the hospital in Pennsylvania for ten weeks. That was the first winter that we started to come down and stay with him in Florida. So when we came down in November 1980, we tried to call Ann in Gulf Breeze, where she lives. And they told us there was no telephone listing under Goodyear. So my husband wrote her a letter. She called me then, and told me she had changed her name to the Indian name because she was working with alcoholics and drug users, and she didn't want them calling her on the telephone at home. I asked her if I could bring my father up to see the children, and she said yes. Then she called me back and told me that Michael had died."

"She didn't tell you that in the first conversation?"

"No. She said that she wanted me to know that Michael had died before we brought my father up. She told me that Michael was in the army and that they were on maneuvers and he got injured during chemical warfare, or something to that effect."

"Did she tell you that Michael had been paralyzed and was wearing braces?"

"No. I knew he was in Walter Reed Hospital, she told me that."

"Did she tell you that he had drowned?"

"No."

"Did she tell you about a canoe trip or a snake falling into the boat, or anything about hitting a submerged log?"

"No."

"When was the first time that you heard that Michael had drowned?"

"When Detective Chamberlain told me sometime last November."

"So, from November 1980 until November 1983, you assumed your nephew had died in the army on maneuvers?"

"Yes."

"Now, after these conversations, there was a visit at Christmas when they came down to your home in Homossassa. Did you discuss Michael's death then?"

"No, she told me that she'd rather we didn't talk about Michael in front of the children, because it upset them so much. And that Michael was more of a friend to them than a brother."

"From Christmas 1980 until the present date, have you had any correspondence from the defendant?"

"No."

"Have you seen her or have the children visited their grandfather?"

"No," Peggy Goeller replied curtly.

"Mrs. John Goeller," Johnston cross-examined, "did you know that your brother had adopted Michael legally?"

"I had heard of it, yes, through my father."

"And you recognize that under the law there is no distinction between an adopted child and a natural child?"

"I know that."

"Did you keep pretty close tabs on Michael prior to his death?"

"Well, I didn't see the boy after he was very young, because we visited him one time before my brother died, and Michael was in the hospital at the time."

"In looking at state's exhibit twenty-seven, I want to read this to you. . . ."

Johnston read aloud selected excerpts from the following letter Judias had written to her sister-in-law from Trinidad, Colorado, on February 9, 1978, twelve days after Bobby Joe Morris's death:

Dear Peggy, Bud and family,
Thank you for your letter of January 22. I called Mr. Goodyear the day I got the letter, and Jim and Kim talked to him. . . .

I am in Colorado going to school. . . . I have, or will in August have my PHN in nursing, which is very hard to get. I go to Denver in August to meet the nursing board. If I answer all their questions properly, I get my PHN judged by my peers. If I don't get it, I will dig a hole and crawl in.

It is very hard doing my internship c̄ three kids. It's demanding for them as well as for me; however, they understand and are a godsend. Mike is home. He has been c̄ us for almost two years, now. He is doing fine; never thought he would. He played football this year and now is playing high school basketball. He is doing fine in a public school, and has a world of friends. He is even learning to drive now. He has a way to go to be as mature as he should, but we are proud he decided to take hold of his life and grow. He's lots of help, very concerned about Jim's and Kim's welfare, and a blessing to our household.

Jim is just Jim. One of the most intelligent children I have ever known. He can do anything an adult can do and he is just 12 years old. He is like the rock, strong and stable. He is almost as large as his father was. . . .

Kim is our brain child and Jim's best friend. She loves chemistry and biology. She is always whipping up one of her experiments. One day she will no doubt blow up the house c̄ one. Kim is a big girl, 5′ 2″ at eleven, and all her parts in the proper places. She is quiet and rather shy yet. She lets Jim be the aggressor, and he makes most of the decisions for the two of them; however, she will give him a good stiff slap along his head if he tries to talk her into doing something that she believes is not right. Most of the time they're like Pete and repeat; one lies and the other swears to it. . . . One day, before I know it, they will be grown and I will be a grandmother. . . .

Pleasant memories is all I have of Jim's family. You all have always made me feel as though I was a daughter. . . . We are going to try to come visit real soon. . . . The kids need to know who their relatives are, and they're big enough now to remember you. . . .

Love,
Jim, Kim, Mike and Ann

Our address is: 1305 Buena Vista, Trinidad, Colorado. . . . It's a little cow town c̄ an 80 bed hospital. . . . We do the transsexual surgery here for most of the world. . . . It doesn't seem natural that a person would want to be another sex. However, there are lots of nuts running loose. Like they say, all the monkeys aren't in the zoo! . . . Most are ugly, ugly homosexuals, and I believe the doctor is just feeding an unnatural and most unusual human desire. . . .

"Did you talk to her about this letter?" Johnston continued his cross-examination.

"No," Peggy Goeller rejoined.

"Have you ever had a relative or a good close friend who died from an accident?"

"No, but I've had a brother and sister die from cancer."

"And if you love someone, sometimes it's kind of painful to talk about that?"

"No, it's not hard for me to talk about it because I loved them, and I knew them. I was very close to them."

"You have no problem talking about the ones close to you that have passed on?"

"No."

"How old is your father?"

"He's eighty-three."

"Did he love the boy, Michael?"

"Yes, he did. He sent Christmas presents and birthday presents every year. He sent presents to all three of them."

"The conversation that you had with Judi on the phone—did you tell your father?"

"Yes, I did. I had to tell him that Michael was dead before we took him up there. That was the reason we went, to take my father to see his grandchildren."

"And Judi told you about the boy dying in the army with chemicals?"

"Ann told us he had just been buried."

* * *

"Just been buried?" Edgar redirected.

"Just been buried two or three days before we got up there," Peggy Goeller repeated.

"In November?" Edgar questioned.

"Yes."

"She didn't tell you he died May 13, 1980?"

"No. No, she did not. And she took my father to the cemetery. My father said if he had known, he would have gone to Walter Reed Hospital to see Michael. He was only two hours away. . . ." Peggy Goeller testified with an accusing glare at the silent defendant.

Following an afternoon recess, the state called its final witness for the day. Don Quinn of the Florida Department of Law Enforcement took the witness stand with professional aplomb. Following an impressive accounting of his training and experience as a questioned-document examiner and forensic scientist, Quinn proceeded to render his expert opinion on the various state exhibits presented by Edgar, including the insurance documents, the handwritten statements purportedly signed by Judias and James Buenoano Goodyear, an employment application purportedly filled out by the defendant, and the letter handwritten to Peggy Goeller and purportedly signed by Judias.

Quinn testified that "Michael Buenoano did not sign the Michael Buenoano signature of the proposed insured on the Prudential form in exhibit nineteen dated October eighth, 1979. I also examined a form in composite exhibit eighteen dated April 5, 1980, which bears a signature of the insured Michael A. Goodyear Buenoano, and Michael Goodyear Buenoano did not sign that form. And I examined a second form in the same Metropolitan group. The signature is Michael A. Goodyear Buenoano. Michael Buenoano did not sign those signatures. Additionally, I examined the statement marked state's exhibit one-A, and I determined that Judias Buenoano Goodyear had written and signed this statement. I examined statement one-B. It's attributed on the face page to James Buenoano Goodyear. I determined that James Buenoano, the author of state's exhibit eight, did not print that statement. The handprinting appearing on the face page of that statement is not that of James Buenoano," Quinn concluded.

"Did you determine whether he signed it?" Edgar asked.

"I had insufficient signatures from James Buenoano to fully determine that he signed it."

"Did you determine who did write that statement?" Edgar pressed, referring to the statement made to the army that James Buenoano had testified was his own.

Quinn replied that the author of Judy Goodyear's employment application also printed James's statement to the army. In addition, Quinn noted that he had found "some evidence that the author of the letter [to Goeller] could have prepared the Michael Buenoano signatures on the two Metropolitan insurance documents."

"If I understand you correctly, Michael Goodyear did not sign those Metropolitan policies, but you have an opinion that Ann, who wrote the letter, probably did?" Edgar queried.

"No. There's some evidence she could have. This is a limited probability as opposed to the full identification, or the full elimination of a person," Quinn clarified. "I can fully determine that it is not Michael Buenoano Goodyear who signed the policies. I cannot fully determine who it is who did."

"If you would look at . . . the application for a Prudential Insurance policy dated October 8, 1979. You cannot say that Judi Buenoano . . . signed the name of Michael Buenoano Goodyear?" Johnston cross-examined the witness.

"No, sir, I can't," Quinn replied.

"And if you would look at . . . the application for a lost policy with Metropolitan Insurance. You cannot say that

Judi Buenoano signed the name of Michael Buenoano to that?"

"No, sir. I cannot."

"And looking at . . . the statement of James Buenoano to the army?"

"It wasn't prepared by him. I don't know whose signature it is."

"You're saying that James did not print that statement?" Johnston questioned.

"That's correct," Quinn affirmed.

"But you're not saying that James did not sign it?"

"No. No."

"Looking at the questioned Michael Buenoano signature, would you say that the person who wrote 'Michael Buenoano' was attempting to trace or forge the signature?"

"It's not a close simulation."

"Not even close, is it?" Johnston emphasized. "So you would deduce that whoever signed this certainly wasn't trying to imitate the signature of Michael Goodyear by tracing or forgery?"

"I find no evidence of that, sir," Quinn agreed.

On redirect examination, Quinn affirmed again that statements of James Buenoano on the Department of Army form were in the same handwriting as Judi Goodyear's notarized employment application.

"And the reason you can't say that one-A, the army statement signed by the defendant, and one-B, the army statement signed 'James Buenoano Goodyear,' were prepared by the same person conclusively . . . is because one is cursive and one is printed?" Edgar resumed.

"That's correct. A cursively written text cannot be compared with a handprinted text for the purposes of identification," Quinn confirmed.

"But you do have one printed example signed by Judy Goodyear, exhibit twenty-four, an application?"

"Oh, yes."

"And she printed James's statement?" Edgar reiterated.

"The handprinting appearing on one-B was by the author of state's exhibit twenty-four," Quinn reaffirmed.

"I just wanted to be sure about that. Yes, sir. Thank you," Edgar concluded the examination of his expert witness.

15

A Policy of Poison

AT NINE-FORTY ON THE MORNING of March 27, this sixth day of testimony in the trial of Judias Buenoano began as prosecutor Edgar called his thirty-fourth witness to the stand.

Robert E. Hill, the short, paunchy, balding, blue-eyed, and fortyish owner of Pensacola's EZ-Rent, reluctantly approached the witness stand. The married businessman and father of two had mortgaged his home to bail Judias Buenoano out of jail on her first arrest for the attempted murder of John Gentry. He had recently rescinded his fifty-thousand-dollar bond following a long talk with Detective Ted Chamberlain.

"May it please the court, ladies and gentlemen of the jury, counsel for the defense," Edgar opened with an unaccustomed flourish. "Mr. Hill, how do you know the defendant?"

In the ensuing examination, Hill testified in his leisurely twang that his business relationship with the defendant, Ms. Judi Buenoano, and her partner, Bobby Joe Morris, went back to the early 1970s. Judi and Mr. Morris had a maid service and contracting business together and rented most of their equipment from Hill's EZ Rent store. Hill said that at the time, Judi lived with Mr. Morris and her three children in a well-to-do neighborhood in Pensacola in an expensive house with an inground pool. At one point, Judi appeared to be hurting financially, and she began selling off many items, such as a trailer home that Mr. Hill bought from her. Then, in 1977, Judi's beautiful home burned

down and she left Pensacola and went west with her three
children. Hill didn't know where Mr. Morris was during or
after that time. When Judi returned to Pensacola in 1978
driving a new car, she was going by the name of Buenoano.
She told Hill that she had been living in New Mexico with
her grandmother, who had passed away, and that she had
sold the water diversion rights on some property that had
belonged to her grandmother. Hill had not discussed Judi's
new affluence. It was obvious, he said.

James, Kimberly, and Michael were with Judi upon her
return to Pensacola, Hill continued. Hill saw very little of
Michael. Judi had told him that Michael was her stepson.
Hill had observed that Michael was a little slow, but Judi
had never discussed what was wrong with him. One time,
after Michael had joined the army, the Buenoanos had
come into his store, and Michael was wearing leg braces.
Judi had said that Michael had been involved in some
chemical accident in the army. Hill had not questioned
her about it; he figured it was none of his business.

On the day of the drowning, Hill was called to the scene
by someone; he could not recall by whom. He did not know
exactly why he was called. He guessed that since he had
been a friend for a long time and Judi didn't know that
many people, she had turned to him in a time of need.
Michael had drowned. Hill had driven the thirty-five miles
or so from his store to the East River bridge. There were a
lot of people there he didn't know. Hill couldn't remember
if Judi was there or not. James and Kimberly were crying
and upset. Hill had never before seen the seventeen-foot-
long yellow canoe that was lying on the shore.

Hill remembered discussing the event with Judi later
that night. Judi had told him that Michael wanted to go
fishing when he came home on leave, and she and James
had taken him fishing in the canoe. They were throwing
the fishing line out toward the bank, the line got tangled
in a tree limb, and while they were jerking on the line, a
snake fell into the boat. In the commotion of attempting
to get the snake out or kill it, the canoe capsized. Hill

did not recall Judi mentioning anything about hitting a submerged log. The canoe, which was taken back to Judi's house that night by one of Hill's employees, ended up in Hill's store attic along with Michael's braces. Judi had told him she didn't want to see them. He told her he didn't want them. She didn't want them, so they just threw them up in the attic out of the way. Michael's braces had remained in Hill's attic for four years, until the Florida Department of Law Enforcement picked them up as state's evidence.

Hill went on to testify that Judi occasionally took her children fishing. They had rented a fish camp for years, before they went out west. Hill had purchased the travel trailer she kept there and removed it. Judi kept a bass boat at the fish camp—a fancy boat with stripes down the side and a steering wheel and seats for three or four people. Hill had seen Michael at the camp once, before he had braces. He did not see Michael go out in the boat. Hill didn't remember Judi ever having a canoe before. His daughter had gone on a canoe trip with the Buenoanos once and she had bought a canoe similar to Judi's. Hill did not rent canoes at his store.

"After Michael's death, there were funeral services, of course. Did you go to the funeral?" Edgar asked the recalcitrant Hill.

"Yes, sir."

"Who was there?"

"There were very few people there. She was there, and James and Kimberly. And my daughter, Pam. And the army had their normal group of people there—honor guard— and fired the rifles. The pallbearers were dressed in army uniforms, and they had a flag over the casket. And after the pastor said a few words, they folded the flag up and gave it to Judi. The normal army funeral, I suppose. There wasn't no outburst or anything. There appeared to be tears," Hill shrugged.

"After the funeral, did you discuss with the defendant the possibility of a loan?" Edgar asked.

"Yes, sir. Because I needed some money to pay income taxes and some other obligations I had."

"Of course, Michael died May thirteenth, and income taxes were due April fifteenth?" Edgar queried.

"I had gotten an extension," Hill rejoined.

"Had you discussed the loan with her before you got the extension?"

"No, I hadn't discussed it with her per se. After she got the money, she asked me if I wanted to borrow some, and I said yes, and I'd be willing to pay her interest on it."

"As a result of friendship, she loaned you some money? Money she received from the life insurance proceeds from the death of Michael?"

"She loaned me some money, yes. I guess it came from that. I don't know."

"Wasn't there a check for fifteen thousand some odd dollars drawn on the account from Prudential Life Insurance Company of America deposited to your account at Liberty Bank in Cantonment on September sixteenth, 1980?" Edgar demanded.

"I didn't know whether she put in a check or cash. I knew she put that much money in. It was not listed on the deposit slip. She made the deposit for me, and it was for one thousand, one hundred and forty-one dollars more than I wanted to borrow. So I turned and wrote her a personal check for the difference, because I borrowed thirteen five from her," Hill explained.

"Did you notice any remarkable change in her life-style after Michael's death?" Edgar continued.

"No, sir. She already had a new car, and she changed cars two or three times after that. I think she got an eighty-model Corvette," Hill answered evasively.

"How about any trips? Did she take some long trips that summer of 1980 after Michael's death?" Edgar pursued.

"She took my two girls and their mother on a cruise that same year."

"How many people went on that cruise?"

"There were eight of them."

"Who paid for it?"

"Judi did."

"The whole thing?"

"As far as I know," Hill drawled.

Edgar next presented the witness with state exhibit twenty-three, a composite of signature cards bearing Robert Hill's and the defendant's signature on several joint savings accounts and certificates of deposit.

"Why were you put on these accounts?" Edgar asked the fidgety witness.

"My understanding was that she didn't have many friends and didn't know that many people she could trust, and if something happened to her, then she felt like she could depend on me to see that her estate or the money was administered properly. And I didn't see anything wrong with that, so I signed them," Hill stammered defensively.

"Did you ever take any money out of those accounts?" Edgar pressed.

"No, sir."

"So essentially, you were sort of an informal executor of her estate?"

"I would assume that."

"She's pretty shrewd in business, wouldn't you say?"

"Well, I suppose so. I've never done any business with her other than borrow this money," Hill lamented.

"Wasn't there one other item you all had at the bank that you shared?" Edgar persisted.

"She had a safety deposit box. My name was on it. I didn't carry the key very long. I gave it back to her."

"If I could ask, what did you all keep in there?"

"I don't know what was in it. I never did go in it," Hill admitted. "Until recently with the police."

"There wasn't anything in it, was there?"

"There was an envelope that had something in it. I don't know what it was. I didn't even look at it," Hill protested.

"Now, Mr. Hill, you made some reference about the defendant coming back to the Pensacola area for visits while she was out west. Did she come back by herself?"

"No, sir. She had all three kids with her when she would come."

"Did she come back with Bobby Joe Morris?"

"I never saw Bobby after she went out west. Ain't seen him since. I don't know whatever happened to him. . . ."

Having presented his chief witnesses, Russ Edgar prepared to introduce similar-fact evidence through testimony showing the common means of arsenic poisoning and pattern of insurance fraud among different events: the attempted poisoning murder of Michael Goodyear in October 1979, the murder of Bobby Joe Morris in January 1978, the murder of James Goodyear in August 1971, and the attempted poisoning murder of John Gentry in October 1982. The proffered testimony, heard outside the presence of the jury, would be used as well in subsequent proceedings in a civil racketeering suit filed against the defendant by the State of Florida in Escambia and Santa Rosa counties.

Dr. Leroy Riddick, a pathologist for the Department of Forensic Sciences in Mobile, Alabama, testified that the symptoms displayed by Michael Goodyear after coming home on leave from the army were consistent with arsenic poisoning. On October 26, 1979, Michael came home on leave and began suffering from vomiting, diarrhea, and dizziness. By November he was suffering from vertigo, a rash on his face, and tingling in his toes and fingers. By December he was paralyzed. Riddick said that arsenic was most likely the cause of the nerve condition that led to Michael's paralysis. On cross-examination, Riddick could not rule out the possibility that the poisoning occurred during Michael's exposure to sodium arsenite in the army at Water Purification School on October 22, 1979.

Dr. Matthew Barnhill, a criminal toxicologist with the Alabama Department of Forensic Sciences, testified that tests performed on liver tissue taken from the exhumed body of Bobby Joe Morris showed a lethal arsenic content. The normal range of arsenic found naturally in any person is from 0.01 to 0.1 milligrams per gram. A lethal amount ranges from 10 to 500 milligrams. Dr. Barnhill's preliminary tests were programmed to show only a minimal lethal range. The results were more than positive.

Louis Girodo, investigator for the district attorney in Trinidad, Colorado, testified that the initial autopsy performed on Bobby Joe Morris was rushed and inconclusive. Girodo said that Judias Buenoano had first wanted to cremate Morris's remains and then had rushed the coroner to ship the body back to Brewton, Alabama, for burial.

Various insurance agents from Colorado testified that Judias had purchased life insurance on Bobby Joe Morris within six months of his death. Claiming that he was too busy to arrange the insurance for himself, Judias had taken the insurance applications with her for Morris to sign, returning the signed applications herself. Judias had collected seventy-seven thousand dollars in insurance benefits on the death of Bobby Joe Morris, which she deposited in a bank in Trinidad, Colorado.

Edgar then called Mrs. Lodell Morris to the stand. The matronly mother of Bobby Joe Morris sank heavily into the witness seat.

"I'd like to ask you if you are familiar with the signature of your son, Bobby Joe Morris?" Edgar asked the formidable Lodell Morris.

"Sure," Lodell responded without hesitation.

"I'd like to show you these insurance applications, state exhibits thirty-three and thirty-four, that purport to be signed by your son, and ask you if you can identify these signatures."

"No, sir," Lodell sternly denied.

"They're not your son's signature?" Edgar clarified.

"No, sir," Lodell repeated.

"Thank you. No further questions," Edgar concluded.

"Mrs. Morris," Johnston addressed the witness in patronizing tones, "you and your son were never very close in the latter years of his life, were you?"

"We were very close," Lodell insisted with stubborn defiance.

"Yet you only went out to visit him in Colorado once, at Thanksgiving," Johnston continued.

"That's right. I had a home too, but we contacted each other often."

"And you've been contacted by the state attorney's office concerning this, and you know this lady is on trial for murder?" Johnston enjoined, his voice rising.

"I saw it on television she was on trial, but nobody contacted me on this 'cause it doesn't concern me," Lodell glowered back.

"Nobody from the state attorney's office contacted you concerning your testimony?" Johnston pressed.

"The signature," Lodell admitted grudgingly.

"The signature," Johnston repeated knowingly. "And you look at those exhibits, and just in a matter of seconds you said that they were not your son's signature. How could you look at something that quick and determine that—unless you already had your mind made up?" Johnston charged.

"Well, if you recognize something, your mind is made up when you see it," Lodell insisted.

"Wasn't your son an alcoholic?" Johnston wheeled.

"No, he was not."

"Well, let me rephrase the question. Did he have a drinking problem?"

"Not to my knowledge. He always went to his job and was there on time. If he had a drinking problem, I didn't know anything about it. And I was close to him," Lodell reasserted as Johnston backed off.

"Ma'am, did you have a conversation with the defendant about the burial of your son?" Edgar delicately redirected.

"My daughter approached her with it, after he was so near dead, and then he got better and we talked it over with him. And he said that if something should happen to him, we had plots in Green Acres in Brewton, Alabama, and that was where he would want his body," Lodell testified, her harsh voice softening slightly.

"Did you ever discuss insurance with your son—about Judi having insurance on him?"

"He told me that she had thirty thousand dollars on him and he wished to hell she didn't. I'm going to say it just like him," Lodell stated boldly. "It was after he come so near dying and then he got all right. He was well aware of what he was saying."

"Mrs. Morris," Judge Lowrey intervened, "what time frame are you talking about that this conversation took place between you and your son?"

"Well, he went into the hospital on the fifth of January. That's when Judi called us and said he was in serious condition and probably wouldn't live 'til we got there. So, my brother, myself, and my sister and her husband drove out there. But he got better. We stayed several days, me and my daughter did. And he got to where he knew what he was doing, and he watched television. We sat around and visited with him in the room. She stayed with him at night and I stayed with him in the daytime."

"Would you tell me the circumstances surrounding those statements he may have made to you at that time that would lead you to conclude he believed he was going to die?" Lowrey asked the witness.

"Well, I don't know if he believed he was going to die. See, we all believed he was at first, while he was unconscious. Then Judi told my daughter we would probably butt horns, because his body would never leave Colorado. And I said, 'Over my dead body, he'd be buried here.' And then, when he got all right, my daughter approached him with it and said, 'I think you'd better get some things straight now.' So he looked up at me and said, 'We have lots, don't we?' He knew we bought them a long time ago, years ago, in Green Acres Cemetery. But he didn't think he was going to need one so soon. . . ." Lodell Morris sighed.

Positioned at his podium, Edgar formally argued his proposed motion for the admission of similar-fact evidence:

"If it please the court, the state intends to offer similar-fact evidence with respect to the main charge of murder to rebut the notion that the drowning was an accident, to serve to explain and put in a better light the motive of the murder, and to establish a pattern of criminality on the part of the defendant.

"The state believes that this burden has been met by clear and convincing evidence that the defendant did poison Bobby Joe Morris with arsenic for the very reason of obtaining life insurance monies. . . . It is clear that the medical cause of Bobby Joe Morris's death was arsenic poisoning. . . . It is evidenced that the defendant stayed in the hospital with the deceased, and it was in the hospital that he took a turn for the worse and died, much to the mystery of several physicians, a mystery that was not solved until recently. . . . It is clear that the defendant requested that the body be cremated so that she might hide the evidence of her poisoning. . . . Prior to the deceased's death, the defendant, knowing that there was thirty-thousand dollars in mortgage life insurance, knowing that she had obtained twenty-seven thousand dollars and twenty-three thousand dollars in additional mortgage life insurance, obtained two more separate ten-thousand-dollar policies, which Bobby Joe Morris did not sign and did not even know that he had. She therefore collected more than seventy thousand dollars' insurance on his life. This money was used to purchase the home in Gulf Breeze. It was used to purchase other things that she arrived in town here with, to set up this life-style of Dr. Judias Buenoano, the mystery lady from out west.

"We say that the defendant changed her name lest those who knew her to be simply a licensed practical nurse who supplies bedsheets and pills understand that this was she. Because they knew what she was, and what she was capable of doing. . . .

"This life-style that she created for herself was frustrated in two respects: One, the monies she obtained soon disappeared. We know from her bank records that she was running pretty close to the line on her finances. Here she is with a job making seven hundred and fifty dollars a month, and every other month, she's bouncing checks. She cannot conceivably maintain the life-style of Dr. Judias Buenoano on the money she obtains from her employment. Now, the second problem with that life-style was Michael Goodyear. She could not be that fantastic, wonderful woman, this doctor from out west with two beautiful children, Kimberly and James, with Michael around. Michael was the odd man out. Michael was the child that she didn't want, was ashamed of, was embarrassed of, because he was less than perfect. Michael was the child that was abused, unloved, singled out for ridicule and hatred. Michael was a child that upset her image. And it was in the solution to the problem of Michael that she found the solution to her pressing problem of finance. We know that in March of 1978 she took out a substantial policy on Michael. It wasn't too long after that that she bought this poor, unfortunate, very awkward child a 500 cc motorcycle. I submit she expected him to kill himself. But he didn't. It wasn't too long after that that she realized, when she shuffled him off to the army, that he would be coming home on a ten-day leave. What soldier in the army does not come home to his mother on leave before his first duty assignment, especially a boy like Michael who desperately wanted to please his mother? She knew Michael was coming, so she took out another insurance policy on him on October eighth, 1979, and forged his name. Just like she forged Bobby Joe Morris's name.

"Again, small policies. Substantial to most of us, but small enough that they would not require a physical and would not be questioned to any great degree. Knowing that Michael was coming home on leave, she purchased the life insurance, and when he came home, she poisoned him.

"There is some idea that perhaps Michael may have accidentally ingested arsenic while he was in the army. But look at the circumstances. This was an army training school supervising raw recruits. Do you really think that the

United States Army would allow that boy to lick arsenic
out of a bottle? There were no symptoms reported in the
army records to indicate that he was poisoned to such a
degree as to cause paralysis before he left the army school.
We know that the army did an extensive investigation after
he became paralyzed, and they were unable to determine
whether or not Michael's toxic condition resulted from
arsenic exposure in the army. We also know that there
was never any claim filed against the army for allowing
this to happen. What we do know is that as soon as he
got home, Michael developed immediate twenty-four-hour
symptoms of acute arsenic poisoning. And we know that
arsenic is readily available in the commercial market. And
the defendant is well versed in the area of drugs. . . .

"So on or about the first of November, when Michael
arrived at Fort Benning, the numbing and tingling began,
and the paralysis began to flow down. It was not discovered
until it was too late that the poison had paralyzed him from
his fingertips to his elbows and from his toes to his knees.

"She had failed. She had failed to poison Michael to his
death because he was only home for a few days. She was
not associated with him closely enough, as she was with
Bobby Joe Morris, for a sufficient length of time to succeed.
Michael went on to the army, and the army discovered his
problem. There, he was away from his mother's poisonous,
venomous grasp, the black widow, who no longer could
attempt to eat her son. . . ."

The prosecutor paused, allowing the full import of his
quietly delivered indictment to take effect.

"Why can't the jury, the people of this community, hear
this evidence? I ask the court this question because it seems
to me, Your Honor, that maybe we, in our laws, are being
too technical. Maybe we are going too much overboard in
the notion of safeguarding the rights of the accused. As a
consequence, we are burying the truth. Why is it wrong
for the jury to hear this evidence?" Edgar challenged Judge
Lowrey with earnest blue eyes.

"Mr. Johnston, do you wish to be heard on behalf of

the defendant?" Lowrey asked, after taking a moment to recover.

"Briefly, Your Honor," Johnston replied with a touch of irony. "Mr. Edgar asked you why this evidence is not admissible. I'll tell you why. Because the law of the Supreme Court of this state, and the law of the First District Court of Appeals in Tallahassee, exclude the evidence.

"The truth of the matter is, Your Honor, that Mr. Edgar and the state have not proved that a crime had, in fact, been committed. There is absolutely no evidence that this jury may infer that a corpus delicti has been established by the state. What Mr. Edgar really seeks to do is to put an inference upon an inference and prove the corpus delicti by saying that she may have poisoned Mr. Morris out in Colorado, therefore she may have poisoned her own son. I have given to the court the case of *Drysdale v. State*, which has never been reversed, and which clearly and unequivocally states that this court cannot permit the state to prove corpus delicti by the proving of a collateral crime.

"What Mr. Edgar further seeks to do is to make the main event not the case of the defendant and the alleged drowning and grand theft, but to make the main event the alleged poisoning of Mr. Morris and the alleged poisoning of her son.

"As I understood the proffer to the court, the test is to demonstrate the existence of an evidentiary connection between the defendant and such collateral facts or events by either direct or circumstantial evidence which cannot be explained by any reasonable hypothesis of chance, coincidence, or innocence of the defendant. The testimony has been such that the court cannot exclude the fact that some type of arsenic could possibly have been used in embalming Bobby Joe Morris that could explain the concentration of arsenic found in the decedent's liver. The other thing is the accidental ingestion of certain pesticides which do, in fact, contain an arsenic compound. . . .

"Then, the question of Michael. There is absolutely no

proof that would suggest that Michael was poisoned by his mother. In fact, the opposite occurs. According to the medical history taken by the doctor at Walter Reed Hospital of Michael Buenoano Goodyear, the patient has eaten dirt, licked storage batteries, and eaten a great deal of paint off wood houses built prior to 1920. A lab course was part of his MOS training, occurring from October first to twenty-sixth, 1979. In this laboratory was a one-pint bottle of sodium arsenite, from which one-ounce vials were decanted for testing purposes. The testimony by Dr. Riddick was that sodium arsenite was the primary cause of peripheral neuropathy, that he could not exclude some type of accidental ingestion by the boy, whom Mr. Edgar describes as 'dull.' Therefore, it is consistent with the records of the United States Army that the great probability and overwhelming possibility is that the boy did contact some type of sodium arsenite between the latter part of October and the time he arrived in Pensacola, Florida.

"Your Honor, there has absolutely, positively been no evidence to connect this lady with the administering of arsenic to her son and to her former husband. The court in *Green v. State*, 1966, held on similar-fact evidence: 'Evidence that merely suggests or tends to suggest commission of an independent crime must be excluded. . . .' In the case of *Dibble v. State*, 1977: 'Prior to evidence of another crime being admissible, it is essential to show that the former crime was committed by the person on trial.' What former crimes had Mr. Edgar shown were committed? There is nothing in the record other than an inference and assumption that this defendant may have committed two other possible crimes. . . .

"In closing, Your Honor, the legal reason the court should exclude this evidence is that it is not relevant. Simply by showing that X and Y may have had arsenic in them is insufficient in itself to connect the accused, the defendant, with placing the arsenic in X and Y. Mr. Edgar wants to prove the corpus delicti by inferring other crimes. This is impermissible. Therefore, the court must, under the law of this state, exclude the evidence proffered in this case," Johnston concluded with a flourish.

Leaning forward, Judge Lowrey rendered his decision in weary tones, fixing his bespectacled gaze on the respective counsels for prosecution and defense.

"As a matter of personal philosophy, I might well agree with counsel that there are too many technicalities in the law. . . . But what separates a good judge from a poor judge, in my opinion, is being able to separate your personal philosophy from your sworn duty to apply the law as you understand it. It is the prerogative of the appellate courts to make the law. It is the sworn responsibility of the trial judge to seek to apply the law, whether he agrees with it or not. . . .

"When you look at the basis of the experts' opinion, construing it in the light most favorable to the state, there was a lethal amount of arsenic found in the body of Mr. Morris. However, neither the toxicologists nor any other competent evidence that's before the court precludes the alternative hypothesis that there may have been used in the embalming process a fluid that contained the compound of arsenic. Further, there is no direct connection in the evidence between the defendant and the arsenic that was found in the body of Mr. Morris. And the court says that 'evidence of a collateral crime is inadmissible unless accompanied by evidence connecting the defendant therewith.' "

Pausing to clear his throat, Lowrey shifted uncomfortably in his seat, avoiding Edgar's intense stare before droning his decision.

"In order for the evidence to be admissible, there must be proof of a connection between the defendant and the collateral occurrences, and in this respect, mere suspicion is insufficient.

"The court concludes that it is, under its oath, obligated to exclude the proffer of evidence for the reasons indicated," Judge Lowrey ruled, leaning back into his oversized leather chair.

Apologizing for the evidentiary deficiencies with respect to the Morris exhumation—deficiencies necessitated by the defense demand for a speedy trial—Edgar informed the court that he would immediately have the laboratory specialist analyze Morris's hair. Living hair would not be exposed to arsenic embalming fluid.

In closing, Edgar put all parties on notice that, should the defendant take the stand, he would be prepared in rebuttal to offer three similar murder attempts or murders committed by the defendant, including the clear connection between the defendant and the poison capsules that John Gentry would testify were personally handed to him by Judias.

With a final bang of his gavel, Judge Lowrey dismissed the court for lunch.

During the break, Judias stood in the courthouse hallway beside her ever-present jail matron, smoking a cigarette in stony silence. The iron shackles on her wrists and ankles, removed in the courtroom for the benefit of the jury, weighed heavily on her high-heeled, stockinged feet.

The jury remained outside the courtroom as the trial resumed on the bright and breezy Wednesday afternoon of March 28, 1984, with the defendant's motion for judgment of acquittal.

Pacing freely before the bench, Johnston pitched the routine defense plea for the court to dismiss the criminal charges against his client due to the state's inability to prove its case, a standard form of insurance for defense attorneys against their client's later claim of incompetent representation.

"I am reminded of what Abraham Lincoln said one time upon a visit to a farm when he saw a horse, and he looked at the farmer and he said, 'That's a fine horse; nice four legs you have. Let's assume that I take the tail, pull it down, and I call the tail a leg. What do I have?' The farmer said, 'You have a five-legged horse.' And the president looked at the farmer and said, 'Just because you call the tail a leg, that don't make it so.'

"And I urge this court: just because the state attorney's office calls this a murder, that certainly does not make it so.

"Three elements must be proved in order to establish corpus delicti in a homicide case," Johnston lectured the court. "Fact of death. There's no question here, Your Honor, that Michael Goodyear Buenoano did in fact die and is dead. Two, identity of the decedent. There's no quarrel that the decedent is, in fact, Michael Goodyear Buenoano. Three, criminal agency of another person as cause thereof.

"That third part, Your Honor: I have a heavy, heavy heart in trying to justify this court letting a jury decide this woman's fate on the electric chair, when there is not a scintilla of evidence to suggest to any reasonable jury that Michael Buenoano died of criminal agency of another person. . . .

"Only in the mind of the prosecutor is there any bad feeling between Mrs. Buenoano and her deceased son. Taking the evidence as a whole, I don't think that the court can conclude that this lady hated her son, that she was ashamed of him. . . .

"In an unbroken line of cases, the courts of this State have held that under such conditions [of entirely circumstantial evidence], the evidence must be not only consistent with guilt, but inconsistent with innocence or any reasonable hypothesis thereof. Viewing the evidence in the light most favorable to the state, we cannot conclude that the evidence excludes all reasonable hypotheses of innocence.

"Your Honor, you may not like to do it, and I certainly was impressed when you said that the difference between a good judge and a bad judge was one that followed the law. You followed the law when you excluded the similar-fact evidence. I only ask you, Your Honor, to follow the law when you direct a verdict of not guilty for this defendant," Johnston heartily concluded.

Edgar's response was short and to the point.

"The pivotal legal issue in this case is whether or not there is a reasonable theory or hypothesis of innocence. I submit, Your Honor, that no reasonable hypothesis of innocence exists. There is substantial competent evidence of a conclusive nature to indicate that the defendant has committed the crime of murder."

Reserving his finding on the motion for a directed verdict until after the defense presented its case, Judge Lowrey recessed the court until nine A.M. the next day.

16

"She Loved Him"

THE STATE HAVING FINALLY RESTED its case the previous afternoon, Johnston summoned the first of his relatively short list of witnesses left uncalled by the prosecution on the Thursday morning of March 19, 1984.

Mrs. Edna Robertson, a former government clerk turned graphologist who had testified as an expert witness for the Holocaust mass murderer Ivan "the Terrible" Demjanjuk, took the stand as the defense's handwriting expert.

Under Johnston's questioning, Robertson testified that the person who signed checks as Judias Buenoano had not signed Michael Buenoano's name to the Prudential insurance application.

"And would you be a little more specific," Johnston continued, "and state to the court and the jury why you have concluded that Judias Buenoano did not sign the name of Michael Buenoano in state's exhibit number twenty-eight, the three signatures?"

"We have two different writing styles. The signature 'Judias W. Buenoano' is a very fast signature, a very skillful hand, and a heavy pressure. And the signature 'Michael Buenoano' is a very light writing, the slant is deep, and it is a less skillful hand. All three of the signatures of Michael Buenoano were written by the same person, because we have the same writing habits," Robertson concluded.

"But they were not written by the defendant, Judias Buenoano?" Johnston reiterated.

"No, they were not."

"Do you have your report with you, your written handwriting report?" Edgar cross-examined the witness.

"No."

"You didn't type a report?"

"No."

"Isn't that customary?"

"No."

"Do you keep notes of your results?"

"Yes."

"May I see those?"

"You surely may," Edna Robertson replied curtly, handing Edgar a set of handwritten notes.

"Thank you," Edgar responded, quickly perusing the jotted notations.

"It says here in your report, 'All signatures of Michael Buenoano were signed by same person. No evidence of being signed by Judias W. Buenoano or Donald Johnson,'" Edgar read.

"That's right," Robertson confirmed.

"Who's Donald Johnson?" Edgar asked curiously.

"It was another name on the insurance policy that I looked at to see if there was any possibility there."

"Now, you determined that Donald Johnson did not sign the insurance application?"

"Yes."

"Ma'am, did you get a good look at the insurance policy? I mean, you did study it carefully under a microscope?" Edgar asked innocently.

"I certainly did," Robertson affirmed.

"Do you think you missed anything?"

"I could have, but if I did, I don't know what it is. . . . I could have. I'm human." Robertson shrugged.

"Would you like to look at it? Would you like to find the name of Donald Johnson on there for me?" Edgar challenged, pointing to the enlarged exhibit before the jury of the Prudential insurance application signed by the insurance agent who had previously testified, Donald Fournier.

"That was not Johnson. That was— At first, it looked like Johnson to me, but it isn't. It's Donald— I cannot read the last name," Robertson stammered.

"Let me see if I can help you. Donald Fournier?" Edgar suggested in patronizing tones.

"Well, the letters were not clear. There was a J, and then F, and then an O, and the writing was not—not comparable in any sense to this. And it wasn't something that I had been asked to do," Robertson explained helplessly.

"Is there anything else you'd like to show the jury on this Donald J. Fournier signature that made you think it was Donald Johnson?" Edgar persisted.

"No.. No," Robertson mumbled.

"Now, the question in the case is whether or not Michael himself signed this application. Did Michael sign this?" Edgar asked pointedly.

"I don't know," the witness replied, glaring at Edgar.

"You weren't asked to determine that?"

"No."

Thoroughly humiliated by Edgar's cross-examination, Edna Robertson left the witness stand in an angry huff.

Johnston's next witness, William Ridenour of Pensacola, testified that Judi Buenoano had appeared distraught when he saw her at the boat landing on the day of the drowning. Later she had told him to get rid of the canoe because "it just tore her and the kids up when they were around it." On cross-examination, Ridenour said he couldn't see how a boy who couldn't use his arms could manage to get a fishing line from a cane pole entangled in a tree.

William McCranie, owner of a local canoe rental business, testified that he had twice rented canoes to a person who wore leg braces. On cross-examination, McCranie admitted it would be unsafe for a person to sit in a lawn chair above the waterline of a canoe. He also said he wouldn't take a family on the East River because it was too deep. Asked by Edgar to point out the front of a canoe, the laconic canoe expert replied with a touch of country humor, "That would depend on which way you were going."

Dawn Fields, a young friend of the Buenoanos from Gulf

Breeze, demonstrated to the jury how Michael Goodyear had put his arms around her to hug her on his first and last night home from the veterans' hospital in Tampa the night before the drowning.

Then Johnston called Kimberly Ann Goodyear to the stand.

The pale, thin, honey-blond youngest member of the Buenoano family, her fragile pallor reflected by a simple pink blouse and wide-set, frightened blue eyes, sat gingerly in the witness seat. Looming over his chief witness for the defense, Johnston began his direct examination with solicitous concern.

"Would you state your name, please?"

"Kimberly Ann Goodyear," the girl, bearing a remarkable resemblance to her slightly older brother James, responded in a barely audible whisper.

"You might have to speak a little louder now. Grab your breath and hold on," Johnston coached. "Kim, how old are you?"

"Seventeen."

The defense had entered into evidence a Buenoano family scrapbook and a school annual. Johnston now asked his client's only daughter to look through the scrapbook. "Is that something that you and your mother kept, Kim?"

"Yes, it was."

"And do any of those pictures show Michael at or near the water?" Johnston prompted, referring to a photograph of nine-year-old Michael sitting on the beach wearing a full life jacket.

"Yes, they do," Kimberly dutifully responded.

"Now, looking at the school annual, do you remember when Michael was going to Trinidad Catholic High in 1978? Did he participate in school activities there?"

"Yes, he did. Football, basketball, anything. He enjoyed mountain climbing. He had horticulture classes he used to go to and study the earth and everything, climbing mountains," Kimberly replied, wide-eyed.

"Did Michael have a deathly fear of water?"

"No, he did not."

"Did Michael have any peculiar relationship with your mother?" Johnston ventured.

"What do you mean by 'peculiar'?" Kimberly asked, lifting her sharply angular cleft chin.

"Was it a relationship of neglect, shame, embarrassment, or hatred?"

"No, sir. It was a loving relationship," Kimberly responded peevishly.

"Was he neglected by you, James, or your mother?"

"No, sir."

"Did your mother not want Michael around?" Johnston persisted.

"She did. She loved him," Kimberly protested, her lower lip trembling.

"Do you need time to get your breath? Do you want some water?" Johnston asked anxiously.

"No, sir, I'm okay," Kimberly mumbled.

"Tell us, Kim, what happened the day of the accident?"

"Well," Kimberly began with a petulant sigh, "I was sitting on the bank fishing, and I had been there a couple of hours—I'm not really sure how long I had been there—and all of a sudden, I saw this guy go by in a boat, and a few minutes later, he came back by and I saw James hanging out the side, and my mom sitting there crying, she was just totally frantic. And I tried to ask them what happened. She couldn't talk; she couldn't do nothing. She told me to go call an ambulance. So I went to go get in the car, and I was too shook up to drive, so this guy that drove the boat got into the car and pushed me over, and we went to call an ambulance," Kimberly recited, her blue eyes shifting rapidly.

"Why did the family decide to go to East River that day?" Johnston directed.

"Because it wasn't so far. You didn't have to drive a long way."

"Did the family take any fishing poles, lunches?"

"Yes, they did."

"Why did you not go in the canoe?"

"Because I'm allergic to the sun. It eats holes in my arms and puts big scars on them."

"Are you under medical treatment?"

"Yes, sir, I am. If I go out in the sun, I have to have an umbrella over me and a long-sleeved shirt, and I can't have any sun on my chest or my arms, my face, or the top of my legs," Kimberly replied.

"After the accident, did James appear to be injured?"

"Yes, sir."

"What was the condition of your mother?"

"She was just totally shook up. She couldn't even talk to you. She was just in hysterics," Kimberly testified with a sidelong glance at her mother staring intently at her from across the courtroom.

"What did your mother tell you about the accident?" Johnston asked, positioning himself between Kimberly and the defense table.

"She told me that they were fishing along the side, and one of the poles got hung up in a tree and a snake fell in the boat, and she was trying to get it out, and she had it out, and with all the panic and everything, they hit a log and the boat turned over," Kimberly haltingly explained, her downcast eyes focused on the twisted tissue in her hands.

"Did you go home that evening after the accident occurred?"

"After we went and got James from the hospital."

"Was there a nice funeral for your brother Michael?"

"Yes, there was."

"Have you been back to the cemetery?"

"Yes," Kimberly answered in a small voice.

"Can you state whether or not the drowning has affected your mother?"

"Yes, it has. It's made her upset. It's really put a lot of pressure on our family," Kimberly answered defensively.

"Does your mother drink?"

"No, she does not."

"Have you ever seen her drink a beer?"

"No, I have not."

"Have you ever seen her drink anything alcoholic?" Johnston pressed.

"No, I have not," Kimberly emphatically denied.

"Your witness," Johnston directed to Edgar.

"Now, Kimberly Buenoano," Edgar politely addressed the young defense witness, "I noticed when you were sworn, you used the name Kimberly Goodyear. Would you prefer that I call you Ms. Goodyear or Ms. Buenoano?"

"Ms. Goodyear."

"Thank you. Try to speak up as loud as you can. I know that because of your age and your feelings for your mother . . . you may be a little upset or a little restless. But try your best, okay?" Edgar empathized. "Now, Ms. Goodyear, do you recall living on Duquane Street in Pensacola?"

"Yes, I do."

"Do you recall your brother, Michael, coming to visit you there?"

"No, sir."

"Did you ever go to visit him in Camp Emachamee?"

"Yes, sir. We talked and visited and hugged each other. There's pictures in here of when we went," Kimberly volunteered, referring to the family photo album, defense exhibit eight-B.

"And after you lived on Duquane Street, you moved to Colorado, and your brother Michael lived in the house with you, didn't he?"

"Yes, sir."

"Well, when he lived in the house in Colorado with you, where did he stay when guests came?"

"He had his own room downstairs."

"In the basement?" Edgar clarified.

"Yes. Well, it's considered the lower floor. They fixed it up really nice. It was big. He wanted a lot of room so he could do the things he wanted to do and put up his CB equipment and have it where, you know, nobody would mess with his room."

"And when you left Colorado, you moved to Gulf Breeze. And at Gulf Breeze, Michael was in high school. How was he received and accepted by his friends?" Edgar asked.

"Well, you know, just like most teenagers. Some people don't like you and some do. He had quite a few friends," Kimberly vouched.

"No one really ridiculed him or made fun of him?"

"Some people did but that's anywhere. I mean, I've had people make fun of me. It's in any school. You're always going to have kids make fun of you." Kimberly shrugged.

"Would you say that Michael was a pretty average teenager?"

"Well, sometimes he did crazy things. He'd ride his motorcycle through the fans at games and stuff. Nothing that any teenager wouldn't do."

"What was abnormal about your brother?" Edgar pressed on.

"I guess it was, pain didn't hurt him. He could wreck his motorcycle and get up from it and be fine."

"Did your mother get on him about it? She didn't like Michael wrecking his motorcycle?" Edgar suggested.

"No, sir, 'cause he'd always ruin his glasses and stuff, and she'd have to buy him new glasses, and she just didn't want to have to pay for all that, and have to get a new motorcycle," Kimberly answered lamely.

"Was Michael ever hurt really bad, that you know of?"

"Not that I can remember."

"You don't remember him getting scalded in Miami?" Edgar rejoined.

"No, sir."

"You don't remember him being put through a glass window?"

"No, sir."

"You don't remember Michael wrecking his motorcycle and getting scarred all over his body?" Edgar crescendoed.

"No, sir," Kimberly replied, her voice shrinking.

"Was Michael what you'd call accident-prone?"

"Not really. Just when he did crazy things."

"Did your mother ever worry about Michael getting killed on his motorcycle? Did she ever talk to him about it?"

"Well, she just asked him if he'd please be careful when he rode it, because motorists seem sometimes not to see you."

Edgar turned back to the album. "There are a lot of pictures in there of Michael at different ages. These pictures of him as a baby, do you see all these bumps and scratches and bruises on his head and face? That's not a birthmark, is it?" Edgar asked innocently, pointing to an open page of the scrapbook spread before Kimberly.

"I really couldn't tell you," Kimberly bristled.

"Do you know how Michael kept getting all those bumps and scratches and bruises? Was it because he was accident-prone?" Edgar asked with a touch of sarcasm.

"Yeah. Because he'd fall over things."

"Yeah. . . . I see that these pictures are kind of out of sequence. They're not in chronological order. Why would that be?" Edgar wondered aloud.

"Well, we just— We just took all— We had all our pictures and everything of Michael, and after he died, we put them all together for a remembrance of him," Kimberly stammered.

"So this was assembled after Michael's death, not before. When was it finished?"

"Quite a long time ago."

"Not recently? Not since these charges have come up?" Edgar crossed.

"No, no, sir," Kimberly protested.

"Okay. Now, when Michael was in Walter Reed Hospital in Washington, did you go see him?" Edgar changed tactics.

"No, sir."

"Did your grandfather, living in Pennsylvania, know that Michael was in the hospital in Washington?"

"I really couldn't tell you."

"When was the last time you saw your grandfather?"

"Right after the accident. We went up and saw him."

"Did you tell your grandfather what happened?"

"I— I— I . . . couldn't talk about it. I didn't . . . It makes me too upset," Kimberly stuttered.

"All right," Edgar relented. "When your mother went down to Tampa to get your brother, did you go?"

"Yes, sir."

"And at that time, Michael was fully capable of walking up and down the stairs and getting dressed by himself?"

"I didn't say he could walk up and down the stairs. He lifted himself up and down the stairs on his arms. And he'd set himself on his bed, and he'd take the hook and lift one of his legs in his pants. . . ."

"He could lift his leg with the hook?" Edgar reiterated.

"Yes, he'd take the hook, and it had a thing on it. . . ." Kimberly tried to explain.

"Could I have the hook, please?" Edgar requested the court clerk. "Is this like the one Michael had?" Edgar asked, presenting a Robbins' Hook device to Kimberly.

"Yes," she replied, her eyes avoiding the painful reminder.

"He'd lift his leg up with this and put on his pants?" Edgar repeated.

"Yes."

"Did he tie his shoes too?"

"We'd have to help him tie his shoes. Because he hadn't figured out how to do it yet."

"Did he put the braces on himself?"

"Well, you'd have to help him slip them over, but he knew how to lock them and everything."

"Did you ever see him fall?"

"Yes, I have."

"So it was important to watch him, wasn't it?"

"Well, we'd just keep an eye on him, to make sure everything was okay and he was okay."

"How long did you think you were going to have to help him out?"

"Until he could do it himself. He was the kind of person that would rather do it himself. He didn't want anyone else to help him."

"But he couldn't ride his motorcycle, couldn't scuba dive?"

"No."

"He couldn't swim?"

"He could. He said he could. He wanted to do things," Kimberly insisted with a plaintive whine. "He didn't want to stay home. He didn't want to be locked up and treated like some person that's just stuffed away. He didn't want that. He wanted to be just like everybody else, after his accident. He wanted to go and be happy just like the rest of the people," Kimberly cried, suddenly collapsing into tears.

"But he couldn't, could he?" Edgar softly rejoined.

Kimberly continued to weep openly into a blue Kleenex, while from across the room, Judias wiped her nose and eyes with a crumpled tissue clutched tightly in one hand.

"Do you feel like you can go on?" Edgar asked the distressed witness. "Would you like another recess, Ms. Goodyear?"

"No, sir," Kimberly shook her bowed head, recovering somewhat.

"Okay. The day that you went canoeing, you don't know what happened, do you?"

"No, sir," Kimberly sniffed.

"How old were you?"

"Twelve, I'm pretty sure."

"Tell us about getting out of the car and getting the canoe in the water. Tell us how that happened," Edgar urged.

"Well, Michael got himself out of the car. He had braces on. He put the lawn chair down in the boat and sat down in it."

"Did he get in the boat by himself?"

"Yes, sir."

"How was he sitting in the lawn chair? Were his feet extended?"

"Yeah, he was just sitting with his legs out. He could bend them upwards too. He could set them up or bend them."

"How were his legs when he took off in the canoe? Were they bent or straight?"

"I don't know. I don't remember."

"Was he strapped into the lawn chair?"

"No, sir."

"Did he have a fishing pole?"

"Yes, sir."

"Which way did they go when they first put in? Upstream or downstream?"

"Up the river. We always canoe up and then float down."

"How long were they gone?"

"About three hours."

"It wasn't anything like thirty minutes, was it?"

"No, sir, it was quite a while, because I had caught six or seven fish. I ate my lunch and sat there. You could just tell by the way the sun was. It was not as high as it was earlier."

"So, you went out and got there about noon and fished till three or four o'clock?"

"I'm not sure what time we got there," Kimberly hedged.

"And there wasn't anyone else around, was there?"

"No, sir, not at the time. When they left, some people drove up and put their boat in, and left in the boat."

"How soon after that did your mother come back?"

"It was a couple hours later, I saw that boat go by, going upstream, and then, all of a sudden, I saw it coming back, and I saw my mom standing up and James laying over the side of the boat with his head hanging almost in the water."

"Was James unconscious?"

"Yes, sir."

"Was your mother hysterical?"

"Yes, sir. She—she just looked at me and started crying. She couldn't say anything else. She just said, 'Go call an ambulance.' "

"She didn't sit down and have a beer, did she?"

"No, sir. My mother does not drink," Kimberly insisted.

"I understand," Edgar condescended. "Did she tell you what happened to Michael then?"

"She told me after the ambulance got there and she had calmed down some; she told me what happened."

"She didn't mention anything about Michael up to that point?"

"No, sir. Except when she came out of the boat, she just looked at me and said, 'I couldn't find him.' I knew something had happened. At that time, all I was worried about was going and getting somebody down there to help. James was hurt. My mom was crying, you know. 'We couldn't find Michael.' "

"When did your mother leave?"

"She left with James in the ambulance."

"And you were still there?"

"I was there waiting with Bob Hill, our good friend, and they were trying to find Michael's body."

"And when they found Michael's body, was your mother there?"

"No, sir."

"Did they take the canoe away before they found Michael?"

"They picked the canoe up and brought it on land, and then when they found Michael, they asked Bob to identify him, and he did, and we left."

"Your mother didn't identify Michael?"

"She was too upset. At the time, with everything that had happened, we were all just in too much of a shock," Kimberly whimpered, her abundant tears suddenly returning. "And it's something that I've never really wanted to remember. I've always wanted to put it behind me, because it's so upsetting for all of us to have to hear about it. It was a total shock to our family. Because you say she didn't love him. I don't understand that, because she loved him more than anything," Kimberly wailed, sobbing into her tissue.

"Do you want to take a recess?" Edgar asked again.

"I just want to get it over with," Kimberly mumbled miserably.

"Okay, let's talk about what happened after Michael died," Edgar resumed. "Now, you used to have a friend named David Lackey, didn't you?"

"Yes, sir."

"How long have you known David?"

"Approximately a year and eight months."

"Did you have a conversation with David one night about your brother, Michael, and the way he died?"

"He asked me about it, and I told him what I knew about it. You know, I wasn't there. I was on the land. I didn't know much about it."

"Did you have a fight with your mother that night about going out with David? Did you get mad at your mother and tell her, when she said she was going to do something to you, 'Yeah, just like you killed Michael?' " Edgar suddenly crossed.

"Yeah!" Kimberly shot back. "I said it to hurt her, to make her angry, to make her quit yelling at me and leave me alone, so I could do what I wanted to do." Kimberly melted into more tears. "She didn't approve of him, because he had been in trouble so much and he had stolen a lot of things. . . ."

"Didn't you have a conversation with David in which you told him that you thought your brother was dying, so your mother tipped the canoe over to get the insurance money?" Edgar pressed on.

"No, sir. Nothing like that at all," Kimberly denied, weeping harder.

"Your mother's on trial for murder, here, and if there's something you think we ought to know that would mitigate the crime she's charged with, something you think she did wrong, that she was negligent or made a mistake or something . . . ?" Edgar coaxed the witness.

"You Honor, I object to that question," Johnston intervened.

"The objection will be sustained," Lowrey ruled.

"Is there anything else you'd like to say, Kimberly?" Edgar concluded.

"She loved him a lot. She really did. And if you would've been there, you'd know the relationship they had together, and you wouldn't be doing this."

With Kimberly's emotional testimony, Johnston rested his case for the defense.

Escaping the neon glare of the confining courtroom for a solitary stroll on the sunlit grassy commons of Milton's courthouse square, Russ Edgar quietly reflected on the exhausting ordeal of the past eight days of trial presentation.

Edgar had tried four other murder cases that year, each averaging nine days with forty-four witnesses for the state. The average murder case lasted two or three days with twelve to eighteen witnesses. "You put on ten a day, nine to five with a mid-morning break, an hour for lunch, and an afternoon break, it's gonna take you two days." He usually worked a murder case from six in the morning till midnight. To date, Edgar figured he'd put over a thousand hours into the Buenoano case. He'd used Judias's statement to the army as the blueprint for the trial, taking every sentence and line by line destroying her credibility before the jury. He introduced her statement last, proving her authorship by comparing it to handwriting samples of checks she'd written for new cars, speedboats, and motor homes. He'd displayed her employment applications showing her occupation as a nurse trained in medical care and first aid. It was a subtle but effective point for the jury. Putting the facts together in the order of proof; highlighting your strengths while minding the weaknesses you must bear in every case; keeping the tempo of the trial moving to hold the jurors while bearing in mind the predicates required for the admission of certain evidence; keeping the message in the forefront of the jury's mind, while understating some things so the jury will have something to work on;

the order that you put it all in—that's the art of advocacy, Edgar reminded himself.

He was disappointed but not surprised that Judias had not taken the stand. He had given Johnston fair warning that should the defendant testify, he would bring out the similar-fact evidence of the poisoning of Morris and Gentry on rebuttal. But he figured it was a mistake on Johnston's part. You don't have a woman accused of being an unfit mother and hating her child before a jury with several women and not have her get up and deny it. By denying guilt, Judias could not enter an insanity plea, which assumes one acknowledges the affirmative acts. Edgar figured Judias was as crazy as they go, but she was not legally insane. Florida, like most states, followed the McNaughton rule, which defines legal insanity as the inability to distinguish between right and wrong. Whatever else Judias thought or felt, Edgar told himself, she knew what she was doing and she knew it was wrong. Still, something inside him wanted to hear her admit it.

Edgar's reverie was broken by the familiar brisk approach of Ted Chamberlain across the dry courthouse lawn.

Continuing to work the original June 1983 bombing case throughout the drowning trial, Chamberlain and Cousson had traced the unusual color-coded wire that connected the leg wires in the dynamite explosion of Gentry's car to a Ford motor car company product. Ford had used the orange-and-white plastic-coated wire for the right-turn signal in their Thunderbirds and Cougars from 1964 to 1966 but had discontinued use of the wire after 1966. Checking the registrations of more than three thousand area Thunderbird owners, Chamberlain traced a 1966 Thunderbird to a teenage friend of James Buenoano in Gulf Breeze. Further investigation revealed the car had recently been removed from the premises. The ATF laboratory in Atlanta, Georgia, had confirmed a match between the two-foot strands of wire used in the detonating device of the car bomb and the wire seized in the search of James Buenoano's bedroom closet.

Indictments against Judias and James Buenoano for the attempted murder of John Gentry by bombing and for grand theft through insurance fraud had been prepared by the state attorney and the US Bureau of Alcohol, Tobacco, and Firearms, but the warrants were held over until after the Milton trial. Edgar did not want charges of a witch-hunt from Judias's attorney to interfere with the jury's pending verdict in the drowning case.

"Hey, Russ, what's the verdict?" Chamberlain quipped, catching up to Edgar's measured stride.

"Can you believe Kimberly's up there saying that her mother didn't drink? And we know she drank. How can we get something on her?" Edgar charged his unofficial top investigator.

"Russ, old boy, trust me," Chamberlain promised, and promptly took off for parts unknown.

"My name's Susan Williams," the former employee of Judias Buenoano's Finger N Faces salon testified meekly, her long, straight honey-blond hair framing her darkly outlined eyes and pretty, slender face.

"Do you know the defendant in this case, Ms. Buenoano?" Edgar asked his rebuttal witness the Friday morning of March 30, 1984.

"Yes, I do."

"Do you recall ever witnessing the defendant take a drink of alcohol of any kind?"

"Yes. It would either be on an occasion, someone's birthday, or perhaps a party we were having. We would go out for a drink after work."

"Did you take a cruise with the defendant once?"

"Yes, I did."

"I want to show you state exhibit number forty and ask you if you can identify that." Edgar handed the witness a photograph of Judias on a cruise ship.

"Yes, that's Judi," Susan Williams affirmed.

"What does she have in her hand?"

"It looks like a Bloody Mary." Susan shrugged.

"What did Judi drink on the ship?"

"Bloody Marys, piña coladas, and they had a tropical fruit drink they served."

"It's your understanding those contain alcohol?"

"Yes."

"No further questions," Edgar concluded, turning on his heels.

Edgar's next rebuttal witness, a thin, dark-haired, mustached young man with a hunted look in his darting brown eyes, slunk into the courtroom.

"Good morning. For the record, would you state your name and address please?" Edgar directed.

"David Lackey. I live in Gulf Breeze, Florida," the youth answered in a deep Southern drawl.

"Do you know Kimberly Goodyear, also known as Kimberly Buenoano?"

"Yes, sir, I do."

"How do you know her?"

"My relations with the family; dating her."

"During the time that you dated her, did you ever have an occasion to discuss with her how her brother Michael died?"

"Uh, yes. It was in my car in front of her house. . . . She had had a fight with her mom and her brother, and she was upset. I came home from work and went over to her house to pick her up so we could go out that night, and she came out to the car, crying. She, uh, said that her mom had drowned Michael," David Lackey testified hesitantly.

"Did she ever discuss why her mom drowned Michael?" Edgar asked.

"Uh, we were discussing it one day, and she thought that her mom had killed Michael for insurance reasons."

"Mr. Lackey," Johnston crossed, "do you have a brother?"

"Yes, sir. John Lackey."

"Where is he employed?"

"Escambia County Law Enforcement."

"Did he tell you it was going to make it rough on him unless you testified?"

"Well, no, he really didn't say that. He called me at work, and he was upset, kind of frantic a little bit, and told me that I need to go talk to the state attorney's office. I told him I didn't want to have anything to do with it. I've had my dealings, I've done my wrongs, I've paid my dues, and I don't want anything else to do with any other court system at all. And he said, well, they would probably get me for perjury if I did not go down there, because I had information that they could use," Lackey said nervously.

"Now, this thing that Kimberly told you, you didn't believe her, did you?" Johnston continued.

"No. She was always upset and having fights with her mom and brother. I just told her I didn't want to hear it. I had my own problems," Lackey mumbled.

"She was upset because her mother objected to her dating you?"

"More or less."

"And would you tell the court and the jury the number of crimes you have been convicted of?"

"A greater number than I can even attempt to think about," Lackey answered, his eyes downcast.

"You served time in the state penitentiary?" Johnston persisted.

"I was there a few months, until my appeal came through."

"And you don't have any idea of the number of crimes you've been convicted of?"

"Well, the last time I went down there, I was a habitual criminal."

"Thank you very much," Johnston concluded.

"Mr. Lackey," Edgar redirected, "since then, have you become gainfully employed?"

"Yes, sir." Lackey looked up.

"Trying to do something with your life?"

"Yes, sir."

"Do you think there's hope for you?"

"Well, I figure in my life all the people that said I would amount to nothing and I would be in prison the rest of my life—I'm here to prove them all wrong. I'm here to prove to them that I can make something of my life and I can work hard, and I can make it through life without having to steal, rob, and do wrong things," David Lackey testified earnestly.

"I wish you luck," Edgar replied sincerely. "Your Honor, the state rests."

In a final gesture, Johnston renewed his motion for a directed verdict of acquittal before Judge Lowrey. Reiterating his argument that the state had failed to prove corpus delicti—the body of evidence showing criminal agency of another person as cause of death—Johnston maintained that the death of Michael Buenoano Goodyear was clearly an accident and not a murder. Lowrey again declined to rule on a directed verdict, allowing the jury to decide the case. The judge dismissed the court for the noon recess.

17

"Hold the Defendant Responsible"

JERRI CHAMBERLAIN CLIMBED PAST the expanding rows of local spectators to resume her seat in the buzzing courthouse gallery the afternoon of the ninth day of the Buenoano trial. She had faithfully attended each day of the unfolding courtroom drama, taking her own notes among the kibitzing crowd that had gathered like a rising storm to witness the concluding episode of a real-life American tragedy.

As the audience speculated noisily around her, exchanging comments on the conflicting testimony of the state's and defense's handwriting experts, the remarkable lack of emotion shown by the defendant, the courtroom folklore that female jurors are harder than male jurors on female defendants, the frequent verbal jabs traded between Johnston and Edgar, Jerri sat quietly and kept her opinions to herself, feeling like a spy.

She had dutifully reported each day's trial events to her husband as he pursued his ongoing investigation of Judias. Ted had not been called as a witness after all. He was more valuable to Edgar in the field. Besides, Johnston would have objected strenuously to Ted's presence in the courtroom. Judias tended to come unglued at the mere sight of the detective she considered her personal nemesis.

Attending the trial had turned Jerri's initial jealousy of Judias into horrified awe, as she watched witness after witness confront the stone-faced mother with the abuse and murder of her own child. Despite the overwhelming circumstantial evidence, if Judias had taken the stand to deny the unthinkable crime, Jerri would have struggled to give her and society the benefit of any doubt.

The fidgeting courtroom fell quiet as Judge Lowrey returned to the bench to reconvene the Friday session. Judias huddled in her chair between the prison matron and her supportive co-counsel, her dark eyes fixed defiantly on Edgar as he took his position at the podium and prepared to deliver his closing statement to the expectant jury. Arranging his notes, Edgar kept his gaze away from the defense table, but he could feel Judias's eyes boring into him from across the room. He'd felt that strong presence of evil in the courtroom a few times before. . . .

"May it please the court, ladies and gentlemen of the jury, counsel for the defense, and all those present," Edgar began solemnly. "In representing the people of the State of Florida, it's necessary for me to present evidence to you to prove the charges of first-degree murder and grand theft laid against the defendant. The defendant, by her plea through counsel of not guilty, challenges the state to prove these charges beyond and to the exclusion of every reasonable doubt. I would like to assist you in reaching your decision by summarizing the evidence for the state and arguing to you what that evidence means. I would like to address the question of how and why and under what circumstances Michael Goodyear met his death on the thirteenth of May 1980, in East River in Santa Rosa County.

"We called the witnesses to testify of their own personal knowledge. We called Mr. Hicks, who testified that while visiting here last May of 1980, he traveled to the river in someone else's car; they dropped him off at the Highway 87 bridge landing and left. It was a quiet day in the middle of the week; he was the only one at the river. He put in his boat, traveled under the bridge, fished awhile, and headed back. He said that he put in between two and two-thirty, fished for some twenty or thirty minutes, and returned. Upon his return, he saw the defendant and her son, James, in the water, approximately four hundred and fifty feet from the bridge. Immediately near them, within twenty-five feet, was an overturned canoe surrounded by debris—sandwich bags floating in the water, an ice chest, two ski belts, a flip-flop shoe. At first he thought they were playing; then he realized they needed help. He pulled them aboard his boat, doing the right thing, and took them ashore.

"The defendant indicated to Mr. Hicks that her son, Michael, had drowned. According to Mr. Hicks's testimony, the defendant was not interested in returning to the scene where Michael had reportedly drowned. Rather, she sat down and drank a cold beer. She seemed more concerned with James's being injured. Kimberly was concerned about James. Mrs. Buenoano was concerned about James. No one appeared to be concerned about Michael.

"After an emergency phone call, the sheriff's department sent Officer Forbie Privette to the scene, who arrived at approximately five minutes after four o'clock. Officer Privette testified that he also saw the overturned canoe and surrounding debris in the general vicinity pointed out by Mr. Hicks. Officer Privette went up the river with Mr. Hicks in an attempt to find Michael Goodyear. In their intensive search of the river, they found no body, no debris, and no evidence of any capsized canoe.

"Now Mr. Roche of the search and rescue team testified that when he arrived, the defendant showed him where the boy had fallen out of the canoe, where he had drowned. It was at the top of the second curve in the river, approximately three-quarters of a mile upstream. Mr. Diamond, the chief diver for the search and rescue team, began a search pattern in that general area, and within a few minutes located first the glasses of Michael Goodyear in the middle of the river. He located the body of Michael Goodyear twenty-five feet downstream from the glasses, also in the middle of the river.

"The body of Michael Goodyear was adorned with these items: two leg braces, a prosthetic device, a wrist support, and a wristwatch which had stopped at three thirty-four.

"If the watch stopped at three thirty-four that would give us an approximate time when the boy drowned. And if the divers found him at approximately six-thirty, as testified, then we can assume that in three hours the body, as a result of the current or whatever movement Michael Goodyear was able to make, traveled only twenty-five feet downstream.

"Now, two important facts were overlooked at the time by the sheriff's department. First, the body of Michael Goodyear, being found in the middle of the river in line with his glasses, did not fall out of the canoe on the edge of the river, as the defendant had described. If he had, and perhaps the current had moved the body to the middle of the river, then the glasses would have been found between the edge of the river and the body, not in line with the body in the middle of the river.

"The second fact was that there was no debris in the area where Michael Goodyear drowned. None whatsoever. There were no fishing poles, no ice chests, no sandwich bags, no life jackets, nothing, from the point where Michael Goodyear drowned to the point where Mrs. Goodyear, or Mrs. Buenoano, or whatever her name is, was found with her son James.

"If the canoe capsized at the point where Michael was found, as the defendant stated to the officers at the scene, then there is no logical, conceivable way for the sandwich bags, the ice chest, the flip-flop, or any of the other articles, including the life belts, to have negotiated the curves in that river in such time as to all end up at the very same place three-quarters of a mile downstream that the defendant and James were discovered in the water.

"When you consider these two circumstances, which are conclusively proven—one, where Michael drowned, and two, where the canoe actually capsized—in conjunction with the time, place, condition of Michael and the supposed medical expertise of his mother, you realize that this was no accident."

Edgar paused to rearrange his notes, allowing the full implications of his points of evidence to sink into the minds of the jurors. With firm deliberation, he continued.

"Let us compare these proven circumstances to the account of the only living witness to this so-called accident. Let us take the account of James Buenoano Goodyear. James testified in court that they were canoeing and his brother Michael, whom he loved so dearly, just unfortunately drowned because a snake fell in the boat while they were trying to untangle the fishing line in a tree.

"We know that's not true. Michael Goodyear didn't paddle that canoe up that river, and he didn't tangle a fishing line in that tree, and he didn't drown when a snake fell in the boat.

"How in the world can James forget what happened to his only brother? He will tell you at one time that a snake fell in the boat. He will tell you at another time, in his statement to the army, that they hit a log and the canoe overturned. He will tell you he did sign the army statement; he will tell you he didn't sign the statement. His testimony is basically that he doesn't recall, doesn't recall, doesn't recall—a broken record. James knows what happened, because he was there. Yet he conveniently forgets and pretends that he was injured and unconscious.

"I submit that is a convenient excuse, because he won't tell you what he really knows. And he really knows what happened. He knows that his mother drowned his brother.

"You remember the testimony of Dr. Dupuis when he said that James told him he had not been rendered unconscious. You remember the testimony of the doctor who carefully examined the X-rays and found no fractures of James's neck. There was nothing wrong with him.

"Ladies and gentlemen, James Buenoano suffers from that basic problem that all persons suffer when they're carefully questioned and they're lying. They can't remember what they're supposed to say. The truth is easy to remember. It may be hard to tell, but it's always easy to remember. And you can tell it time and time again, and it will come out the same way. But a lie—a detailed, complicated, fabricated lie—when carefully examined and dissected, won't come out the same way every time it's told. Because that's the hardest thing to remember, a fabricated story."

With a deep sigh, Edgar turned slightly toward the defense table.

"The only other living witness to the drowning is the defendant. Examine her statements to the witnesses. She first told Mr. Hicks that a snake dropped into the boat while they were trying to retrieve a fishing line, causing a panic, and that caused the canoe to capsize. As soon as she found out that Michael's body was found in the middle of a flat-bottomed river, as were his glasses, that story was shoved off into the corner. She told Mr. Black, the insurance investigator, and Major Carmichael, the army investigator, that they were returning to the dock when they hit a log and the canoe turned over. This is her statement to the army, submitted in her own hand, and proven to have been written by her: 'I thought the ski belts were safe. I really do not know why we capsized. Maybe there was more weight on one side so when we hit the log, it turned.' There's not a single word in her statement about a snake. . . .

"In her panic at the scene, before they found Michael's body, the defendant said a snake fell in the boat. To those she wanted money from, she created what she thought was a fairly plausible story: they just hit a log in the river and the canoe overturned. Yet to those who knew her well—her sister-in-law, Mrs. Peggy Goeller—she made up a completely preposterous story that Michael died of chemical poisoning in the army . . . and the lie lived on. . . .

"That's the long and short of the river. Now, I know you have to consider Kimberly's statement. Kimberly didn't see it. And Kimberly is very upset about Michael drowning. James knows what happened and won't say; Kimberly suspects what happened, but she's afraid to say. She believes in her heart that her mother drowned her brother, but she just can't come to accept it, because it's just unimaginable that a mother would do this to a boy in Michael's condition. And that's the long and short of Kimberly.

"So in determining what happened on the river and whether this was an accident or not, you have the circumstances of the witnesses who have nothing to gain or lose, who are simply reporting what they found. On the other hand, you have the statements of the defendant, her son, and her daughter, and they're hanging together."

Edgar shuffled through his papers as jurors shifted uncomfortably in their seats. A small wave of restlessness rippled through the hushed courtroom. Edgar cleared his throat and continued.

"I submit to you that under the circumstances, considering the statements of all the witnesses, there is no reasonable explanation for this particular drowning to be an accident. Therefore, it is homicide. But I further submit to you that it is also a premeditated murder. A fraud in this case has been perpetrated on the insurance companies, the military, the sheriff's department, and on this court. And that is the collection by the defendant of over a hundred thousand dollars in insurance on the life of Michael Goodyear. The handwriting expert has established that the particular policies on Michael's life were not signed by Michael. These policies were, indeed, signed by Mrs. Buenoano. I say to you that to concoct fraudulent insurance policies, to have reissued insurance policies, and to cause to have the insured's name falsely placed upon those documents when he was not even present, is evidence of fraud. Proof of the fraud is proof of the premeditation. I say to you that this homicide is a premeditated homicide, for there is no other reason to go to such great lengths to fraudulently procure the insurance.

"It was very clever of the defendant not to take out one single policy of one hundred thousand dollars. That would have triggered a health physical, a credit check, a background check, and all those other inquiries that insurance companies are supposed to do. A few small policies aggregated together, which may amount to one hundred thousand dollars, would draw no particular attention from the various insurance companies. It's not worth their while to investigate. Just pay it. They'd spend more in legal fees contesting it. But it was very stupid of her to forge Michael's signature on a day he wasn't even present. But in her plan she wasn't counting on getting caught.

"She had all the insurance lined up. She had everything lined up to check Michael out of the VA hospital, bring him home, take him out of there, put him in a canoe, take him up the river beyond the sight of everybody but James, and pitch him out of the canoe. I don't know how she did it, I really don't. We'll probably never know exactly what happened that day. All we know is that Michael ended up at the bottom of that river. Whether he was rolled out or thrown out, or whatever, the fact is, ladies and gentlemen, that he's dead, and he's dead at her hands."

Edgar turned and looked Judias right in the eyes before returning his attention to the jury.

"And she planned it well. . . . After Michael was pitched out, she headed down the river to get back to her car. . . . But the best-laid plans sometimes go awry for the littlest things, and the littlest thing was a man named Ricky Hicks. Here comes Ricky in his boat, just having a good time fishing. Like he said, he fishes every chance he gets. He sees her. She pitches that canoe over. She capsized that canoe right in front of the bridge. She does it quicker than you can believe, because she had to get that canoe over. And that's probably how James sprained his neck, if he was hurt. She didn't know anything about currents or fishing, and that's what messed her up. Because there's no way you can believe that canoe capsized up that river. It didn't. It capsized right where Ricky Hicks found her.

"And I submit to you that's what made her panic and make up the story about the snake, and threw her off her plan. . . . The best thing she could think to do was hide. So she jumps in the ambulance with James and goes to the hospital with him. She didn't even wait for Michael to be found. They bring her back to identify the body and she disappears again. She's supposedly off changing clothes somewhere. They still can't find her.

"Is that the way a mother acts when her boy drowns? They're looking for her firstborn, crippled child in the river, and she's off changing her clothes? I don't know what she was doing. It doesn't really matter. The point is she wasn't where she should have been, and that was waiting at that riverbank for her boy.

"I submit to you that this is premeditated murder," Edgar charged the rapt jury, his deep baritone wavering with suppressed emotion.

Edgar paused to sip some water and continued. "I don't have to prove a reason why. It's not required by law that I prove why. But proof of motive is oftentimes compelling and often most potent. And I think it's necessary in this case to present to you all the facts, because I don't really believe that you could make a decision to convict the defendant of first-degree murder of her own child unless you understand how in the world a mother who gave life to a child could take that life. . . . The proof has to do with two things: one is pride and ego; the other is greed. Her pride could not let her accept Michael as less than perfect. Her pride refused Michael the right to a normal life like any other little boy who may be a little slow. She did not want him; she neglected him; she abused him; she was ashamed of him; she ridiculed him. So here's Michael coming home. And this time, it's not little Michael that loses his glasses or is hyperactive. This is Michael a grown man, who's going to require someone to wait on him probably the rest of his life. . . . She found a solution to the problem of Michael by drowning him. And this solution. . . . was presented to her at the same time that she had every opportunity to turn a profit.

"Not to say that Michael didn't try. Lord knows he tried. Even when he was eighteen years old, he was trying in his heart to please her. He never quit. When Michael got into that canoe that day, the last thing he ever thought was that his mother would let him drown, pitch him out of that boat. He trusted her. Michael must have thought after all those years of neglect, 'Gosh, I've grown up and they do love me; they're going to take me canoeing.' And it was the last thing he ever did. He'd spent one night at home.

"I don't know how long it took him to die. It must've been several minutes. It must've been going through his mind that any second now, she's going to reach down and pull me out of this water. But she didn't pull him out. She got that canoe and she was heading for home to get herself a cold beer. And that's what she ended up doing, sitting there drinking a cold beer. He was probably dead by then. I don't know, maybe he wasn't."

Edgar turned his penetrating gaze directly on Judias. "Yeah, it's conceivable she'd do it, the way she treated him all his life like he didn't count. Or what's more, it fit in real good with her plans. Her plans to maintain that life-style she was leading. That Dr. Judias Buenoano from out west. That mystery lady with all the money. Buenoano, Morris, Welty, Goodyear, whatever her name is. Whoever she is. She's sitting right there. She won't look at you. She's covering her face up. I would too."

Edgar turned and faced the enthralled jurors. "It didn't take her long to ask for the money, either. The first policy she cashed in was eight days after he died. Within a matter of weeks all the blood money was coming in. Over a hundred thousand dollars. What did she do with it? She gave fifteen thousand dollars to Bob Hill. She set up accounts in her children's names. Maybe that made her feel better. Maybe they didn't ask any more questions about what happened to Michael. She spent the rest on such things as a motor home, powerboat, new furniture, a Caribbean cruise. It was a life of fun, of Caribbean cruises and big fruit drinks. It was a life without Michael.

"She enjoyed the times after Michael died. I suppose with the right attitude and enough money, you could forget about that boy. But we are not going to forget about him. We're going to carry this around with us for the rest of our lives. And I'll venture to say, every time you hear the words 'East River' or see anybody with braces, or if somebody tries to sell you any insurance, or you see some little kid with thick glasses who seems kind of goofy or maybe a little slow, you'll hope that as he grows up, his mother will not take him out canoeing and let him drown. You will remember Michael, and you will never forget him.

"The law is simply letters on paper, unless you understand what is behind the law. And what is behind the law are those values that we're all taught. It is when we know those values and have the courage to apply them and the spirit to embrace them that we know we're going to do the right thing. And the right thing is to hold the defendant responsible for the most horrible crime, the murder of one's own child. Thank you."

"The court will be in recess for about twenty minutes," Judge Lowrey ordered, breaking the stunned silence.

18

"Guilty of Murder"

ESCHEWING NOTES, JOHNSTON STOOD ALONE before the reassembled jury, his large, florid face flushed with the heat of the moment. In a loud voice full of moral outrage, he delivered his closing argument to the unsuspecting jury in the freewheeling manner of a man who prefers to think on his feet.

"Ladies and gentlemen of the jury, you have heard a warped, twisted, poisoned version of what one man says about how this accident happened. I want to tell you what the facts are. Not what my interpretation is. I want to tell you what the law is, and what you, as jurors, said that you would do."

Johnston stopped to glare at Edgar, seated with folded arms behind the prosecution table.

"As I sat back and listened to the prosecutor's closing argument to you, I heard the misrepresentation of a sick mind spewing forth falsehoods, improper innuendos, trying to get your emotions so stirred up that his poisonous venom would get to you and you would convict an innocent lady of murdering her son.

"He said to you that Judi and James pitched this boy out of the canoe in the middle of the stream. I ask you, ladies and gentlemen, what witness did you hear say that to you? The only statement like that was made by this man," Johnston charged, pointing his finger at Edgar. "He would have you believe that because she didn't say anything about a snake in the boat to somebody, therefore she's guilty of murder.

"I know that this lady comes in with a cloud over her head, because the average person says, where there's smoke, there's fire. And I know some of you may have read some unfounded remarks about this lady in the paper. You said that you would not consider those and that you will judge this case on the evidence from the witness stand and the law the court will give you. I believe that. . . .

"Now, let's get to the scene—not of this remote place which Mr. Edgar has described—but the popular place for recreation that the evidence said it was. One of the most amazing things that I have learned in twenty years in the courtroom is how someone could remember something from four years ago that was really insignificant at the time. I can't even remember what day of the week it is now—I think it's Friday—or whether or not I wore a blue suit or a green suit or a brown suit Monday. So I don't believe any witness got up here and said a deliberate lie. I do believe, though, that they could not remember some of the things that they did. I subpoenaed Mr. Hicks to testify because I wanted him here. Mr. Edgar, because he is required to put on evidence first, used him first.

"Mr. Hicks said that he heard this lady screaming for help. That the boy, he thought, was unconscious. He was moaning and groaning. He rescued them and brought them back to the landing. Then he called for help. And while the help was coming, Mr. Hicks said this lady asked him for a beer. I don't think it makes any difference whether she asked him for a beer or not. The prosecution would have you believe that as soon as Mr. Hicks picked this lady and her child up, she says, forget it, give me a beer. That's not what Mr. Hicks said.

"One man says that because the glasses were in front and twenty-five feet down was the body, they must've thrown him out. There is no circumstance whatsoever pointing to that. All the circumstances point exactly what this lady said to the police officers: 'We were out canoeing and a line got hung in the tree. We were fishing near the bank.' Nowhere does she say the snake caused the boat to capsize. And nowhere does James say the snake caused the boat to capsize. James and she both said what caused the boat to capsize was that it hit a log or stump or limb or something.

"And the state infers—would have you believe—that Michael didn't have a life jacket on. . . . The evidence is that this lady, James, and Michael all had a belt on. Two were recovered. But because something wasn't recovered, that doesn't mean, and you are not permitted to infer, that Michael didn't have a life belt. He did. Perhaps when he hit the water, it came unbuckled, something happened, and it floated to the top. And because his life belt came off and the poor child could not swim, he unfortunately drowned. And do you know what today is, of all days? Maybe it's a good omen. Today is Michael's birthday. Today is his birthday. . . ."

Johnston paused dramatically, resting a pitying gaze on his expressionless client.

"If this lady was going to kill her son— Do you imagine what this man has said? That her own son, Michael's brother, was a principal with her, in conspiracy with her. James was fourteen years old. What kind of a fourteen-year-old beast is that? I don't think you're going to say that James was part of it. He seemed like a nice, well-mannered kid; yes sir, no sir. I asked him, 'James, do you remember signing the statement?' 'You know, I don't really know.' This is a bad memory for the kid. I said, 'Is it your signature?' 'Yes, sir.' 'Is everything true?' 'Yes, sir.'

"Now, Mr. Edgar says, we didn't have all this information that we've got now. Well, what information didn't they have? They had exactly where the body was located; exactly where Judi said the fishing line was; exactly the testimony of Mr. Tom Roche, who said that Judi went there and showed them where it happened; exactly the statement of Mr. Hicks; exactly where the glasses were found; exactly where the body was found; the autopsy. They knew of the insurance, because the army investigated. And after the Santa Rosa County Sheriff's Office investigated, Captain Boswell says on August 11, 1980, 'Dear Sir, our investigation reveals that the above-captioned subject died accidentally, when the canoe in which he was a passenger capsized in East River. There is no evidence of criminal negligence in this matter.' That is . . . what they said then. They had the same facts then that they have now.

"Now, he says it was for insurance. Had all this insurance on him. The truth of the matter is, this lady only had, I think, around thirty-seven thousand dollars' worth of insurance on the boy. Because it was an accident . . . they paid double what the policy was. And I know that if she had it to do over again, she would give up the hundred thousand, the house, the boat, and everything else to have her son back.

"He said she bought the policies to kill Michael. And do you know what the man from Prudential said? That for another forty cents she could've bought another twenty thousand dollars' worth of insurance. Ladies and gentlemen, is it reasonable to believe that this fine lady was going to murder her son and collect all the insurance, and for another forty measly cents she would not get another twenty thousand dollars' worth of insurance? Does that sound like somebody that's going to murder her son?

"You know it doesn't. And more importantly, he knows it doesn't," Johnston accused, pointing emphatically at the silent prosecutor.

"You will have defendant's exhibit number eight-B, a photo album which he suggested and implied was put together hurriedly overnight. These are the pictures of Michael. These are the cherished memories that this lady had of this child, which will forever be blackened because of one person. You go through and look at these and see. The lady that hated her son, and she saved his valentine— 'To the most beautiful woman in the whole wide world, my mom. Be my valentine.' A letter from Michael, July fourth,

1979—'With love, please come to Fort Leonard Wood. . . .
I appreciate the personal letters. . . . I need at least sixty
dollars in twenties. . . . Please, I don't get paid until July
31, 1979. That is at least four weeks away. . . . Please. . . .
Love to my little Kimmie-pooh and James.' These pictures
tell the story. You don't need to see anything but this.

"No woman could murder her own child and keep this
at home. . . .

"As you look at Judi right now, the law says that you
have to presume that lady is innocent. That presumption
of innocence abides and carries with Judi when you go back
to the jury room. It never leaves her until and unless you
say, 'Beyond all reasonable doubt, I'm satisfied from all of
the evidence that on May 13, 1980, she committed the
cold-blooded murder of her son, and on May 21, 1980,
she stole from the insurance company.' Only then does
that presumption of innocence ever leave this lady.

"You are a chosen few. There are not too many people that ever have the opportunity to sit and determine
whether someone gets the electric chair or not. I know
that you do not take that responsibility lightly. . . . Don't
think the worst and make that the best of your reason. Let
this lady go home tonight with her daughter and her son.
Apply the law to the facts. And may God help you in your
deliberations."

With a solemn bow to the jury and a parting glower at
Edgar, Johnston retired to the defense table.

A collective sigh accompanied the general exodus of the
courtroom as the stiff-necked spectators shuffled for the
exit, led by the hastily retreating members of the press.
Whatever the ending, the show was over. The final drama
of the jury's deliberations would take place behind closed
doors. The faces of the jurors as they stretched and yawned
in place gave no clue as to what their decision might be.
The defendant, heedless as ever of the crowd now dwin-
dling behind her, huddled in whispered conference with
her attorneys as Edgar wearily assembled his prodigious

stacks of files and documents on the opposite side of the emptying room.

Following the other spectators filing slowly out of the gallery, Jerri Chamberlain turned to view the courtroom scene one last time, almost sorry to be leaving. Her role as unofficial court reporter had given her a sense of mission over the past ten days, a feeling of importance, for a change, to her workaholic husband. For once, Ted had allowed her to share in his consuming work. She wondered if she'd ever get that chance again.

With simple ceremony, Judge Lowrey delivered his final charge to the restless jury, reading the instructions in a slow drone. To prepare them for their task, the judge outlined the duties of the jury, reviewing key aspects of the law and how it applied to interpreting the evidence. Then, at last satisfied with the formal explanations, he dismissed the jurors to their deliberations.

At six forty-three P.M. on Friday, March 30, 1984, on what would have been Michael Buenoano Goodyear's twenty-third birthday, the jury began its deliberation on the guilt or innocence of Judias Buenoano on the charge of murdering her son.

At nine thirty P.M. that night, James Buenoano was taken into custody by Escambia County Sheriff's deputies while drinking beer with his friends on the hood of his mother's Corvette on Pensacola Beach. James, a juvenile at the time of the violation, was arrested for the attempted first-degree murder of John Gentry by car bombing on June 25, 1983.

At the same time, as she waited in her cell at the Santa Rosa County Jail for the jury's decision, Judias Buenoano was served with a warrant for her arrest on the charge of the attempted first-degree murder of her former fiancé, John Gentry, and grand theft through insurance fraud. The papers were served personally by Special Agent Dewitt Fincannon of the Federal Bureau of Alcohol, Tobacco and

Firearms and Detective Ted Chamberlain.

Struggling against her lawyer's restraints, Judias lunged in rage at Chamberlain.

"I'll see you rot in hell!" she screamed after the grinning detective.

Driving directly to the Escambia County Jail, Ted Chamberlain paid a long-anticipated visit to James Buenoano, held in detention at the juvenile center across the road under $500,000 bond.

"Gotcha, motherfucker!" he told the ever-smirking James through the iron bars of the holding cell.

Shortly before one A.M. on March 31, 1984, having rejected the judge's earlier offer to recess for the night, the weary jury reached its verdict on the drowning trial of Michael Goodyear.

Amidst a scattered gathering of the media and the insatiably curious, court was reconvened at the Milton courthouse in the wee hours of the morning.

"Let the record reflect the defendant, her counsel, counsel for the state, the jury, and all necessary court personnel are present," Judge Lowrey announced, dispensing with further ceremony. "Members of the jury, have you reached a verdict?"

"Yes, we have," the foreman rejoined.

"Would you give the verdict to the bailiff, please?"

The foreman complied, handing the folded form to the waiting bailiff, who in turn, delivered it to the court. Without expression, Judge Lowrey quickly perused the verdict and handed it to the expectant clerk.

"Mr. Clerk, would you publish the verdict?" Lowrey routinely instructed.

"Under count one of the indictment, we the jury, find the defendant, Judias Buenoano, guilty of murder in the first degree. As to count two, guilty of grand theft, as charged in the indictment. So say we all," the court clerk read in a nasal monotone.

Her face an expressionless mask, Judias moved closer to her co-counsel, turning away from the zooming television cameras.

Outside the courtroom, standing alone in the empty hallway, Kimberly Buenoano let loose deep sobs.

19

Life

"My name is Judias W. Buenoano."

"Your age?"

"I'm forty."

"Have you ever been convicted of a crime?"

"No, I have not."

"Did you murder your son?"

"No, sir. It was an accident."

"What else do you want to tell the jury?"

"I don't see how I've been convicted of murder when there was no murder that took place. True enough, I might have been negligent in not insisting that he wear a full life jacket, but I honestly believed the ski belt that he wore was sufficient. I have lived with guilt every day since he died that it was my fault. But I did not murder him. I loved my children. I would have never harmed any one of them."

"Your witness."

Turning abruptly to the waiting prosecutor, James Johnston concluded the final direct examination of his client on the Monday morning of April 2, 1984. The penalty phase of Judias Buenoano's murder trial, during which the jury would hear mitigating and aggravating circumstances before issuing a nonbinding recommendation of either life imprisonment without possibility of parole for twenty-five years or death in the electric chair, had begun.

Russ Edgar, having decided to argue for the death penalty before the court, approached the convicted defendant with his usual quiet confidence. Judias, coiffed and dressed for the occasion in tailored gray slacks, low black heels, and a demure white Kitty Foyle bowed blouse, her harsh pallor softened by a touch of pink lipstick and a blush of rouge, sat defensively in the witness chair and squarely faced her accuser for the first and last time.

"Did you feel guilty when you spent the money, the one hundred thousand dollars that you collected on Michael's death?" Edgar fired.

"Yes, sir, I sure did. Every—" Judias started to fire back.

"You feel guilty now?" Edgar interjected.

"Yes, sir, I sure do," Judias retorted with conviction, her narrowed eyes glaring at Edgar.

"When did you start planning to collect insurance on your son's death?"

"I never planned to collect insurance on my son," Judias interposed defiantly. "The insurance was purchased for his future. If my parents had done that for me, when I became old enough to realize I needed insurance, it wouldn't have cost me an arm and a leg to get insurance. So I planned for my children's future. I had it done for all of them. Not just for Michael, but for every one of them, for their future. Not for murder. Not to go off and kill one of them. I mean, what kind of a mother would kill one of her children? I love my children," Judias protested, her voice rising in indignation.

"That's what we're trying to find out, ma'am. . . . That's what we're trying to find out."

"Well, no one has ever said that I ever killed anyone but you, Mr. Edgar. You have hunted me; you have witch-hunted me, sir," Judias charged loudly.

"You don't consider yourself a witch, do you?" Edgar baited.

"No, sir, I sure don't. And I don't think I've been treated fairly by you, either!"

"Do you want to explain that answer?" Edgar replied coolly.

"Well, sir, you explained it in court the other day. You said this was the direct result of the fact that I would not talk to you, and therefore my silence was an admission of guilt."

"I did ask you to talk to me, didn't I?"

"Yes, sir. So, what do you do? You go out and witch-hunt me, sir. It was not murder. It was an accident, and it appalls me that twelve members of this jury could find me guilty when you didn't parade any evidence through this court that I was a murderer."

"Well, they made their decision that you are a murderer. . . ."

"Yes, sir, they sure have. And they're going to have to live with that decision too," Judias snapped back.

"Yeah, you've said some pretty nasty things about the people in this case, haven't you? You said that you would like to see all of us fourteen feet under and the worms eating our bodies."

"No, sir, I have not! I have never said anything nasty about anyone!"

"Do you want me to bring a witness on?"

"You bring whoever you want on. I mean, you've hatched all this up anyway," Judias retorted, striking the air with an angry wave of her hand.

"I made it all up myself?"

"Yes, sir, you sure have. And I have not had a chance to defend myself in this whole case. And we really didn't think it was necessary, because you had not produced any evidence to the fact that I had killed anyone."

"You didn't have a chance to explain your side of the story?" Edgar echoed.

"No, sir. I didn't have a chance to go before the grand jury and explain my side. I haven't had a chance to explain nothing. All I have been done is be threatened by you, sir!"

"You were here that day, weren't you? You came running up the hallway looking for your daughter and your son the morning the grand jury—"

"I have never run up and down the hallway looking for anything. I stood right outside Judge Lowrey's door waiting for my daughter."

"You sat out there in the truck after James and Kimberly testified, yelling at them and pointing your finger at them, didn't you? 'Cause they'd messed you up, and you didn't know what they said!" Edgar responded, his composure slipping.

"No, sir, I did not do any such thing."

"We caught you by surprise, didn't we?"

"I won't even answer that question. I don't think it's even worth an answer. That's bizarre. If I wanted to run, sir, I could've run a long time ago, because of some other circumstance, and you know," Judias retaliated.

"Because of what?"

"Mr. Gentry told me what was going on in your office, sir."

"He was your spy?"

"Whatever you want to call it."

"What did he tell you?" Edgar queried, curious.

"I don't think we need to discuss that at this time. I'm sure it'll come up at another time," Judias smirked knowingly.

"Why are you so sure?"

"Why shouldn't it? That's not pertinent to this case anyway, Mr. Edgar. Get on with your questions, please," Judias demanded with an impatient gesture. "You've already got a conviction."

"Yeah, and right at this point, I'm just like the police officer that arrested you. I'm about finished. It's going to be their turn." Edgar looked in the direction of the riveted jury. "Do you want to tell them something to mitigate this crime?"

"When they realize, and they have to live with the fact that they have convicted an innocent woman. . . ." Judias's angry eyes remained fixed on her prosecutor. "It was an accident, Mr. Edgar. No one went through this court and said anything other than the fact that it was an accident, other than you! And you gave an awful accounting, and you weren't there! And you don't know!" Judias shouted, her fist pounding the witness rail.

"Do you want to tell us how it happened then, from the beginning?" Edgar challenged.

"It was an accident, Mr. Edgar. James explained it to this court, how it happened in the beginning. . . ."

"Excuse me, Judi." Johnston stood to address his distraught client.

"No, I am upset, Mr. Johnston," Judias shot back, unable to quell her fury.

"Well, just don't say anything. Let me make an objection." Johnston looked up at Lowrey in exasperation. "Your Honor, that was not brought on direct examination, and I would object to the line of questioning. It's not relevant."

"She said she didn't murder her son; it was an accident. I want to hear, Your Honor, from her what happened that day," Edgar argued.

"She will not be required to speak if she doesn't want to," Lowrey ruled.

"You don't wish to? Can you remember?" Edgar turned his steel-blue gaze on Judias.

"Oh yes, sir, I remember what happened." Judias glared back.

"Just a minute, Judi," Johnston intervened. "Your Honor, I would like to advise my client in front of the court and jury that she's given a statement. There's no sense in going into it. . . ."

"Which statement do you want us to consider?" Edgar demanded. "The one to the army? The one to Roy Black? The one to Major Carmichael? The one to Ricky Hicks? Or the one to Billy Jenkins? Which one of the five? Don't look at him. He can't help you," Edgar charged as Judias glanced sidelong at her attorney.

At Johnston's renewed objection, Edgar approached the bench, addressing Judge Lowrey outside the hearing of the jury with hushed intensity.

"My conscience is not going to be clear, fully, until I get her to tell me what happened. I've heard five different stories. I want to hear it from her."

"Counsel, she's not required to discuss the guilt phase of the evidence in any way. The objection will be sustained, unless she exercises her right to discuss it as a factor of mitigation," Lowrey ruled.

His frustration mounting, Edgar returned to his hostile witness.

"Ma'am, about this money you collected. Did you sign your son's name to the Prudential policy?"

"No, sir, I did not," Judias answered evenly.

"Well, who did?"

"Your Honor, just a minute," Johnston objected. "I didn't know we were going to try the case again. Apparently, Mr. Edgar does want to retry it. I'm certainly willing to do that."

"I want answers to questions," Edgar persisted.

"The objection will be sustained," Lowrey replied in monotone.

"She said that she did not profit intentionally from her son's death, and a factor that's to be considered by the jury as an aggravating factor is that this was cold, calculated, and premeditated," Edgar protested.

"The evidence is before the jury on those matters already. I'm going to sustain the objection," Lowrey repeated.

"Well, why did you get the reissuance of the lost policy that you signed?" Edgar tried again.

"Why? Because my son had been hurt, Mr. Edgar," Judias replied, taking the offensive.

"Did you expect him to die?"

"No, sir, I did not expect him to die. I did expect that I had to get all of his insurance policies together because the VA wanted to know what kind of life insurance we had."

"You didn't think that you were going to kill him?"

"Why would I kill my own child, Mr. Edgar? Would you kill one of yours?" Judias countered.

"Unfortunately, ma'am, I don't have any."

"I know that you don't, but if you did have children, would you want to kill them? They're the most precious possessions that we've got."

"And that's the way you treated Michael?"

"The only thing I ever did for Michael was for his own good."

"Was Michael your real child?"

"Yes, sir."

"Why did you tell people he was your stepchild?"

"I did not tell anybody that he was my stepchild."

"Who was Michael's father?"

"That really is none of your concern," Judias replied icily.

"Was it Sergeant Michael Schultz, an air force member stationed in New Mexico?" Edgar pursued.

"That still isn't any of your concern. It wasn't brought into this trial," Judias stonewalled.

"Do you disagree with the testimony of the witnesses in this case as to your relationship with Michael?"

"I heard a lot of people testify," Judias said sharply. "How would you look at it if you were thirteen? Every time you correct a child, they don't think it's a problem. They don't think it's right. And let's face it, it's a sad world when we cannot tell one of our own children something that they've done wrong, or we cannot discipline them without people hollering child abuse. . . . No one told you that I had abused my child, ever!" Judias expounded heatedly.

"How about Constance Lang? Do you disagree with what she said?"

"Yes, sir, I most certainly do. I haven't seen Constance Lang since 1971, and she was dismissed from my employ, if you want the truth."

"That's what we want," Edgar rejoined.

"Why didn't you ask for it long before now? I have never had a chance to answer any questions. . . ."

"Be careful when you say that. Do you recall Ted Chamberlain asking you questions?"

"No, sir, Ted Chamberlain never asked me any questions," said Judias bitterly.

"You didn't volunteer anything either, did you?"

"Why should I? You had already convicted me in your mind; you are the one who put me on trial!"

"Was Michael lonely?"

"No, sir, Michael wasn't lonely. Michael was friendly. Michael talked to everybody. He loved everybody. He had a very positive attitude. He had all kinds of friends. Anytime Michael wanted to talk, I'd sit down and talk to him. Just like I do my other two children. There was no difference. In fact, I loved Michael more than I did the other two children," Judias attested.

"Was Michael awkward and uncoordinated?"

"No, not necessarily. Michael did have a visual perception problem, which did make him a little uncoordinated. But over the years of Michael running—Michael ran—I used to run right alongside of him."

"Chasing him or following him?" Edgar rejoined.

"Why would I chase him, Mr. Edgar? Now, that's bizarre."

"How come Michael didn't stay at home?"

"Because Michael had a behavioral problem when he was young. And a doctor in Orlando suggested—told us—that this was the best thing for Michael because we were too protective—we were overprotective parents. We never allowed him to grow up."

"After Michael went to the Montanari school, where did he go?"

"Chattahoochee. And would you like for me to explain why? Because Montanari had taken such good care of him that they had made a drug addict out of him. So he had to be weaned off the drugs."

"You were capable of curing him of his drug problem, weren't you?"

"No, sir, I was not."

"After Chattahoochee, where did he go?"

"He went to Camp Emachamee. And that's the best place in the world for anybody to have ever gone. I would love for James to go there, and would love for Kimberly to spend a year there."

"Are they emotionally disturbed too?"

"No, sir, they are not. But not all the children there are emotionally disturbed. And Michael was not emotionally disturbed; he had a behavior problem."

"What do you mean?"

"He just would not mind; he would not do anything he was told to do. You'd say, 'Don't touch that,' and he did it anyway."

"So what did you do?"

"I just talked to him. I didn't have the heart to ever spank him or do anything like that. And I never have James or Kimberly either."

"You never touched him?"

"I slapped him one time in his whole life, and then it was because he dared me!"

"What about all those bruises and marks in Michael's pictures in the photo album? Where did they come from?"

"Different places. I think most of those pictures were all taken one Christmas. Those pictures in that album are my favorites."

"Yeah," Edgar said sarcastically.

"I have pictures of Michael from every age. And I'm so tired of your insinuations. Your insinuations!" Judias cried, her fist hitting the rail. "This whole murder case is your idea!"

"Ma'am, I didn't take him in the canoe. . . ."

"No, sir, you didn't take him in the canoe, so therefore you don't know what happened in that canoe! But you sure gave the jury a real good show of what I did, and my God, you don't know! You weren't there!" Judias raved, her voice trembling with outrage.

"Well, tell me what you did then. I want to know!"

"I don't have to tell you!"

"Then I don't have any more questions."

"Great!"

Edgar's closing argument for the penalty phase was mercifully brief. Citing two aggravating circumstances—that the defendant had "profited from the execution at her own hands of her firstborn child," and that "the particular murder was done in a cold, calculated, and premeditated manner without any pretense of moral or legal justification"—Edgar stood unmoving behind his podium and quietly asked the jury to return a recommendation of death in the electric chair.

"I realize that she is a mother and she is a woman, but half the population of this country are woman and a good percentage of those are mothers. You told me when you were selected to sit on this jury that that alone would not persuade you to vote against a verdict of first-degree murder or against the death penalty," Edgar calmly reasoned.

"I've become tired, and I've become weary, and I just want to walk away and forget it, because I've had enough of this case. But I can't do that," admitted Edgar, his quavering voice betraying mental exhaustion. With a final nod to the all-too-familiar jury, Edgar retired to his seat, an expression of relief playing across his features.

James Johnston rose wearily to his feet, determined to make his final plea for mercy for the unfortunate client who sulked silently beside him. His ruddy face heavy with undisguised emotion, Johnston addressed the long-suffering jury in the desperate tones of a man deeply shaken in his beliefs.

"I quite frankly find myself in a very awkward position— since having known Judi personally for a number of years, knowing the kind of person she is—never talking about anybody, never putting a heavy hand on anybody, giving always more than she would take—and believing sincerely in my heart, my mind, and every fiber of my body that this lady is completely innocent— To be in a situation of talking to twelve people who have said that she's guilty of first-degree murder— Then listening to the state attorney ask you to execute her in the electric chair . . ." Seemingly at a loss, Johnston paused to shake his head.

"I know that the question of capital punishment is a personal matter with each of us," Johnston resumed. "And when the Supreme Court declared the execution of people unconstitutional, I had the fortune of being elected by the people of four counties to represent them in the Florida senate. And, you know, the first thing that we took up was the restoration of capital punishment. Do you know that I helped write the law that the judge will give you? And reflecting back to 1972, on the senate floor there were a lot of people who did not believe in the death penalty. And I got up on the senate floor with a microphone in my hand, and I said to the other thirty-nine senators, the press, and the public, 'What I do not want to happen in the imposition of the death penalty is for a judge to make that determination without the benefit of the jury. We have to build some protection in this thing. Then, at least, an innocent person may not be executed.' Because unfortunately, in our system there are some who do things because they appear to be popular with the press. And after hearing all the arguments, the senate unanimously said, 'Let's also say to the jury, you make a recommendation to the court; the court is not bound to follow the recommendation, but it's still another check and balance between tyranny and democracy, between dictatorship and democracy.' Because you, twelve citizens, have some input into your government," Johnston preached, moving in on the jurors.

"Isn't there some possibility . . . that you could be mistaken? . . . If there is, don't you think that under our law you should give the benefit of that doubt to this lady? . . . It would be an awful, horrible thing to sentence someone to death and find out that you made a mistake—something most human beings couldn't live with.

"I don't want to argue the case over. I, too, am tired and weary," Johnston segued, moving back toward the defense table. "My client is exhausted. Can you imagine going to twenty funerals? Every day that she sat in this courtroom was a funeral for her. She is so numb that she can hardly talk!" Johnston spluttered, gesturing toward the sullen Judias.

"Let's talk about mitigating circumstances. One that you are bound to consider by law is the fact that this lady has no prior criminal activity. None. Never in her life has she ever had a speeding ticket. She's forty years old. That's the second mitigating factor. To me, it would be far worse punishment to spend life imprisonment without possibility of being paroled for twenty-five years. She'd be sixty-five. What could she do? Nothing.

"Do you know what the third mitigating factor is? . . . The defendant's character. . . . You may have wondered why I did not call her to the stand. That was the decision that I made, a legal decision, nothing that I wanted to hide. That's the decision I stuck with. The state can call any other witness they want to show that she's got bad character. They called none. I have to assume that they don't question her character.

"I called three witnesses to the stand that testified to this lady's character. Two of them worked with her, and one was a young girl who knew her. . . . These people were not bound to come to court. They came because they wanted to say something good about this lady. They said, we considered her our 'mom.' And I know that you feel the same way about your mom, that your mother's character is above reproach. For people who needed a place to stay, she had an open door. For a hungry stomach, she had some food. For loneliness, she had some love. And in return, she asked nothing except for them maybe to take out the garbage.

"When I went home to get my bologna sandwich at lunch, I was talking to my wife, Rebecca, and I said, 'You know, I've never been canoeing. I don't think I ever want to go in one after this.' How in the world could somebody believe that this lady and a fourteen-year-old boy picked up the son and brother with his braces on, and just *phewww*, pitched him out in the river. It seems to me if the canoe was that unstable, it would turn over. Got to be some reasonable doubt. . . ." Johnston appeared to be wrestling with his own doubts. With a final plea for life imprisonment for his client, Johnston hastily concluded.

After less than an hour's deliberation, the jury returned a recommendation that the court sentence Judias Buenoano to life imprisonment without possibility of parole for twenty-five years.

"The court will set this matter for sentencing on June sixth, 1984, at three-thirty P.M. The defendant will be remanded to custody without bond," Lowrey announced, dismissing the court with a resounding bang of his gavel.

Satisfied that the guilty verdict would not be overturned on appeal, Edgar in the end had agreed to the court's stipulation that the jury would return a recommendation of life imprisonment. He did not want the case tied up for the next ten years in appeals over the death penalty. He knew there were more trials ahead for Judias Welty Goodyear Buenoano. Besides, he was tired of pronouncing her names.

"Geronimo, take a look at this. Got it back from Washington the other day. Looks like Judi's not a relative of yours after all." Bob Cousson grinned, handing Ted Chamberlain a letter from the Bureau of Indian Affairs dated April 4, 1984.

Chamberlain, seated beside Cousson in an unmarked official vehicle in the deserted driveway at 2812 Whisper Pine Drive, a signed search warrant for the vacant Buenoano home in his inside jacket pocket, read the letter in silence.

In reference to your telephone request about the descendants of Geronimo and the Mesquite Apache tribe, there is no indication that any of Geronimo's family have the name Welty or Northam or that any carry the first name of Ann Lou or for that matter either Ann or Lou. Tribal members of the Mescaleno and Fort Sill Apache tribe, wherein Geronimo's descendants are members or close associates, are unfamiliar with the above names. Ms. Welty Northam is not listed on the Chiricahua claims payment lists which include Geronimo's descendants, and her name does not appear in any of the research on Apaches which I have accumulated over the past twenty years.

There is no Mesquite Apache tribe.

"So the bitch was lying again—Geronimo was her great-great-granddaddy. I knew she couldn't be one of my people. Boy, what an ugly woman!" Chamberlain whistled, handing the report back to Cousson.

"Let's get in there and see if we can find some dynamite," Cousson said, climbing out of the driver's seat.

"They were stupid enough to leave the wire in James's closet. Maybe they stashed the dynamite in the dishwasher," Chamberlain quipped, unlocking the front door of the confiscated house.

"We never did check out the attic," Cousson replied, following his partner into the empty foyer. "There were a lot more than two sticks of dynamite missing from Johnny Rowell's Brewton purchase. We got enough evidence with the matching wire to charge James and Judi with the bombing, but without Rowell's testimony, I'm not sure we've got enough to convict them."

"Five hundred thousand dollars in insurance money is one hell of a motive. Gentry will swear to that," Chamberlain retorted on his way to the kitchen.

"I reckon the bank took all the furniture when they confiscated the house," Cousson remarked, his voice echoing through the abandoned rooms. "You know, Judi managed to sell her fingernail business to some woman back in January for ten thousand dollars or thereabouts. She got away with that much anyway."

"Well, they got James's truck and Kimberly's Camaro. She transferred the Corvette to her lawyer before the state could get their hands on it," Chamberlain called back, slamming kitchen cabinets and drawers. "Johnston was cruising by the county jail in it the other day, waving up to Judi in her cell—ta ta!" Chamberlain quipped, joining Cousson in the hallway. "The kitchen's clean. Let's try upstairs."

"I'll take Kimberly's room. That's where we found the pills on the first search," Cousson volunteered. "It's gotta be rough on that kid, with her mom and brother both in jail. Where do you think she is now?"

"Probably hanging out with 'the troops'—James's and her friends over on the beach. Remember when we asked her her name?—She had to look at her driver's license. 'What's our name today, Mommy?' That's one mixed-up kid," Chamberlain cracked, heading for Judias's bedroom.

Standing alone in the empty, carpeted room littered with the flotsam of a hasty evacuation Chamberlain felt for the first time like an intruder in Judias's personal space. A stray April breeze wafted through the half-open window, gently fluttering the ruffled polyester curtains and casting a play of pale shadows across the stained baby-blue walls. Tossed carelessly in a far corner, a blue-green scrapbook lay facedown and open. Chamberlain seized the discarded memento and cautiously turned the thick cardboard pages, like an explosive expert dismantling a bomb.

The torn gray pages were childishly pasted with magazine cutouts of contented babies, frolicking puppies, flower stickers, and kindergarten cartoons. Bizarrely juxtaposed with this maternal collage was a full-color close-up of a monstrous spider, staring black-eyed above the caption, "All about spiders." On the opposite page was an enlarged photograph of a black widow spider gorging on an insect trapped in her web. The caption asked, "What Are Webs For?"

In the middle of the strange collection of children's art, carefully cut glossy magazine illustrations of Norman Rockwell families, and clipped articles titled "There's a New Law to Help Your Handicapped Child" and "Did You and Daddy Stop Loving Each Other Because I Was Bad?" was a display of snapshots devoted to Jim and Kim, ages two through twelve. A handmade Mother's Day card signed by Kim at age eight read, "I like my mother because she lets me go to the bank with her. She buys me lollipops. She lets me give the check to the lady." A pressed birthday corsage from Jim when he was twelve graced a single page.

There were no photographs of Michael. No letters, no cards, no school projects. Not one.

Beneath an array of happily nursing mothers were scrawled the line, "Breast-feeding your baby is quite a treat, until he gets some teeth"; "Caring for your baby is a lot of fun, it's like a mountain rose, with care it will surely grow"; "Have the kids driven you crazy and you have a migraine? Well, take a pill, my dear, and simply settle back."

Opposite a clinical diagnosis form detailing the medical symptoms of a one-month-old patient suffering from acute rectal bleeding was pasted a handwritten poem:

> The Pediatric Nurse is like a clown that must wear two faces; She sees the joy and sorrow that some children bring; she sees the bright, healthy, loving child and those with future dim; she feels the anger, hurt, joy, pride and sometimes even cries; the pediatric nurse is really human inside.
>
> It was signed "Judias."

Stapled onto a subsequent page was a poem entitled "Masks":

> Don't be fooled by me, Don't be fooled by the face I wear, for I wear a thousand masks, masks that I'm afraid to take off, and none of them are me. . . . My surface may seem smooth, but my surface is my mask. Beneath this lies no complacence. Beneath dwells the real me in confusion, in fear, in aloneness. But I hide this. I don't want anybody to know it. I panic at the thought of my weakness and fear of being exposed. That's why I frantically create a mask to hide behind. A nonchalant, sophisticated façade to help me pretend, to shield me from the glance that knows. But such a glance is precisely my salvation, my only salvation, and I know it. . . . But I don't tell you this. I don't dare. I'm afraid to. I'm afraid your glance will not be followed by acceptance and love. I'm afraid you'll think less of me, that you'll laugh at me, and your laugh would kill me. I'm

afraid that deep down I'm nothing, that I'm no good, and that you will see this and reject me. So I play my game, my desperate game, and so begins the parade of masks, and my life becomes a front. . . . I idly chatter to you in the suave tones of surface talk. I tell you everything that is really nothing, and nothing of what is everything, of what is crying within me. So when I go through my routine, do not be fooled by what I'm saying. Please listen carefully and try to hear what I'm not saying, what I'd like to be able to say, what for survival I need to say, but what I can't say. . . .

On the last page, a dark-haired woman sat rigid in a formal straight-backed armchair, almost as if she were strapped into an electric chair. Beneath this picture Judias had written the words, "This is a mother who is at wit's end; she has a handicapped child she says will never win."

Slamming the book shut with an involuntary shudder, Chamberlain tossed the haunting memento away from him back into its forgotten corner.

Cousson returned from the attic empty-handed.

"Let's get the hell out of here," Chamberlain said. "This place gives me the creeps."

Flanked by two armed guards and clad in a brown prison jumpsuit proclaiming "Santa Rosa County Jail" in large white letters across her back, Judias sauntered through the side entrance of the near-empty Milton courthouse on the afternoon of June 6, 1984. James Johnston, ever courteous in his pink shirt and white linen suit, held the door for his about-to-be-sentenced client.

Rubbing her handcuffed palms lightly together, Judias slumped into her familiar seat beside her counsel at the defense table and waited with apparent nonchalance for the judge who would sentence her to life or death.

Within moments Judge Lowrey, his black robes billowing behind him, swept onto the raised bench.

"Would the defendant and counsel come forward at this time?" Lowrey mumbled, wasting no time.

Following her somber lawyer, Judias strutted boldly up to the unsmiling judge, and slumped seductively against the chest-high wall of polished walnut. She swayed one white-sneakered foot coyly on tip toe, fidgeting slightly, as Johnston, hands clasped militarily behind his back, repeated his routine plea for mercy. He was interrupted. From the far side of the room, Russ Edgar's deep baritone, devoid of any emotional inflection, reverberated through the courtroom.

"The defendant did commit the crime, and if you believe that the punishment should fit the crime, she should be thrown out of the canoe herself, with her arms and legs bound. That's my personal belief."

Without further comment, Judias was led by a silent guard to the defense table and fingerprinted once again for final identification before receiving sentence. Judge Lowrey's small black eyes stared intently at Judias as each of her manicured fingertips was rolled tediously on the pad of black ink.

Led back before the bench, Judias stood in a practiced slouch, her weight shifted provocatively to one side, as Judge Lowrey donned his horn-rimmed glasses and, without looking up, read the prescribed sentence in a mechanical monotone.

"It is the sentence of law that the defendant is hereby committed to the Department of Corrections to be imprisoned for a term of natural life without parole for twenty-five years."

Judias quietly shifted her weight to the other side.

Her dark eyes darting rapidly, her shackled hands gesturing with urgency, Judias conferred in hurried whispers with her lawyer before her prison guards whisked her unceremoniously from the courtroom.

Prancing past the waiting television cameras, a coy smile imprinted on her face, Judias descended the back stairs of the courthouse, gingerly wiping the black ink from her polished red nails, and disappeared through the swinging glass doors.

One month later, Okaloosa County officials exhumed the body of Gerald Dossett of Fort Walton Beach, a onetime boyfriend of Judias's who died in an area hospital under sudden and mysterious circumstances in 1980. An autopsy had been ordered to test the remains for traces of arsenic.

20

"Ta ta!"

JOHN WESLEY GENTRY SHIFTED UNCOMFORTABLY on the hard wooden bench at Pensacola's Escambia County Circuit Courthouse on the bright Tuesday morning of October 16, 1984, and wondered if he wouldn't be better off if he hadn't survived the bombing after all.

He'd taken some antibiotics the last few days and was feeling a little better. His guts still flared up every once in a while. The medicine wasn't going to prolong his life, though. Hell, the doctors had told him he'd be lucky to live till sixty. There were a couple of pieces of metal lodged pretty close to his heart; a couple of scars up near his jugular vein. Between that and the shrapnel he still carried in him from that mine explosion in Vietnam, he was a walking target for airport metal detectors. Still, he figured he was luckier than the rest of Judi's victims. Gentry looked sidelong at his new wife, Pat, seated close beside him, and gave her hand a reassuring squeeze. Her shoulder-length, straight black hair eclipsed the expression of resigned weariness on her attractive face. The most innocent victim of all, she had stuck by him through the whole miserable ordeal of the past year, waiting in drafty courtroom hallways for her husband to testify against the woman who had repeatedly failed to murder him but had nevertheless succeeded in destroying his life.

He and Pat had gotten together about six months after the bombing, shortly after the bankruptcy. With all the negative publicity, his carpeting and wallpaper business had dropped from six thousand to two hundred dollars a day, almost overnight. Within three months, he had lost over $6 million.

Once before, several years ago, he and Pat had been a very hot item. But his first wife had just run off with his best friend, and Pat's husband had taken off, leaving her with a seriously ill six-month-old baby. Neither one was ready to trust anybody. Then along came Judi.

After he got out of the hospital, he had felt totally alone and abandoned. The only person who had never let him down when he needed her was Pat. He called her. Within a few weeks they were married.

Two months later, police officers appeared at their door with a warrant from the State of Georgia on bad check charges. A two-thousand-dollar check written to a Dalton, Georgia, supplier for Gentry's carpet business had bounced. Gentry tried to explain that his Pensacola attorney, Gerald McGill, was handling his bankruptcy proceedings, but the people in Dalton, a carpet town, were determined to get somebody. They got a governor's warrant issued for a fugitive from justice. Gentry was taken away in handcuffs in front of his seven-year-old stepson and held in Escambia County Jail without bond pending extradition to Georgia. His arraignment before the judge ran for five minutes on the local evening news. Pat, a former legal secretary, went down to court and managed to get her husband's bail set at three thousand dollars. They borrowed the three hundred dollars for the bondsman from relatives.

The constant negative publicity in the local media had made it impossible for the "notorious" John Gentry to get a job in the Pensacola area. When Pat tried to sign a check at the local grocery store, they asked if she were married to *the* John Gentry before refusing her credit. In increasingly dire financial straits, they applied for food stamps but were refused because Pat received fifty dollars a week in child support from her ex-husband. When Gentry applied to Florida's Victims Compensation Fund for help with unpaid medical bills, he was told that he did not qualify because he had been living with Judias at the time of the bombing and was therefore not considered a victim of a violent crime.

It was as if he had been tried and found guilty of being an accomplice to his own attempted murder. Even his own mother seemed to blame him. Just in the way she talked, he got that feeling.

But it was James Buenoano's bombing trial that had driven the final nails into the coffin of Gentry's murdered reputation.

Michael Patterson, Pensacola's new young assistant state attorney, had tried to combine the trials of Judias and James Buenoano for the attempted murder of Gentry by bombing. "In the interests of justice, it is essential that both defendants be tried together," Patterson had argued before Circuit Judge Joseph Q. Tarbuck. But Judge Tarbuck, wanting to ensure that Judias's prior murder conviction did not reflect on her son, had ordered separate trials.

In his opening statement before the six-member jury at James Buenoano's trial on the morning of August 5, 1984, defense attorney James Johnston, taking the offensive, alleged that "John Wesley Gentry is a drug dealer. Drugs, pot. A dope dealer."

"Gentry Is a Drug Dealer," proclaimed the evening headlines of the *Pensacola News Journal*, quoting Johnston.

Called as the prosecution's first witness, Gentry recounted for what seemed the hundredth time the events of the day of the bombing, explaining how he had left his car along with the keys to his trunk with James that afternoon so that the boy could mount some stereo speakers.

"I went to get in my car, turned the key in the ignition, turned the lights on, and the car exploded." He shrugged. "Basically, it jumbled up my insides and turned them inside out."

He explained how Judi had insisted on purchasing a $500,000 life insurance policy with him, paying for the down payment and premiums. He described how four days before the bombing, Judi borrowed three hundred dollars from him to send her son, James, to Brewton, Alabama, to buy some drugs from "Uncle" John Daniel Rowell, who was known to have purchased dynamite a few days before. He said he believed James was responsible for planting the dynamite in his car, adding that, "If he didn't do it, I hope to God this jury lets him off."

On cross-examination, James Johnston attacked Gentry with religious fervor. Wasn't it true that a judgment of fraud had been won against him by his former business partner in Mobile, Jackie Morgan? Wasn't it true that he had made a lot of enemies in his past business dealings? Wasn't it true that the night of the bombing the police had found marijuana in his coat pocket? Wasn't it true he was a "drug king" of Pensacola?

"I would call any such testimony a lie," Gentry flatly denied, overwhelmed by the irony of his situation.

Judi had set him up perfectly. Having failed to poison him on schedule, she had arranged a car bombing that would automatically scream drugs or Mafia to the provincial citizens of Pensacola. Then, for good measure, she had planted the evidence of drugs in his own pocket. No wonder she had called out Jackie Morgan's name at the scene of the bombing. Johnston had been his defending attorney on the Mobile lawsuit, recommended by Judi.

Gentry smiled ruefully to himself. If he were a drug king he'd be sipping piña coladas in Jamaica instead of sitting there defending himself from his own former attorney. The court system was set up to protect the accused, and rightfully so. But who in hell protected the rights of the victim?

Classically tall, dark, and handsome, prosecutor Michael Patterson, looking out of place in his double-breasted pin-striped suit against the drab courthouse setting, did his best to implicate James Buenoano in the bombing through circumstantial evidence and expert testimony. Lloyd Erwin, a forensic chemist with the Federal Bureau of Alcohol, Tobacco and Firearms, testified concerning the unusual strands of wire found in James's bedroom closet that matched identically the wire used in the bombing device that exploded Gentry's car.

On cross-examination, Erwin stopped short of saying the matching wires were cut from the same roll. "Nowhere is there a test in the whole world that will tell you if these wires were ever joined," the forensic expert admitted. Johnston succeeded in making the point that the wire was found in a paper bag along with tools and items belonging to other members of the household.

Telephone calls made from the Buenoano home to the Brewton, Alabama, residence of John Daniel Rowell one week before the bombing were submitted as state's evidence. Johnston established in cross-examination that it could have been Gentry himself who placed those calls.

Hilda Jordan, a latent print examiner with the Pensacola Police Department, testified that a palm print belonging to James Buenoano was found just below the trunk on Gentry's exploded car. No prints were found belonging to John Gentry, Judias Buenoano, or John Rowell.

Dale Otterbacher, an explosives and arson investigator with the Florida Fire Marshall's office, demonstrated how easily the car bomb could have been made. "You can go to the library and get a book that tells you exactly how to do it in a safe manner," Otterbacher said.

Subpoenaed once again by the district attorney's office, Kimberly's former boyfriend, David Lackey, reluctantly testified that James had told him once that if he got mad at somebody, he would shoot him, burn down his house, or blow up his car. And Rayford "Ray" Odom repeated his polygraphed testimony that he had purchased fifty sticks of Hercules dynamite and six electrical blasting caps of the same type used in the detonating device placed in Gentry's car for John Daniel Rowell in Frisco City, Alabama, on June 17, 1983, one week before the bombing.

Subpoenaed as an impeachable court witness, the portly heavily bearded John Daniel Rowell lumbered painfully to the witness stand. His six-foot-four frame towering above the bench, Rowell asked to remain standing due to recent back surgery.

"Do you know the defendant in this case, James Buenoano?" Patterson began his examination.

"I refuse to answer, Fifth Amendment. Might incriminate me," Rowell mumbled sullenly.

Patterson and Johnston did simultaneous double takes. Neither was prepared for Rowell's taking the Fifth. Patterson had hoped to prove Rowell had purchased the dynamite and given it to James. Johnston had planned to suggest that, due to failed drug dealings with Gentry, Rowell had planted the bomb himself.

Amid a hubbub of kibitzing lawyers and buzzing press, the jury was ushered out of the courtroom. A thirty-minute recess was called as the judge and lawyers pondered the situation. Judge Tarbuck could give Rowell use immunity, preventing his testimony from being used against him in any other case, but that would not prevent federal authorities from charging Rowell on other evidence. The chief assistant public defender was brought in to advise Rowell. An assistant U.S. attorney was called to advise Judge Tarbuck on pending federal charges against Rowell. Tarbuck wanted to make sure federal authorities would not charge Rowell before compelling him to testify. Finally, the jury was recalled and the witness resumed the stand.

Admitting to having purchased the dynamite, the laconic Rowell stuck stubbornly by the story he had given when originally questioned by the police in Brewton, Alabama.

"For what purpose did you purchase the dynamite?" Patterson crossed.

"I was going to blow beaver dams up," Rowell answered shortly.

"What happened to the fifty sticks of dynamite?" Patterson pressed.

"They got stolen out of my truck," Rowell drawled back.

"Why didn't you report the theft to the Brewton police?" asked Patterson.

"I've reported several things to the police in the past, and they never did find out who did it. You just keep quiet in that small town and see who has it, then I was going to go see them," Rowell said ominously.

"Those people up in Brewton know you really well— the chief of police, the deputies. If they say you have a reputation as a known drug dealer, they are mistaken, aren't they?" Johnston asked facetiously.

"Yes, sir, they sure are," Rowell replied dryly.

As his final witness for the state, Patterson called Jason Robert Middlebrooks, James Buenoano's former jailmate, to the stand. Middlebrooks testified that James said he planted the dynamite in Gentry's car in the restaurant parking lot the night of the bombing. James told him that he got the dynamite from "Uncle John" and that he made the bomb because Gentry had not paid back a loan from his mother, so they were going to collect seventy-five thousand dollars in insurance on his life. "He just said he wished he had killed him the first time when he had a chance," said Middlebrooks.

Johnston hotly accused Middlebrooks, charged with the stabbing death of his cousin, of fabricating the story to get his own first-degree murder charge reduced to manslaughter. Middlebrooks flatly denied it.

The state having rested its case, Johnston made his routine motion for a directed verdict of acquittal, charging that the state had failed to exclude every reasonable hypothesis of innocence.

"I would give your motion serious consideration had it not been for the testimony of Mr. Middlebrooks," Judge Tarbuck replied, denying the motion.

In his presentation for the defense, Johnston brought forth several of James's teenage friends, who gave him an alibi for the day of the bombing, swearing that James had spent the entire day and evening watching television and frolicking on a houseboat on Pensacola Beach. But during cross-examination, the young witnesses gave conflicting testimony as to details, hedged on their original strong statements, and ended up saying they weren't sure about much.

Johnston presented a forensic scientist from Tallahassee, Florida, who stated that had he been in charge of the bombing investigation, he would have examined the wire used in the bombing for fingerprints. On cross-examination, the scientist admitted that in twenty years of analysis he had never found a fingerprint on a wire.

Johnston produced an individual who said that once he had purchased a small bag of marijuana from Gentry. Apparently Gentry had rented the man space in his store and later evicted him for nonpayment.

Then Johnston called Michael Barfield to the stand.

James Buenoano's twenty-two-year-old Escambia County Jail cellmate sat nervously in the witness seat. Johnston expected him to say that Detective Ted Chamberlain and Federal Agent Bob Cousson had coerced him into testifying that James had made a jailhouse confession to him, admitting that he planted the bomb in Gentry's car. But Johnston was visibly shocked when Barfield suddenly reversed his story, stating instead that Johnston had offered him free legal services in exchange for his testimony against the state.

"You are a liar!" Johnston accused his own witness, his face reddened with outrage.

"I was under a lot of intimidation and coercion from you and James Buenoano," Barfield replied shakily. "James told me if I testified for him, things would be all right, and that I would suffer the consequences if I didn't."

"Mr. Barfield, don't you have any respect for the truth?" Johnston demanded in exasperation.

"I'm telling the truth," Barfield replied evenly.

"God save your soul!" Johnston ejaculated.

Cross-examined by Patterson, Barfield said that James had confessed to fashioning the bomb and placing it in Gentry's car. James and another inmate had beaten him, Barfield said, sending him to the jail infirmary, when they found out he was on the prosecutor's witness list.

With the confused jury again ushered out of the courtroom, Johnston moved emotionally for a directed verdict of acquittal, saying that he could not effectively represent his client because now he as well would be on trial in the eyes of the jury.

"My character, my integrity, has been directly put at issue," Johnston railed, demanding Judge Tarbuck order polygraph tests for himself and his co-counsel wife, Rebecca, who sat at the defense table with her hands covering her face, weeping quietly.

"I want to cry," Johnston choked, "but I'm so mad I can't."

Patterson calmly informed the court that he had warned defense counsel several days earlier that Barfield was saying Johnston had offered him a bribe.

"I didn't want that issue to muddy up this trial," Patterson said, explaining why he had not called Barfield as a witness for the state. "The defense called him; let the defense be saddled with him." Agreeing with the prosecutor, Judge Tarbuck denied Johnston's motion for a directed verdict of acquittal. James Buenoano, who had sat expressionless throughout Barfield's testimony, buried his head in his hands.

"Your Honor, I need a little break here," Johnston sighed, the color draining from his florid face. "I'm just kind of sick."

The following morning, Johnston called his final two witnesses to the stand.

Kimberly Buenoano, her blue eyes flashing with anger, ardently defended her accused brother. James had been watching movies the day of the bombing; he had not had any dynamite, nor had he fashioned any bomb, Kimberly insisted scornfully. The items found in the bag along with the suspicious wire in James's closet belonged to Gentry, not James, she said. The house had undergone remodeling and the closet held things that belonged to all members of the family, Kimberly testified, her tremulous voice tinged with righteous indignation.

Next James Buenoano smoothly mounted the stand and politely denied all the charges against him. His light brown curls cropped close around his smooth young face, James spoke softly, his brow creased in consternation. Occasionally he wiped his tear-filled eyes and sniffled. He didn't even know his mother had a $500,000 life insurance policy on John Gentry, he said in wide-eyed wonderment.

Under cross-examination, James quietly denied he had told friends that Gentry was going to die and that he was going to come into a lot of money. Yes, he did own a .45 caliber submachine gun. But it did not have automatic fire, he added.

"James, you are afraid to handle dynamite, but not a submachine gun, uh?" Patterson crossed sarcastically.

"Yes, sir," James replied with ingenuous charm.

Flanking their glum young client at the defense table the Friday evening of August 10, 1984, James and Rebecca Johnston sat in grim repose, awaiting the imminent return of the jury—three men and three women—after just two and a half hours of deliberation. Experience told them that a jury who had their minds made up usually brought back a verdict of guilty.

No one was more surprised than the defendant himself when the clerk of court pronounced the verdict, "not guilty." Recoiling as if he had been slapped in the face, James collapsed into the surprised embrace of his counsel. Kimberly, seated in the front row of the gallery with a cheering squad of their teenaged friends, jumped up and down with squeals of joy.

Mobbed by his gang of rowdy young loyalists, James Buenoano disappeared into the deserted streets of downtown Pensacola, a crooked smile on his lips. There was no doubt in John Gentry's mind that James would do his best to get even with those who had testified against him.

Gentry got up from the unyielding courthouse bench, stretching his long, cramped legs, and lit a cigarette. At least he'd lost the weight Doctor Lucy had recommended when he first checked himself into the hospital two Christmases ago, bent double with a daily dose of Judi's poisoned vitamins.

Yeah, Judi and James made a good team, all right.

With a sickening jolt, Gentry remembered when he first came to live in the house with blue shutters. Judi's double bed was grooved out on his side, where she said James had slept till he, Gentry, moved in and displaced him. She always left the door to the bathroom at the top of the stairs wide open when she took a bath. The sixteen-year-old kid sat there on the commode and watched her. By the time he was fourteen, Judi had corrupted James beyond her own ability to control him. He called her "whore" and other foul names to her face, and there was nothing she could do about it. Anything James wanted, no matter how expensive, he got. She gave him a submachine gun for his fourteenth birthday to add to his growing gun collection. He was, after all, more of a partner than a son.

Gentry remembered driving to the military cemetery out on the Pensacola naval base with Judi, James, and Kimberly to visit Michael's grave. James and Kimberly had walked over to the grave site, one of thousands among the endless, regimented rows of white crosses. Judi had remained in James's truck, parked two hundred yards away, never bothering to get out. She'd go to her grave denying it, but he'd bet she never felt any real grief for Michael. James, on the other hand, was probably sorry he helped her do it.

Gentry was certain that James and Kimberly knew their mother had killed their brother. He had been lying next to Judi on the couch the day Kimberly had angrily accused her mother, "What are you going to do, kill me like you did Michael?" He had waited with Pat in the hallway at the Milton courthouse all day, ready to testify in the drowning trial, but they never called him. They didn't want to hamper his credibility in the upcoming bombing trials. As it turned out, there wasn't much left of his credibility anyway.

But here he sat again, trying to be a decent citizen and testify against a woman who had killed without mercy those who cared for her most. He had never been a strong proponent of the death penalty before, but for what she had done to her own flesh and blood, Judi deserved it if anybody did. He and the others may have been fools. That poor kid, Michael, was totally defenseless. If the day ever came, Gentry told himself, he wanted to be one of the witnesses at her execution. He'd blow her a kiss good-bye.

Lighting another cigarette, Gentry paced restlessly in the stuffy green-walled witness room, not daring to meet the look of silent reproach in Pat's eyes. Ever since he was arrested on those bad check charges, Pat's seven-year-old son, Jeff, whom he had come to consider his own, would ask anxiously each time he left the house, "Is Daddy in jail?" The other kids were beginning to harass him at school—"Your daddy's a drug dealer!" He wasn't excited about the prospect of leaving his hometown, but this guilt by association thing was so powerful, it looked like they'd have to leave the Pensacola area if his newfound family was to survive.

Wherever he went, Gentry knew the haunting sense of betrayal would follow him, along with his permanently scarred credit rating.

The civil suit he'd filed against Judi back in March 1984, seeking damages for the pain and medical expenses he suffered when she twice attempted to murder him, had only served to heighten his notoriety. Denying all charges, Judi promptly countersued him for the more than fifteen thousand dollars she had lent his business to cover outstanding checks while he languished in the hospital with his bombing injuries. Even if he won the pending civil suit, there would be little left of Judi's financial assets for him to recover.

Soon after her conviction in the drowning trial, the court declared Judias partially indigent. Whatever resources she had would likely go to her defense on the upcoming Orlando trial, scheduled for January 1985. An Orlando grand jury had indicted her for the first-degree murder of her first husband, James Goodyear, in 1971, after the autopsy report on his exhumed body concluded that he had died of arsenic poisoning. An indictment against her in Colorado for the arsenic poisoning of her common-law husband, Bobby Joe Morris, was still pending, awaiting the outcome of the Orlando trial. After drawing additional headlines and raising more eyebrows, the autopsy results on the exhumed body of Gerald Dossett of Fort Walton Beach had tested negative for arsenic, clearing Judias of charges in his death.

Judi had probably tried paraformaldehyde on Dossett too, thinking that because formaldehyde was used in the embalming process, it would never be discovered. What she apparently didn't know was that, unlike arsenic, paraformaldehyde was not retained in the body tissues. Dossett's death certificate stated he died of cancer, but no sign of cancer was found in his autopsy either. Whatever killed poor Dossett, he had ended up in a cheap pine box. Judi had ended up with his classic model Thunderbird.

Gentry's stomach lurched as he recalled the agonizing sensation he had experienced with each paraformaldehyde-laced capsule Judi had given him—like his guts were turning inside out. It took an especially heartless cruelty to inflict that kind of torment on someone who loved you and watch him slowly die. Treachery was such a cowardly act. What easier prey than the one who trusted you the most and suspected you the least? He didn't think Judi had ever hated him. Emotion didn't factor into the matter: she just wanted the money. Greed was the only thing Judi understood. In a way, she was almost screaming for someone to catch her. Had he not survived, she might have gotten away with it all, Gentry told himself. Maybe it was worth the price he had to pay to stop her. Just to think she might have met up with someone else's son . . . It was the only way he could look at it and keep his sanity. He just thanked God he had saved those two capsules.

By the Monday afternoon of October 15, 1984, a jury of five women and three men, including two alternates, had been chosen from the Pensacola area to hear Judias Buenoano's trial for the attempted murder of her fiancé by car bombing. Of eighty jury prospects, only four had not recognized the Buenoano name; only a third said they could truly consider her innocent until proven guilty. Escambia County Circuit Judge Joseph Tarbuck had denied defense attorney James Johnston's motions to move the trial from Pensacola and to sequester the jury.

Again representing the state, prosecutor Michael Patterson planned to present much of the same evidence brought out in James Buenoano's earlier bombing trial, with the additional proof of Judias's attempt to poison Gentry six months before the bombing. Patterson's opening statement, however, was cut short when Judge Tarbuck, responding to Johnston's strenuous objections, excluded any mention of the attempted poisoning of Gentry until he could rule on the admission of the poison capsules as similar-fact evidence.

Johnston's opening remarks again focused on Gentry's failed business transactions and alleged drug dealings. He accused Gentry of bilking a Mobile woman out of her life's savings and of having run-ins with his former employees. Judias had been visibly upset at the bombing, passing out "cold as a cucumber," said Johnston, and she had mortgaged her home to help Gentry cover outstanding checks just after the explosion. While not disputing the state's evidence of the dynamite purchase by John Rowell and the matching wire found in James Buenoano's bedroom, Johnston contended there was no proof directly linking his client to either the dynamite or the wire, nor any testimony that she had asked anyone to plant the bomb for her.

Judge Tarbuck's exclusionary ruling had left Patterson's first witness, Detective Rick Steele, limited to testifying only that he had retrieved two orange-and-white capsules from John Gentry's unlocked briefcase after interviewing the victim in the hospital, and that a background check on Judias had led to a search of her home and business and her arrest. He was not permitted to elaborate charges.

The following morning, Judge Tarbuck, agreeing with the prosecution that the poison attempt did show a pattern or motive, allowed Patterson to include testimony and evidence relating to the poisoned capsules Judias had given Gentry. Roger Martz, a forensic chemist with the FBI lab in Washington, D.C., testified for the state that the Vicon-C vitamin capsules retrieved from Gentry's briefcase contained paraformaldehyde, a toxic substance commonly used in fungicides and disinfectants. Enough of the substance could kill a person, said Martz.

Dr. James Potter, a pathologist, testified that ingestion of paraformaldehyde could cause severe stomach disorders and the other symptoms Gentry had suffered while taking the capsules. But one would have to consume about one hundred capsules for a fatal dose, Dr. Potter said. The two to four capsules a day Gentry had taken could only have killed him by causing a bleeding ulcer.

Billy Don Johnson, a local wholesale beauty supplier, testified that tablets containing paraformaldehyde were commonly used to make cleaning solutions for beauty shop utensils. He did not know if Judias had purchased paraformaldehyde from him for her Fingers N Faces salon. There were about ten wholesale suppliers and fourteen thousand beauticians in the Escambia County area, he added.

Vicki Buggs, formerly a manicurist at Judias's Fingers N Faces salon, testified that while Gentry was in the hospital in December 1982, Judias had told her "John was very ill and had cancer. She said it was very bad and she didn't expect him to live." Judias had also told her that she was pregnant in June 1983, some months after she had said she had her fallopian tubes tied.

Susan Williams, Judias's former employee and cruisemate, testified that in April 1983 Judias had brought in cruise books for a world cruise she was planning that cost twenty thousand dollars per person. Judias was planning on taking her two children but not Gentry, Susan added. The night of the bombing, Susan witnessed Judias's fainting spell at the restaurant. "She just jumped up and grabbed her heart and her eyes rolled back in her head," Susan described. But since then, Susan said she had seen Judias, who had claimed to be a "scientific pathologist," fake emotions, and she now believed the fainting spell was a put-on.

Barbara Corwin of John Broxson and Associates testified that she had sold Judias and Gentry $500,000 in straight term life insurance policies, paid for by Judias. The policies weren't worth a penny unless one of the insured parties died, said Corwin.

"The state calls John Wesley Gentry," announced Patterson.

Exchanging a last weak smile with Pat, Gentry took a final drag on his cigarette and followed the bailiff into the waiting courtroom.

"Do you know the defendant in this case, Judias W. Buenoano?" Patterson directed.

"Yes, I do," Gentry nodded.

"Is that person present in this courtroom today?"

"She's seated at the table in front of me, beside the lady in the pink dress," Gentry described, pointing an accusing finger at his would-be murderess.

After describing in detail the day of the bombing, Gentry calmly told the jury about the poisoned capsules Judias had given him six months earlier.

"Each night after we finally retired to the bedroom, Judi would reach over to the nightstand on her side and give me the Vicon-C vitamins. I started getting extremely ill and nauseous and couldn't hold anything on my stomach. When I refused to take the capsules, Judi said something to the effect, 'If these aren't doing you any good, maybe you should double the dosage.'"

Asked by Johnston on cross-examination if he believed Judi could conspire to kill him, Gentry replied yes without hesitation.

"Why do you say that?" crossed Johnston.

"Greed would be the only reason. Judi tried to kill me for the half million dollars in insurance. I didn't think that way up until the day it happened," Gentry drawled, his eyes straying toward Judias as she stared serenely ahead.

"What caused you to change your mind about her?" Johnston wanted to know.

"Six months in the hospital," Gentry answered dryly.

Shortly before noon on Wednesday, October 17, Patterson rested his case.

Before presenting his case for the defense, Johnston argued at great length that Judge Tarbuck should accept his motion for a directed verdict of acquittal. Citing Florida law prerequisites in circumstantial evidence cases that required the state to exclude every reasonable hypothesis of innocence, Johnston charged, "Isn't there another hypothesis which may be true? This is really, Your Honor, a trial of speculation and assumption. . . . There is no evidence this lady is guilty of chicken thievery, much less attempted murder!" By allowing testimony of the attempted poisoning of Gentry into the trial, the judge had committed reversible error that would cause the trial to be thrown out on appeal, Johnston told the balding, bespectacled Tarbuck.

"We haven't had a bombing case here, Judge—we've had a poisoning case. . . . If this lady is guilty of this crime, there is a higher being she will have to answer to," Johnston preached.

Rebutting Johnston's motion for a directed verdict, Patterson quietly cited the most recent Supreme Court decision that the question of whether evidence fails to exclude all reasonable hypotheses of innocence is one for the jury to decide.

Saying that he would rule on the motion before the case was given to the jury, Tarbuck ordered Johnston to present his case for the defense.

Johnston called his three witnesses.

Syd Schafer, a former employee at Judias's salon, said she had never seen paraformaldehyde there.

Detective Rick Steele reiterated his testimony concerning the search warrants issued for Judias's home and business.

"The defense calls Detective Ted Chamberlain." Johnston announced his final witness.

Mounting the stand with customary verve, Chamberlain looked directly at Judias.

"State your full name, sir," Johnston began bluntly.

"Theodore Chamberlain."

"Where are you employed, sir?"

"Pensacola Police Department."

"How long have you been one of Pensacola's finest?"

"Six years."

"Were you assisting Mr. Steele in the investigation of the car bombing of John Wesley Gentry on June twenty-fifth, 1983?"

"Yes, sir."

"Did you subsequently obtain a search warrant for the residence of the defendant in Gulf Breeze, Florida?"

"Yes, sir."

"When did you go on the search?"

"I believe it was on the twenty-seventh of July."

"Did you call her up and tell her you were coming?"

"No, sir, I didn't."

"The truth of the matter is, Mr. Chamberlain, the element of surprise is one of the key factors in serving a search warrant?"

"It helps, sir."

"When you reached the residence of the defendant, did you find any paraformaldehyde?"

"No, sir, we didn't."

"Did you find any dynamite?"

"No, sir, we didn't."

"Your Honor, the defense rests," Johnston concluded abruptly.

Dismissing the jury to await further instructions, Judge Tarbuck leaned forward, peering intently at Judias, who sat with jaw clenched.

"Mrs. Buenoano, would you state your full name, please?"

"My name is Judias Buenoano," she answered darkly, remaining firmly rooted in her seat.

"You are represented in this case by James Johnston, is that correct?"

"That is correct," Judias nodded curtly.

"At the conclusion of the state's case, Mr. Johnston took a thirty-minute recess in order to decide how he was going to proceed with the defense. During the course of that recess, he decided with you, evidently, that you should not take the witness stand. Is that correct?" Tarbuck asked pointedly, leaning further over the bench.

"Excuse me, just a minute," Johnston interposed. "I appreciate what the court is doing, but this invades the attorney-client privilege."

"I'm not going to ask about the substance of the conversation that you may have had," Tarbuck addressed Johnston testily. "All I want to know at this point is whether she knowingly declined to take the witness stand. I want to hear it from the defendant."

Johnston protested. "I can represent to the court that I did discuss this matter with my client, and that it is my judgment that my decision not to put the defendant on the stand is in her best interest."

"Did you discuss with her what right she is giving up by declining to take the witness stand, what the consequences of her failing to testify could be?" Tarbuck persisted.

"No, I did not, because I know of nothing under the law that she's giving up by not taking the witness stand," Johnston stated defensively.

"I'm going to ask your client a question. You may object if you want to," Tarbuck rejoined, turning his gaze deliberately on Judias. "Mrs. Buenoano, have you heard and understood everything that's been said so far?"

"Yes, sir," Judias affirmed.

"Are you satisfied with the advice counsel has given you during the course of this trial?" Tarbuck wanted to know.

"Your Honor, I will object to the court asking her that. If she wants to voluntarily answer, that is certainly her right," Johnston spluttered.

Casting a sidelong glance at Johnston, Judias sat and said nothing.

"All right. We'll be in recess until nine in the morning," Tarbuck concluded with a short bang of his gavel.

"This is a cunning, cold, calculated attempt to collect an easy half million dollars," Patterson told the jury in his closing argument early the next morning. "Use your common sense; have the courage to trust your common sense that this defendant attempted to kill John Gentry."

"Follow the law," Johnston exhorted in his final statement. "Say to the king and his men, 'We want proof.' The benefit of the doubt should go to the defendant and you should find her not guilty."

At 11:40 A.M. on Thursday, October 18, the jury retired to deliberate its verdict. They returned at 1:35 P.M.

Seated cross-armed between her counsel and co-counsel, Judias tapped her foot lightly on the floor as she waited, scarcely breathing, for the verdict to be read.

"The defendant will hearken to the verdict," the security officer pronounced. "We, the jury, find the defendant, Judias Buenoano, guilty of attempted first-degree murder."

With a short intake of breath, Judias increased her foot-tapping, but otherwise remained cool. She managed a wan smile for the crowd of reporters who immediately converged upon her.

"I just don't really feel in this area I have gotten a fair trial in this case or the last case," Judias complained to the press. "The last trial should have been moved to anywhere but Milton. I'm certain I won't receive a fair trial in Orlando either," she predicted. "I don't think I will ever get a fair trial because of the publicity," pouted Judias with a tilt of her stylishly bobbed head.

"My client was convicted on a big guess. We'll appeal this verdict in a New York second," quipped Johnston, whose prompt appeal of Judias's first conviction was still pending.

"The conviction is a result of the tenacious efforts of the Pensacola Police Department and the Federal Bureau of Alcohol, Tobacco and Firearms, and it was through their efforts we were able to obtain justice," the pleased young prosecutor told the press.

Judge Tarbuck, who had not yet ruled on the defense motion for a directed verdict of acquittal, set sentencing for November 6.

"I thought about this case long and hard," Judge Tarbuck began reluctantly, peering down from his elevated position on the altar of justice. "I must admit, I seriously toyed with the defendant's motion for a directed verdict of acquittal."

From behind his wire-rimmed glasses, Tarbuck's pale eyes searched Judias's wan, impassive face as she stood before him by her lawyer's side. Only the night before, after concluding that there was enough circumstantial evidence for a jury to have found her guilty of the attempted murder of John Gentry, had he decided to deny Johnston's motion to acquit his client, Tarbuck confessed, his bland features compressed into painful resolve.

"Your Honor, the state has shown in a previous conviction that the defendant poisoned her own son—" Patterson began arguing for a thirty-year sentence.

"That's a lie!" Judias blurted out, suddenly breaking her stony silence.

"And then she placed the paralyzed boy, weighted with braces, in a lawn chair in a canoe, and drowned him," Patterson quietly continued.

"That's two lies!" Judias loudly protested, visibly agitated by the prosecutor's remarks.

"In my judgment, I don't see how in the world the First District Court of Appeals is going to affirm that conviction," Johnston asserted with false bravado.

With obvious hesitation, Judge Tarbuck sentenced the defendant to an additional twelve years in prison, to be served consecutively with her previous sentence.

Judias's face paled.

As she was led away once again in handcuffs and prison garb, Judias's stormy eyes met the steady gaze of Ted

Chamberlain, leaning casually against the back wall of the deserted courtroom.

"Ta ta!" Chamberlain waved good-bye, flashing her a boyish grin.

Unable to contain her long-suppressed rage, Judias lurched violently in Chamberlain's direction, straining against the firm grip of her two armed escorts.

"I'll see you in hell!" she screamed after the grinning detective as she disappeared, still struggling, through the swinging courtroom doors.

21

Acute Arsenic Intoxication

"GOOD MORNING. IN JUNE OF 1971 Sergeant James Edgar Goodyear returned home to Orlando, Florida, after a tour of duty in South Vietnam. He returned home to his wife, the defendant, Judi Goodyear. . . ."

On October 22, 1985, Assistant State Attorney Belvin Perry, diminutive, dapper, and black, delivered his opening statement to the twelve jurors seated stiffly before him in the cavernous ninth Judicial Circuit Court for Orlando, Orange County Florida. After months of postponements and a series of arguments for dismissal and motions in *limine* by defense counsels James and Rebecca Johnston, the trial of Judias Buenoano, aka Judi Goodyear, for the 1971 first-degree murder of her husband, James Goodyear, had begun.

Speaking with the short, quick jabs of a bantamweight boxer, the unsmiling Perry continued. "Sergeant Goodyear was a mechanic Supervisor in the air force and was reassigned to the McCoy Air Force Base here in Orlando at that time. On the twenty-fifth day of August 1971, Sergeant Goodyear felt some discomfort in his stomach. He went to the dispensary at McCoy Air Force Base. From the twenty-fifth of August to the thirteenth of September 1971, he continued to have the stress in his stomach. He was nauseated, vomited a lot, and had some periods of hallucination. On the thirteenth day of September, Sergeant Goodyear was admitted to the Naval Hospital at the naval base here in Orlando and was treated until his death on September sixteenth, 1971."

Perry pointed out that in March of 1984 the body of James Edgar Goodyear was exhumed, and an autopsy showed that he had died in 1971 as a result of arsenic poisoning. "The evidence," he went on, "will show that prior to James Edgar Goodyear's going to South Vietnam, he and his wife were experiencing marital difficulties. The evidence will show that while he was away in South Vietnam, his wife carried on an affair with another gentleman. The evidence will show that after Mr. Goodyear died, Judi Goodyear came into approximately twenty-eight thousand dollars in life insurance benefits and Veterans Administration benefits totaling in excess of sixty-two thousand dollars. . . . The evidence will show that Mr. Goodyear died as a result of arsenic poisoning at the hands of his wife, Judi Goodyear, and this evidence will convince you beyond and to the exclusion of every reasonable doubt. Thank you."

Content with Judge Thompson's prior ruling excluding any similar-fact evidence unless and until the state had proven corpus delicti—that James Goodyear had died as a result of the criminal agency of another—James Johnston declined to make an opening statement for the defense until the close of the state's case. Johnston and Perry both knew that if the state failed to produce a corpus delicti independent of the similar-fact evidence of poisoning of Bobby Joe Morris and the attempted poisoning of John Gentry, the court would rule a directed verdict of acquittal. Johnston also knew that a directed verdict was probably his only chance of saving his client from a guilty verdict and a possible death sentence.

Perry called his first witness, Investigator B. B. "Dusty" Rhodes of the state attorney's office in Orlando. Responding in kind to Perry's no-nonsense questioning, the leathery veteran investigator described his involvement in the James E. Goodyear case in clipped, official tones.

He began his investigation into the death of James Edgar Goodyear on November 22, 1983, in response to a telephone call from authorities in Pensacola. Obtaining certified copies of Goodyear's death certificate and the health records compiled during his hospitalization, Rhodes consulted with the chief medical examiner and other witnesses and obtained a court order for the exhumation and autopsy of James Goodyear's body. On March 14, 1984, the body was exhumed from the grave site in the veterans' portion of Chapel Hill Cemetery in Orlando, Florida. Along with the medical examiner and representatives from the Florida Law Enforcement crime lab, Rhodes located the plot, dug up the vault, took soil samples from the head, center, and foot of the vault, removed the casket, sealed and marked the closed casket with evidence tape, and escorted it to the morgue. The following day, March 15, 1984, the seals were broken, the body was removed from the casket, and the autopsy was performed. Rhodes had observed a well-preserved thirty-seven-year-old white male in a United States Air Force sergeant's uniform decorated with various ribbons. On the left hand, which still held a withered rose, was a gold wedding band inscribed with the initials JEG.

Johnston declined to cross-examine the witness. In the interest of sparing the jury and court the ordeal of viewing the state's graphic slides taken of the corpse during the various stages of the autopsy, Johnston agreed to stipulate to the identity of the individual in the casket as being James Edgar Goodyear.

Perry called his next witness, Dr. R. C. Auchenbach. Accepted by the defense as an expert witness in the field of internal medicine, Dr. Auchenbach, a faculty physician with the Pittsburgh University School of Medicine, had been the attending physician for James E. Goodyear upon his admission to the Orlando Naval Hospital on September 13, 1971.

Referring to his medical records, Dr. Auchenbach testified with professional alacrity as to the medical condition of James Goodyear upon his presentation to the active duty ward. Sergeant Goodyear had been seen at the McCoy dispensary two weeks prior to his admission to the Naval Hospital, complaining of nausea, vomiting, and light-headedness. He had difficulty maintaining liquids and had a temperature of 100 to 101 degrees. He complained of some tingling in his arms and legs as well as numbness. He was treated for nausea without effect. Laboratory tests done at the McCoy dispensary revealed some abnormal liver injury or tissue damage.

When Sergeant Goodyear arrived at the Orlando Naval Hospital, he appeared chronically ill, although his previous health history had been essentially that of a normal, healthy thirty-seven-year-old male, Dr. Auchenbach testified. Upon examination, Goodyear's blood pressure and temperature were normal, but his heartbeat was rapid. He was in some distress and complained of abdominal pain. He had a dry tongue and dry skin, symptoms of dehydration. There was a faint rash on his trunk and he had recently lost weight. He had distal weakness in his legs and his gait was somewhat unsteady, but he could maintain equilibrium. His reflexes were normal. At the time of admission, Dr. Auchenbach could not render a diagnosis of Sergeant Goodyear's symptoms. His medical history and military duty revealed nothing that accounted for his illness. He had taken his antimalarial drugs while in Vietnam and had not been ill during his prior year's tour of duty. Since his return from Vietnam in June 1971, he had felt progressively more fatigued and weak.

Sergeant Goodyear was hospitalized on the fifteenth of September 1971. At 5:17 the following evening he died.

An autopsy performed the following day confirmed the immediate cause of death as pulmonary congestion, cardiovascular collapse, and renal failure. "But it didn't really give us a precise diagnosis," Dr. Auchenbach admitted. "It didn't answer the specific question as to why this previously healthy man became acutely ill and died within four days."

Perry asked Dr. Auchenbach if he had reviewed the 1984 toxicological report from the medical examiner's office in Miami, the autopsy report from the Armed Forces Institute of Pathology, and the autopsy report of the court medical examiner, Dr. Thomas Hegert, performed on the exhumed body of James Goodyear. He had.

"Now, Doctor, based upon those findings, and within the bounds of reasonable medical certainty, do you have an opinion now concerning the cause of Sergeant Goodyear's clinical presentation to you as your patient back in September 1971?" directed Perry.

"Yes. Mr. Goodyear's complaints and physical findings were probably related to acute arsenic intoxication," Auchenbach firmly replied. The circulatory collapse, renal damage, and hallucinations were all manifestations of acute arsenic poisoning. "I believe his progressive illness, culminating in pulmonary vascular collapse, was secondary to his arsenic intoxication that was documented by the toxicological studies," Auchenbach concluded.

"Dr. Auchenbach, how many cases of arsenic poisoning and deaths have you personally dealt with?" Johnston opened his cross-examination of the state's expert witness.

"None to my knowledge prior to this case," Auchenbach replied, stiffening slightly.

"Your opinion as to the cause of death is predicated on the information that you received from the toxicologist in Miami, the autopsy by Dr. Hegert, and the toxicology report from the Armed Forces Institute being accurate. If those reports are inaccurate, would your opinion be different?" Johnston challenged.

"If I knew the information to be inaccurate, certainly, it would influence my opinion," Auchenbach retorted huffishly.

"Can you tell the jury what the average lethal dose of arsenic would be, based upon your own medical experience?"

"Arsenic is in our environment. We excrete a certain amount of arsenic every day. The range of toxication may depend many times upon the remedy with which arsenic would be administered and how much is absorbed and excreted."

"Well, what tissue is the most significant in examining the average amount of arsenic poisoning?"

"If someone is chronically poisoned with arsenic, probably an examination of the hair and nails is one of the more reliable tools for measuring levels. Toxic concentrations greater than zero point one milligrams per hundred grams of hair are considered indicative of poisoning. That's twenty times the normal concentration."

"Referring specifically to Mr. Goodyear, what is the significance of the different levels of arsenic found in his hair?"

"In the toxicology report, the arsenic level at the hair root was ninety-five milligrams per kilogram. At the medial shaft of the hair it was thirty milligrams per kilogram. At the distal end it was one point zero. Because the hair grows—I think it's been estimated at half an inch to three-quarters of an inch per month—the higher exposure was the more recent exposure."

"How long was Mr. Goodyear's hair when the toxicologist took the sample?"

"Approximately two inches in length."

"So that would mean that he had been exposed to some type of arsenic four months earlier?"

"Possible, if his hair grew at the rate of half an inch per month, but we don't know that."

"Four months earlier he was in Vietnam; is that correct?"

"Yes."

"Now you indicated that Mr. Goodyear had an acute exposure to arsenic before he came to the hospital; is that correct?"

"I think his clinical course was entirely consistent with that, yes. Acute in the sense of getting a large amount in a relatively brief period of time to cause the toxic gastrointestinal symptoms as well as the circulatory collapse."

"Can you exclude the possibility that he got the acute dose of arsenic from the environment?"

"That's a loaded question. Are you talking about industrial exposure in the sense of pollutants in the atmosphere, or what are you talking about?"

"Can you exclude the fact that he could have gotten arsenic from the atmosphere?"

"Yes. If it was in the atmosphere in that concentration, we would have seen other individuals with the same type of poisoning."

"Doctor, can you state to the jury that there was no other such person in Orange County that turned himself into the hospital in 1971?"

"No, I can't say that, but there weren't any other cases that were admitted at the Naval Hospital at that point in time."

"Do you know that in 1971 they sprayed the citrus trees in Orange County with a substance that contained lead arsenate?"

"No, I didn't know that. I know that arsenate is used in insecticides, yes, but specifically did I know that. No, sir."

"Can you exclude the possibility that the air force used some type of insecticide or chemical that contained some type of arsenic where this man would be exposed to it in his day-to-day work as an air force mechanic?"

"I can't exclude that, but I think his presentation would have been entirely different if it were mere chronic poisoning. The acute manifestation of arsenic toxication is consistent with the gastrointestinal distress and cardiovascular collapse. The chronic manifestation usually involves the perirenal and nerve and central nervous systems."

"Would it be fair to say that some individuals can tolerate higher doses of arsenic than others?"

"That is probably true. If they are in the normal range of tissue concentrations."

"Is it also true, Doctor, that different arsenic compounds are more toxic than some other arsenic compounds?"

"That's probably true."

"Dr. Fox performed the autopsy of Mr. Goodyear's body in 1971. What did he do with the organs?"

"He took pieces of the tissue and examined them under a microscope. He examined part of the kidney, liver, lung, and brain. Samples of each organ were preserved in a paraffin block, and the organs were put back in the body cavity and the cadaver was sewn up and sent back to the undertaker."

"Now, Dr. Fox took the liver, kidney, brain, and lung and put them in a Ziploc bag all together and put them back in the body, is that correct?"

"That's correct."

"Doctor, does not the literature say that you cannot and should not ever mix an organ with another organ if you want to test for arsenic poison?"

"I don't know that to be a fact."

"My question is, wouldn't all the organs be contaminated? If one, for example, had arsenic, wouldn't it contaminate the others?"

"No, I don't really think it would. I'm not sure, but certainly his fingernails and hair were not contaminated."

"You are not sure if these samples would be contaminated?"

"Right."

"Dr. Auchenbach, you gave no indication or evidence that arsenic could have been involved when you treated Mr. Goodyear in the hospital?"

"No, we didn't, because we did not have any clinical suspicion of arsenic intoxication."

"Doctor, would it be a fair and accurate statement to say that you would simply be guessing as to how Mr. Goodyear got this arsenic, which you say the experts now discover?"

"Yeah, I think that would be true."

In his redirect of the witness, Perry introduced into evidence the Armed Forces Institute of Pathology toxicological report on the paraffin block tissue samples of Goodyear's organs performed in 1984, directing Dr. Auchenbach to read a portion of the report to the jury.

" 'A review of the symptoms,' " read Auchenbach, " 'the clinical record, and the autopsy report indicate that the symptoms and death are consistent with arsenic toxication. Symptoms caused by arsenic frequently mimic natural diseases and may easily be misdiagnosed unless suspected.

Postmortem toxicology was not performed in 1971. The acid-fast stain of the kidney revealed nuclear inclusions consistent with lead. The scanning electron microscopy revealed traces of both lead and arsenic. The amounts of these metals did not appear large. However, the examination was performed on glass slides prepared from paraffin tissue blocks. The tissue had been washed several times with various solutions as a part of the preparations of the blocks. . . . ' "

Upon recross, Johnston asked the witness to read the last paragraph of the toxicological report, which had previously been omitted.

" 'This death is suspicious for arsenic and lead intoxication. However, there is not sufficient information to determine the cause or manner of death from the materials examined,' " read Auchenbach.

"You say he died from arsenic poisoning and they say there is not sufficient information to determine the cause or manner of death?" Johnston asked archly.

"That's their opinion," shrugged Auchenbach. "I say his clinical presentation is entirely consistent with arsenic intoxication."

"In my opinion, this man died as a result of arsenic poisoning or excessive exposure to arsenic," echoed the state's second expert witness, Dr. Thomas Hegert. Designated an expert in forensic pathology by the court, Dr. Hegert had performed the autopsy and toxicological examination of the remains of James Goodyear's exhumed body in March 1984.

Hegert based his opinion on the concentration of arsenic in Goodyear's hair. "The length of the hair, and the fact that there was continuing arsenic, would suggest that he had some continuing exposure of either multiple small doses or occasional large doses that were not lethal that would replenish and keep the arsenic in the body so that it could be deposited in the hair follicles. . . . The most common way for that to occur is by ingestion," concluded the thirty-year veteran medical examiner.

"You can't tell the jury as a matter of fact that Mr. Goodyear received arsenic as a matter of homicide, suicide, or accident?" Johnston cross-examined.

"No, I cannot," Dr. Hegert answered in a low voice.

"Now, Doctor, as a medical examiner, wouldn't it be important to study Mr. Goodyear's environment?"

"Yes."

"Are you familiar with the fact that the air force used Agent Blue in Vietnam?"

"Yes. It was a compound of dimethylarsene acid used primarily as a herbicide."

"Would you say that Agent Blue would be a source of arsenic contamination to an air force mechanic if he were, for example, to clean the tanks from which this chemical was sprayed?"

"I would think that would be a possible source of contamination if he worked with that equipment."

"If he were exposed to Agent Blue, could that account for the arsenic found in the distal end of Sergeant Goodyear's hair?"

"Yes. Agent Blue is arsenic, so if you were exposed to it, it would deposit itself in the hair. I think that would be a possibility in the time frame we are talking about."

"He gets back home to Orlando, and from what you say, he gets another dose, and this additional dose could have tipped him over into the lethal range?" queried Johnston.

"Yes. I think the exposure had to be over a period of time. He could take smaller doses more frequently and gradually build up to a toxic level. Certainly it wasn't a single-dose exposure," insisted Hegert.

"Doctor Hegert," Perry re-directed, "did you specifically determine what type of work Sergeant Goodyear did as a mechanic in the Air Force?"

"Yes. My understanding was that he was a supervisor in the mechanic section—a managerial position."

Following the hair-splitting testimony of the state's expert witnesses, Perry called Constance Lang, Judias's self-proclaimed "best friend," to the stand. Identifying the defendant as "the brunette in the white blouse" seated at the table, the former Connie Gilmore, now residing in Dover, Delaware, proceeded to testify that she had first met Judy Goodyear, a neighbor, in Orlando, Florida, in 1969 through her former husband, George Gilmore, who was very sociable. When her factory job got cut back, Lang said she jumped at the chance to work for Judi at her Conway Acres Child Care Center for fifty-five dollars a week. Over the next year, Judi and Connie became "as close as sisters." They often discussed their common marriage problems. Judi was unhappy in her marriage to James Goodyear. They had grown apart. They didn't have the same interests anymore.

"Prior to James Goodyear going to Vietnam in 1970, did the two of you have any discussions about poisoning?" Perry went straight to the point.

"Yes," replied the thin-lipped Lang. "We would joke about it. Something to the effect, we can solve our problems by lacing their food with arsenic, or we could poison them and that would solve it all."

"The defendant brought that up first?"

"Yes, sir. It was just a running joke that women have. A lot of women fantasize about things like that."

"After James Goodyear went to Vietnam, did she ever bring the subject up again about poisoning?"

"Yes. Several times. We were still joking about it."

"And during that time, did you continue to confide to Judy about your marital difficulties?"

"Judy helped me through a very difficult period. She gave me the courage to leave my husband."

"Did she ever talk to you about separating or getting a divorce from her husband?"

"No."

Perry proceeded to ask Lang about Judi's relationship with a man named Bob Crawford, who lived in Pensacola. Crawford and Judi had a business relationship, according to Lang. About twice a month they would go together on business trips while James Goodyear was away in Vietnam. Sometimes Judi packed a nurse's uniform for the weekend, saying she was going as a nurse. Once or twice Lang accompanied Judi and Crawford on their trips. They would stay in motels. Crawford had one room and Judi and Lang shared another. Lang fell asleep watching the late show on TV before Judi would return from her nightly business meetings with Crawford. At times, Lang said, Crawford would spend the night at Judi's home, sleeping on the couch in the den.

"Would you tell me to the best of your recollection some of the things the defendant said to you after Sergeant Goodyear returned from Vietnam concerning her unhappiness with her marriage?" Perry interjected.

"Words to the effect that they don't have the same interests anymore; things are different now; 'I'm tired of this,' " Lang remembered.

"Did she ever mention to you how she proposed to solve her problems with her marriage?"

"Only in that context of the joke about the arsenic or poisoning. One way out would to put it in macaroni and cheese or tomato juice."

"And how many occasions did she say that or words to that effect after Sergeant Goodyear's return from Vietnam?"

"I don't know, maybe five."

"Did there come a time that you learned Sergeant Goodyear was ill and subsequently died?"

"Yes."

"How many days before he died did you learn that he was ill?"

"A week or two before Judi had mentioned that he was sick. And then he got sicker, and he went into the hospital and died."

"Did she tell you what was wrong with him?"

"She said he died of the Black Death. Right before he and some other men came back from Vietnam they were inoculated against the plague, and some terrible error had been made and the people who were inoculated actually contracted the disease and had died from it," Lang attested straight-faced.

"After Sergeant Goodyear's death, did you move in and live with Mrs. Goodyear?" Perry asked the increasingly flustered witness.

"At the grave site, Judi had a grand mal seizure," Lang explained earnestly. "As far as we knew she had never had them before, but she was very, very upset with Jim dying. And after we had talked, she was afraid that it would happen again, and she needed someone to be there with her to take care of her and the children, and I moved in with her and helped her with the children, and when she did have the seizures, I helped her to keep her from swallowing her tongue, and in exchange she paid me weekly," rattled the gullible Lang.

Not very long after her husband's death, Judi traded in her old station wagon for a new two-seater MG sports car, Lang continued her direct testimony. The MG wasn't very practical for Judy's two preschool children plus Michael, so in a short while she traded the MG for a brand-new pink Cadillac. She bought Lang a new MG Midget too. Then Judi and the kids and Lang drove out west in the pink Cadillac to visit Judi's family.

After Sergeant Goodyear's death, Judi continued to see Bob Crawford. Judi and Crawford introduced Lang to Bobby Joe Morris, who lived in Pensacola. Lang liked Bobby Morris—he didn't like to be called Bobby Joe. He was nice and he was fun. At one point, Judi expressed an interest in Bobby Joe. She told Lang she was falling in love with him and wanted to marry him. Before Christmas of 1971, Lang moved with Judi and her kids from Orlando to Pensacola. Lang, who had been dating Bobby Joe, soon saw that he preferred Judi over her. In January 1972, Lang moved away from Judi and went about her own affairs.

"As I understand what you are saying, Miss Lang," Johnston opened his cross-examination, "Judi got your boyfriend?"

"Well, you can't marry everybody you date. Bobby drank too much for my liking anyway." Lang shrugged defensively.

"And were you upset by his preferring Judi to you?"

"Of course. Upset but not angry. I do have some pride."

"Now, you said that Judi brought up the subject of arsenic to you. I asked you in a deposition on June 18, 1985, Do you remember who might have mentioned it first, you or her? and in June you said you didn't have any idea, and today you say it was Judi."

"It was," Lang replied firmly. "I can remember the very instant when we first started joking about it. We were making macaroni and cheese for the kids. It must have been 1970, just before he went to Vietnam."

"This bothers me. You say this girl talked about giving poison to her spouse?" Johnston asked incredulously.

"Spouses. Mine too," Lang replied matter-of-factly. "I bet most women do, either that or a shot or something. You ever hear anybody joke about it if somebody breaks in your house? Shoot them and drag them in the house so you don't get in trouble?" posed the outspoken witness.

"I have heard a client say that, but I haven't heard my wife say that," retorted the abashed Johnston.

"People joke about things like that and nobody takes them seriously," shrugged Lang.

"That's the whole point, Miss Lang," Johnston rejoined with a note of irony.

"That's the point I'm trying to make too," replied the witness, obviously missing the point.

"That it was always a joke, you considered it a joke and Judi considered it a joke?" Johnston clarified.

"That's the point I'm trying to make," Lang repeated firmly.

For his next witness, Perry called another female companion from Judias's long-buried past. Debra J. Sims of Jacksonville, Alabama, haltingly related that she had been taken from her alcoholic mother and placed in Judi Goodyear's custody in Orlando under court order at the age of twelve, one month before James Goodyear left for Vietnam in June 1970. Judi had asked that Debra, who lived next door, come live with her and help take care of the house and her two children, James and Kimberly, while Judi worked at her child care center during the day. During Mr. Goodyear's absence, Debra did not remember Judi mentioning that she missed her husband.

Debra was still living in the Goodyear household when James Goodyear returned from his tour of duty in Vietnam one year later in June 1971. Debra remembered that James Goodyear had returned home in good health, but a couple of months later he became sickly. He was weak and acted like he might have the flu. There was a time that he began hallucinating, saying that he saw rabbits in his bed, and picking at the bed linens. He seemed not to be aware of her presence in the room.

One afternoon in September 1971, Judi and Debra walked into the front yard, discussing Mr. Goodyear's illness. Debra asked Judi why she didn't take her husband to the navy hospital in Orlando. Judi said that he had been given medicine by the doctors, who had told her that her husband had contracted hepatitis from shots he had received upon returning from Vietnam. Judi told Debra she would take Goodyear to the hospital if he didn't get any better.

A couple of days after that, Debra moved out of Judi's house. James Goodyear was still ill and confined to his bed when Debra left. A few days later, Debra returned to pick up her clothes. There were cars in front of the house. Mr. Goodyear's family was gathered in the den. Judi was in the living room with a gentleman that Debra did not know. It was then she learned that James Goodyear had died.

Asked by Perry who had prepared the meals at the Goodyear household, Debra Sims answered that Judi had. There was a den with a bar. The children usually ate dinner at the bar; Judi and James Goodyear would sit around as people do in a den. There was no set dinner hour at the dining table. Mr. Goodyear drank coffee like most people smoked cigarettes. Judi drank a lot of coffee too. Mr. Goodyear also liked chocolate milk. Debra couldn't remember Judi administering any special care to Goodyear during his illness. She couldn't remember if Judi had taken her husband to the hospital more than once.

"What was Judi's relationship with her husband?" Johnston cross-examined the noncommittal witness.

"I always thought Judi had a good relationship with her husband," Debra Sims responded with a small shrug.

"Did she ever appear to be unhappy with her marriage?"

"No. We never discussed her marriage."

"Did you see any men coming into her home?"

"No."

"She had a good Christian home, is that what you are saying?"

"I'm not going to say she had a good Christian home, because she never attended church and religion was never mentioned."

"But there wasn't any arguing; there weren't any men staying there?"

"No."

"And she was a working mother, taking care of her children, and you were assisting her?"

"Yes."

"Do you know if Mr. Goodyear drank?" Johnston asked his concluding question.

"No, he didn't," Judias's former live-in ward primly replied.

Perry called Robert Crawford, also known as Earl Howard Spence, to the stand. The burly scowling state's witness, who had previously refused to testify or appear in court out of his prison uniform, mounted the stand in an ill-fitting civilian suit with obvious reluctance. Brusquely stating that he was currently an inmate serving time on a felony conviction at the federal penitentiary in Danbury, Connecticut, Crawford told the unsmiling jury how he had come to know the defendant.

He had met Judi Goodyear in the early part of 1970 at a used car lot in Orlando. He and two other guys were wholesaling cars on Colonial Boulevard, and Judi answered an ad one of them had placed for a secretary. Judi got the job and worked several months for Crawford. Judi was a good worker. One time, the married Crawford took her out and bought her an evening gown, which made Judi very happy. He told her if she ever wanted to go out or needed anything to give him a call.

In 1970, about the same time that James Goodyear left for Vietnam, Crawford moved to Pensacola. Before long he got a call from Judi asking him to come down to Orlando. A few days later, Crawford met Judi at an Orlando bar. They spent the next few days together at Judi's house, sleeping in the front bedroom. Crawford made several trips to Orlando over the next few months, staying with Judi. On a few occasions they would take trips out of town together. Once they went to St. Petersburg. Crawford did not remember if Judi's friend, Connie Gilmore, had accompanied them or not. Crawford did not have any business relationship with Judi at that time.

In the summer of 1971, right after James Goodyear returned home from Vietnam, Crawford stopped seeing Judi. A couple of months later, Judi phoned Crawford and told him that her husband was very ill. She didn't think he would live, she said. Soon after, Judi called Crawford again and invited him to Orlando to attend her husband's funeral. Crawford didn't feel right about going to the funeral, but he did. During the funeral services, Judi had what looked like an epileptic fit. She told Crawford that her husband died because he had become addicted to narcotics in Vietnam and the doctors had given him a drug to counteract the narcotics.

Over the next couple of months, Judi and Crawford resumed their intimate relationship. Then Crawford introduced Judi to Bobby Joe Morris, a business acquaintance from Pensacola. Judi seemed to like Bobby Joe, and Bobby Joe seemed to like Judi. Subsequently, Judi moved to Pensacola and started living with Bobby Joe, and Crawford was just phased out of the picture. That's really all he knew about it, the recalcitrant witness drawled.

Before Perry could call his next witness for the state, Johnston reiterated his charge to Judge Thompson that, thus far, the state had failed to prove that there was a criminal act involving his client.

"What is the evidence that they have shown here?" Johnston demanded. "They have put on three expert witnesses. Two of the witnesses said that, in their opinion, Mr. Goodyear died of arsenic poisoning. I asked each of those witnesses could they say how the arsenic was administered. I can represent to the court that in each answer they could not, that there were only three possibilities—homicide, suicide, and accident. Are we to infer now because of a joke that it was a homicide? That's not the clear and convincing evidence required by the appellate courts of this state."

Maintaining that previous Supreme Court rulings had merely prescribed that for similar-fact evidence to be admissible, there must be proof of the connection between the defendant and the collateral occurrences, Perry summarized the evidence in the Bobby Joe Morris case before the court.

The evidence concerning Mr. Morris showed that he and the defendant were involved in a close personal relationship, and that the defendant, in fact, had represented herself in Trinidad, Colorado, as Mrs. Bobby Joe Morris, Perry brusquely related. They had purchased a home together in Trinidad. The defendant met with an insurance man when Morris was not present, and purchased a ten-thousand-dollar life insurance policy on Morris. That evening, with Morris at home, another insurance man came to the house and they purchased a thirty-thousand-dollar life insurance policy. Perry noted that when the first insurance man asked to speak with Morris, the defendant indicated that her husband was out of town and that she would handle all the necessary papers. The following morning, she went to the insurance office and picked up the application, saying that she would bring the application to Mr. Morris at work and have him verify and sign it. That afternoon she returned to the insurance office with the signed application.

The evidence will show, continued Perry, that on December 2, 1977, the defendant went to another insurance agency and repeated the procedure, returning an application for a third life insurance policy worth ten thousand dollars allegedly signed by Morris. By mid-December of 1977, Morris entered the hospital displaying the same symptoms that James Goodyear had exhibited just before his death. The doctors attributed Mr. Morris's sudden illness to his alleged alcohol problems, as reported by his wife.

Mr. Morris's health stabilized and he was released from the hospital into the care of his wife, said Perry. Three days later, he was back in the hospital displaying the same symptoms as before. The doctors could not attribute the cause of his illness to alcohol consumption this time, since he had spent the previous three weeks under hospital care. Within a few days, Bobby Joe Morris died of cardiovascular collapse, pulmonary congestion, and renal failure, the same causes of death listed for James Goodyear. The defendant collected over eighty thousand dollars in insurance benefits and promptly left town. Morris's body was later exhumed and autopsied, and it was determined that he had died as a result of arsenic poisoning.

"Three men in her life develop illness with the same symptoms; they die; she collects on life insurance; then toxic levels of arsenic are found in their bodies. These are the basic reasons for the relevancy and admissibility of the evidence," Perry concluded briskly.

"My question to Mr. Perry is this," rebutted Johnston. "How can he prove that a crime was committed in the first place, when we have basically the same set of facts in Morris that we have in Goodyear? We have a man who died in the hospital; we have a man whose body was exhumed, and they found a lethal dose of arsenic in his body. What witness has come forth in this trial and said that the defendant ever in her life possessed arsenic? There is none, and there will be none. I will tell the court this, that living with this lady and Bobby Joe Morris were two sons and a daughter. Now who are we going to say gave the man the lethal dose of arsenic? Was it the defendant? Was it her two sons? Was it the daughter?

"This is the very thing that the courts are talking about when they say . . . it's improper to make an inference and then tack it onto another inference. . . . If the court lets this evidence in, there is not a ghost of a chance of this lady getting a fair trial," Johnston blustered.

"All right," Judge Thompson interjected, clearing his throat. "I think Mr. Johnston is correct when he indicates that it's a defense-directed verdict of acquittal at this point, because if the Williams Rule [similar-fact] evidence is not admissible, then the state's case as to the death of Mr. Goodyear rises or falls on the evidence presented up to this point. . . .

"What we have, in essence, is a family with marital problems, a discussion of killing husbands by arsenic, a husband returning home healthy, taking ill, symptoms consistent with arsenic poisoning, exhumation of the body, arsenic from sources unknown found in the body was sufficient to cause death, did cause death, and that the arsenic did not come from atmospheric or environmental conditions. That is sufficient to establish corpus delicti of homicide.

"Because of the nature of poisoning," Judge Thompson continued, clearing his throat a second time, "it's very much like the crime of burglary. It's done surreptitiously. No one can actually testify in this case that they saw her put arsenic in the food, they saw him eat it, or they saw her put arsenic in the coffee, they saw him drink it. We do know that she said she should poison him by using arsenic, and we know that he died by arsenic ingested from some source. If someone says I'm going out to shoot him with a three-fifty-seven magnum and they are joking, and later someone turns up dead and it's the person that they indicated, and he had been shot with a three-fifty-seven magnum, that is sufficient in my opinion to establish a cause of death that is homicide." The judge paused and adjusted his spectacles.

"That brings us to the similar-fact evidence. If you have a burglar who has a particular mode of operation, that he always leaves a particular sign or symbol, or always enters during certain periods of the day, that is sufficient to establish a modus operandi. In this case, we have all those things present: same kind of death, same content of poisons, prior conversations as to the death, and prior purchase of insurance to the death, to indicate a similar-fact pattern. I don't know how much closer you can get in similar-fact evidence. It shows modus operandi, motive, lack of mistake, and a similar plan or scheme.

"The ruling will stand . . . to admit the presentation of similar-fact evidence. Bring in the jury," Judge Thompson ruled with an air of finality.

Mary Beverly Owens, a fragile dishwater blonde, approached the witness stand with the trembling fortitude of the condemned about to ascend to the guillotine. Mary Beverly tried hard to shut the persistent image of Judias's coldly furious face from her pale, watery eyes as she sat gingerly on the hard edge of the oversized witness chair.

"Do you know a person by the name of Judi Goodyear?" Perry asked his seventh witness for the prosecution.

"Yes, I do," answered Mary Beverly in a small, clear voice.

"Is the person that you know as Judi Goodyear present here in this courtroom today?"

"Yes, she is. She's the brunette lady with the cream-color top on," described the witness, avoiding Judias's cool, steady glare from across the expanse of the courtroom.

"Approximately when was it you first met Judi Goodyear?"

"It was either the end of September or some time in October of 1971, at my home in Pensacola Beach. I had a friend named Bobby Joe Morris. He was a good friend of mine, and had been for eight or ten years, and he brought Judi to our home. . . ."

Mary Beverly shuddered as she remembered Bobby Joe's easy, good-natured grin. That last time he called from

Colorado that late December, she knew he feared for his life. She had tried to warn him about Judi back in 1972. Bobby Joe had sort of laughed about it, but he knew even then that Judi had killed her husband for the money. He must have known right up to the day he died, the same way James Goodyear had died. When she tried to call him back at the hospital, Judi answered the phone. She said Bobby Joe was too sick to talk to anyone. His condition was critical. Then she went on about her big position there at the hospital. Judi was always a real talker. She came on so fast, you either liked her or you just couldn't stand her.

Mary Beverly had liked Judi the first time she met her. For about two months she saw Judi almost every day. Judi knew Mary Beverly was having money problems, and she would bring over bags of groceries and even buy her dresses. She was very generous with her money. Judi said she had gotten a lot of her money from selling real estate in Orlando near Disneyworld. Then she said that she had collected forty thousand dollars from insurance after her house burned down.

Judi was different from anybody Mary Beverly had ever known, always telling stories about the things she had done. It was fascinating to be around her. Judi said she had grown up on an Indian reservation and that she had killed her stepmother with a hatchet. She was sent to reform school until she was sixteen and then moved to a women's penitentiary. There, Judias said, she read books voraciously and educated herself. She said she was in the Mafia and that she and Bobby Joe were into smuggling dope. One time Mary Beverly went over to Judi's and there was a huge boat sitting on a trailer in the back. Judi said the boat was stolen and they were hiding it until they could move it somewhere else. Judi had acted proud of the things she had done.

Mary Beverly was scared. She didn't know whether to believe everything Judi said, but she knew Judi was serious as a heart attack that afternoon in the grocery store when she told her that she had poisoned her husband and wanted to help Mary Beverly kill hers.

Mary Beverly had hoped Bobby Joe would reassure her when she told him what Judi said; he just laughed it off. But then Bobby Joe was dead.

Years passed. Then one night, she turned on the TV, and there was Judi looking right into her face from the ten o'clock news. Then she knew. She always felt she should have come forward, but she was afraid of what Judi might do. Ever since she had seen that wild look on Judi's face as she described how she had killed her first husband, she knew Judi was capable of doing just about anything to anyone who got in her way. Mary Beverly now realized that this woman had murdered a lot of people. That's when she finally made that anonymous call to the police. . . .

"When you first met the defendant," Perry continued his direct examination, "did she tell you anything about her husband in Orlando, James Goodyear?"

"Well, she told me she had recently become a widow, and that her husband had been a Green Beret in Vietnam, and that he had picked up a virus over there and died after he got home," Mary Beverly earnestly testified.

"Did there come a time that she told you how her husband died another way other than the way she previously told you?"

"Yes, there did. This was after Christmas, in January of 1972. My husband, David, and I were having problems about money, and we were separated. I was on the phone at home one Saturday morning in an argument with David when Judi came over. Judi and I had become pretty good friends, and she saw how upset I was. We talked some, and then I went to the grocery store, and Judi went with me. We were still talking about my marital problems with David, when Judi told me that what I should do is kill the S.O.B. I said, 'Judi, I could never do that!' Then she said that she had done it. I was shocked that Judi told me that she had killed her husband.

"Then she said," Mary Beverly continued, " 'if you want to do it, we can get the poison right here in the fly bait department.' She said that it has arsenic in it. She went on, and I don't know if she told me whether it was fly bait or roach poison or rat poison, but I do remember her telling me that it had arsenic in it, and that arsenic was something that builds up in your system and that you never throw it off. She said they give it in small doses to people who have parasites. She said there is no way they could ever find out, because an autopsy won't show up arsenic unless they are really looking for it.

"So that's how Judi told me that she killed James Goodyear with arsenic. She told me I would have to have the stomach to do it, because it was a really bad thing, and how sick it would make him. She asked me if David drank a lot of milk, which he did, and she said that I would have to give it to him in milk or in a milkshake. She told me she had to give it to James several times. She didn't let James go in the hospital because she treated him at home, and I could probably do that too. Then she told me to take out more insurance on David.

"I don't remember whether Judi told me that if I didn't have the stomach to do it, she could do it to David, but I do know that I went directly to my children's father and told him what Judi had said. 'David, don't drink anything or eat anything that woman gives you!' I told him, and he said, 'Well, you just get away from her because she always acted like she was crazy.' I tried to stay away from Judi after that. . . ."

On cross-examination Johnston asked the witness why she hadn't gone to the police.

"Because I did not know for sure whether or not Judi was telling the truth," Mary Beverly answered. "Also, I was scared of Judi and the people she said she was associating herself with. She told me she had burned her house, Mr. Johnston, and collected on the insurance."

"And yet you told it to a husband you couldn't stand to live in the same house with?"

"I didn't want him dead."

"And you told it to Bobby Joe Morris. Did you ever make a statement to his mother?"

"No, I never did."

"You and Mrs. Morris now are the best of friends, aren't you?" Johnston accused.

"My God, I never saw the lady, until yesterday, since 1973 New Year's Eve! I didn't even recognize her," Mary Beverly Owens insisted in clear, plaintive tones.

The imposing Mrs. Lodell Morris planted her ample frame firmly in the witness seat.

"Mrs. Morris, can you tell this jury how you first met Judi Goodyear?" opened Perry.

"It was at a New Year's Eve Party at the White Horse Inn. It's a club outside of Brewton, Alabama. It was 1972 or seventy-three, somewhere along there. I don't remember the exact date," Lodell Morris tersely testified.

"Now, at that time, did you know of any relationship between Bobby Joe Morris and the defendant, Judi Goodyear?"

"Well, they were living together."

"Did there ever come a time, Mrs. Morris, after you had met the defendant that she mentioned anything to you concerning the death of her late husband, James Goodyear?"

"Yes, she did, at a time when she was at my house in Brewton. She had her two kids with her."

"Would you relate to the court and the jury what she said to you, and you to her, in that conversation concerning the death of her husband?"

"Well, I don't know exactly what all was said. What I can remember is asking her was her family from Orlando, where was she raised. She said she had no family and she married at a young age, and he was no good. She said she had to work her butt off, and every time her back was turned he was in bed with a thirteen-year-old, and he was no help to her. So she killed the son of a bitch, that he didn't deserve to live," blurted the blunt Lodell.

"Mrs. Morris, did you call the police?" Johnston cross-examined.

"No, I didn't call the police. I was absolutely in shock. I had no proof that she killed him."

"You weren't afraid of Judi, were you?"

"Oh, no."

"And you weren't inquisitive enough . . . to say, how did you do it, why did you do it, what did you get out of it?"

"My thought was if she did it, why would she tell me? And if she didn't do it, why would she tell me? I mean, it was absolutely no concern of mine. I don't even know the man."

"But ma'am, this lady was going with your son, and she had confessed to a murder."

"Well, don't think it didn't upset me."

"And you did not make any statement of this to any law enforcement agency?"

"Well, I made a statement to my neighbor. I talked it over with her. Then I talked it over with my son. I told him I did not want him associating with a person guilty of murder, if she was so guilty."

"Don't you think that's a matter for the police?"

"There was nobody present but her and her two kids. It would have been my word against hers. I didn't think it was my place to do it. I wasn't concerned with Goodyear and I wasn't concerned with her."

"You don't think it's your duty as a citizen to report a murder, whenever somebody confesses a murder, to the authorities?"

"Maybe it was, but I neglected it. I didn't do it," admitted Lodell Morris with curt candor.

Over the next two days, Belvin Perry paraded a succession of out-of-town insurance agents, doctors, and prosecutors before the overwhelmed jury, expanding the register of insured victims allegedly poisoned by the defendant with a plethora of similar-fact evidence and testimony.

Veterans Administration officials testified that Judi Goodyear had collected on two life insurance policies worth $13,000, a government insurance policy worth $10,000, and dependency compensation benefits totaling $62,642.46 upon the death of her husband, James Goodyear.

Various insurance agents from Trinidad, Colorado, confirmed the fact that Judias had purchased three separate life insurance policies on Mr. Morris in his absence, claiming her husband was too busy, and returning the signed applications to the agencies herself. Judias collected a total of $80,000 in insurance benefits on the life of Bobby Joe Morris.

Dr. Charles Raye, the physician who treated Bobby Joe Morris during his hospitalizations in Trinidad, Colorado, stated that he thought that Bobby Joe's first presentation to the hospital on January 4, 1978, could very well have been the result of arsenic poisoning. While many of his symptoms during his first hospitalization were also consistent with pancreatitis due to alcohol consumption, toxicological tests for alcohol were negative upon his second presentation to the emergency room in severe shock. While postmortem tests revealed the mysterious presence of phenothiazines in his blood, Dr. Raye thought that the cause of Bobby Joe's profound state of shock and subsequent death was most likely arsenic poisoning.

Dr. Leon Riddick, the forensic pathologist of the Alabama Department of Forensic Sciences in Mobile, who performed the autopsy on the remains of Bobby Joe Morris's exhumed body, testified that, in his opinion, Morris died from acute arsenic poisoning.

Dr. Mathew Barnhill, toxicologist for the Alabama Department of Forensic Sciences, stated that the concentrations of arsenic found in Morris's liver and kidney were indicative of acute arsenic poisoning. Dr. Barnhill could not test the samples of Morris's hair and fingernails for arsenic content since the tissue samples had accidentally been discarded during a routine cleaning of the pathology freezer.

Joseph Zielman, chief chemist for the Royal Bond manufacturer of embalming chemicals in St. Louis, Missouri, testified that a federal statute prohibiting the use of heavy metals and arsenic in embalming fluids had been in effect since the late 1930s. The basic ingredients of most embalming fluids were a mixture of formaldehyde and methanol.

"Arsenic is an excellent preservative," said Zielman. "It doesn't have the distortion as with formaldehyde, but there are heavy fines if you're caught using it."

Mr. Baldwin of the Fairchild Funeral Home in Orlando, who had embalmed the body of James Goodyear for burial, stated that the embalming chemical he used was either Powertone, a mixture containing 36 percent formaldehyde, or Formcel, with 55 percent formaldehyde. Arsenic had been prohibited in embalming fluid as long ago as 1907, said Baldwin.

Assistant State Attorney Michael Patterson gave testimony concerning the trial and conviction of Judias for the attempted murder of her former fiancé, John Gentry, by poisoning and car bombing.

John Gentry took the witness stand one more time to tell the jury how Judias had given him paraformaldehyde-laced vitamin capsules that failed to kill him. During this time she had secretly made payments on a $500,000 mutual beneficiary term life insurance policy.

At 10:46 A.M. on Monday, October 28, the state rested its case.

22

In Her Own Defense

WITH THE JURY REMOVED FROM THE COURTROOM, Johnston immediately asked that the court declare a mistrial because of the introduction of similar-fact evidence pertaining to Bobby Joe Morris. Since the state had failed to prove that the defendant had administered the lethal dose of arsenic to Mr. Morris, the defendant was prejudiced by the admission of such evidence. The motion was swiftly denied.

Johnston moved for a directed verdict of acquittal on the grounds that the state had failed to prove that the alleged poisoning of James Goodyear had occurred in Orange County, Florida. Furthermore, Johnston argued, the state's expert testimony conflicted as to the exact fatal dose of arsenic ingested by the deceased. The state had failed to exclude every reasonable hypothesis of innocence.

Standing by his previous ruling, Judge Thompson once again denied the motion for a directed verdict of acquittal. Declining to make an opening statement to the returned jury, Johnston dejectedly began his case for the defense.

Dr. Robert Braman, an analytical chemist from Tampa, Florida, called the toxicological tests performed on the remains of Goodyear's and Morris's bodies "virtually useless" and "subject to suspicion." The test for arsenic content on Goodyear's remains should have been run at least three times for an average valid result, said Braman. The test showing a low end level of arsenic content in Goodyear's tissues had been run only once. Braman also pointed out that, according to the National Academy of Science, the 4.5 level of arsenic found in Goodyear's liver was within the average person's body load of 4.2 to 5.5 milligrams per kilogram of arsenic taken in each day.

On cross-examination, Dr. Braman, who had not analyzed the tissue remains, said that Goodyear would have to have inhaled at least twelve pounds of arsenic contained in any pesticides sprayed in Vietnam for the exposure to be lethal.

Dr. Ted Loomis, a Washington toxicologist with forty-two years of experience and a recognized expert in arsenic poisoning, said the amount of arsenic found in Goodyear's remains was too small to conclude that the poison caused his death. In order to get a true reading of arsenic level, said Loomis, one needs a good sample. The fact that Goodyear's organs had been intermingled in a plastic bag for thirteen years could throw off the accuracy of the readings and leave the tests subject to suspicion. The levels of 4.5 for the liver and 8.8 for the kidney in Goodyear's remains were the reverse of the usual results of arsenic poisoning, in which higher concentrations were found in the liver and lower concentrations in the kidney, Loomis stated. In his opinion, the hair and fingernail test for arsenic was not a good test, since the hair was subject to external contamination from arsenic content in shampoo and water, and after death, arsenic molecules are attracted to the part of the body with the highest concentration of sulfur—the hair and fingernails.

The expert defense witness agreed with the prosecution, however, that the symptoms Goodyear suffered shortly before his death were consistent with arsenic poisoning.

Late into the stormy Monday afternoon, Johnston called Kimberly Buenoano to the witness stand in a final desperate attempt to save his beleaguered client. At eighteen, she was no longer the awkward, frightened teenager who had whined her testimony between sniffles and sobs at her mother's previous trial. A more grown-up Kimberly approached the witness stand wearing high heels, an innocent shade of pink lipstick, a becoming two-piece suit, and as much dignity as she could muster.

Kimberly began her testimony in a muffled voice between furtive glances at her mother. Judias, leaning forward intently in her seat behind the defense table, fixed her penetrating gaze on her only daughter.

"Do you remember living in Orlando, Florida, in 1971?" Johnston directed his young witness in condescending tones.

"No, sir," Kimberly respectfully replied.

"Do you remember anything about your father, James Goodyear?"

"No, sir."

"Do you remember living in Pensacola after 1971?"

"Yes, sir."

"When was the first time you met Mr. Morris?"

"In Pensacola, when I was about six."

Kimberly remembered Mr. Morris living in her home with her mother and two brothers, James and Michael. In 1978, the family moved to Colorado to live with Mr. Morris. Michael, institutionalized for quite a few years, came too.

"How did Mr. Morris and Michael get along?" posed Johnston.

"Michael did not like him at all."

"What about you and Mr. Morris?"

"I hated him," Kimberly blurted forcefully.

"Why did you hate him?"

"Because he tried to abuse me very bad. He did abuse me very bad. Every time I turned around, he was trying to do something to me. . . . He sexually abused me very bad," accused Kimberly, suddenly melting into tears.

"How old were you?" Johnston gently probed.

"About ten," Kimberly murmured between sobs.

"What did Mr. Morris do?"

"He made me have sex with him," Kimberly whimpered, breaking into more tears. "He would come home and he would come through the house and try to snatch my clothes off me. My brother James caught him one time. I would suck my thumb at night, and when I would get up in the morning, he would pour hot sauce in my mouth. He would take the dress I had to wear to school. He beat on me. Bobby was very cruel to me. I hated the man more than anything in this world," she cried.

"How did Michael react?" Johnston inserted.

"Michael was going to do something about it. He didn't like me having to go through the pain and suffering I was going through." Kimberly sniffed.

"Did Michael ever do anything?"

"I saw Michael put stuff in a bottle that was setting on the medicine cabinet that Bobby always drank out of."

"Whose medicine was that?"

"Michael's. I'm not sure of the name of it. Some was for being hyper. Some was because he would not think straight, and at times it was to calm his nerves and stuff."

"Do you recall when Mr. Morris went to the hospital and then was later discharged and came back home?"

"He came home from the hospital and he still looked real bad. We were sitting down inside, and he went to the store and got some booze, and he came back. He started hounding Michael very bad. Michael walked in the bathroom and put something in Bobby's beer and handed it to him. Bobby got real sick and went back to the hospital. Michael was happy. He was glad the pain was going to be over with soon. . . ." Kimberly sighed heavily.

"When did Bobby J. Morris first start abusing you sexually?" Perry cross-examined.

"He started out playing games with me. Every time I would walk by, he would pinch me or grab me or something. It did not go far then," Kimberly explained.

"So we can understand how far it did go, specifically tell this jury what Bobby Joe Morris did to sexually abuse you," Perry demanded.

"He would grab me and take my clothes off me, and when I would try to leave, he would pull me back."

"Did you ever tell your mom?"

"No," Kimberly replied, looking down as Judias sat sphinx-like, covering her mouth with her hand.

"Were you close to your mom?"

"Yes, sir, I was very close to my mom," said Kimberly defensively.

"You didn't tell your mom about this drunk sex molester who was living there with you and your brothers?"

"No, I didn't."

"Do you recall my taking your deposition back on the eighteenth day of June, 1985, up in Pensacola, and at the time asking you the following question about Bobby Morris: 'He didn't try to sexually assault or molest you?' Do you recall what you told me?" charged Perry.

"I told you no."

"So you lied then, didn't you?"

"I sure did."

"What was the reason for you to lie at that time?"

"You have to understand that this is something I have to live with the rest of my life. I tried to hide this. Now everybody has to know about it."

"You tried to blame this on Michael, isn't that correct?"

"That is not, no."

"Do you love your mom?"

"I love my mother very much."

"You love your mother enough to lie for her, don't you?"

"No, I would not lie."

"You lied when I took the deposition," accused Perry.

"Because I have to live with it. Now everybody is going to know. People are going to talk about it. It is so hard for me to get over it now. It took me so long to get over it. We moved because of all of it. Now I am going to have to live with it again," Kimberly cried miserably. "I didn't want people to look at me and say, well, her father abused her, look at her. I know people already put me down for this, and I am now going to be knocked down even worse."

"All this time, you never told anybody about Michael putting something in Bobby Joe's medicine?" Perry pressed.

"I swore to Michael I would never say anything because he was helping me out. He was getting the pain off me," Kimberly testified in hurt confusion.

"Were you there the night Bobby Joe went into the hospital the last time?"

"I got the ambulance for them to put him in."

"You testified he went and got some alcohol to drink. When did he get all this alcohol in reference to the time he was taken to the hospital?"

"I don't remember. It may have been a couple of hours before."

"Was he pretty well drunk by the time they wheeled him out and took him to the hospital?"

"I have no idea. Bobby could drink four cases of beer and still walk the same."

"Ma'am, how do you account for the fact that when they performed an examination on his blood they found no alcohol?" challenged Perry.

"I have no idea," Kimberly rejoined with a note of defiance.

James Buenoano Goodyear, the early growth of a light brown mustache adorning his upper lip, sauntered to the witness stand to verify his sister's testimony. Describing Bobby Joe Morris as a violent drunkard given to fits of rage, James said that Michael and Bobby Joe frequently argued and came to blows a couple of times. Michael would not mind Bobby and resented the way he treated James and Kimberly. Michael had a punching bag on which he had drawn Bobby Joe's picture and he would often practice on it. While he was never physically abused by Bobby Joe, James remembered coming home to their house in Colorado one afternoon in December 1977 to find Bobby Joe holding Kimberly down on the carpet while she struggled to get away. James rescued his sister from Bobby Joe's sexual abuse. Michael had sworn to kill Bobby. James never told anyone of the incident. It was something between his sister and brother and nobody was ever to know, said James.

"Do you recall my taking your deposition back on the eighteenth day of June 1985, and asking you, 'Did Bobby Joe Morris ever mistreat you, your sister, your brother, or your mom?' Your answer was 'Never.' Do you recall that response?" Perry cross-examined the unperturbed James.

"Yes, sir," James replied calmly.

"So, in other words, you didn't tell me the truth then?"

"Yes, sir."

"It was convenient at the time not to tell the truth, as it is convenient for you to tell us the answer you are telling us now; is that correct?"

"Yes, sir. I feel it needs to be said."

"Do you love your mom?"

"Yes, sir."

"You love your mom, and you would do anything to help her, isn't that right?" accused Perry.

"Yes, sir," James coolly responded with a smug smile.

"Mr. Johnston, do you have any other witnesses to call?" Judge Thompson asked after James was dismissed.

Johnston approached the bench to confer outside of the hearing of the jury.

"I don't have any others except possibly the defendant, Your Honor. I will need time to talk to her. I asked her about it earlier, whatever she wanted to do after her children got through. She shook her head no. I will ask her again," confided Johnston.

Thompson ordered a short recess to allow defense counsel to confer with his client.

Fifteen minutes later, court was reconvened without the presence of the jury. Leaving Judias seated cross-armed at the defense table, Johnston again approached the bench.

"I spoke to the defendant. She indicated to me she would prefer to testify tomorrow because she feels she may have one of these seizures," Johnston explained to the judge.

"Is she taking any medication?" queried Thompson.

"I don't know," replied Johnston.

"Yes," Judias interjected from behind the defense table.

"Well, if there is any medical reason for it, I wouldn't want her to have a seizure if she were to testify today," commented the judge. "Court will be in recess until tomorrow morning at nine A.M."

"Your Honor, we would call the defendant," announced Johnston the morning of October 29, 1985.

"Come forward and be sworn in," Judge Thompson formally addressed the defendant seated stiffly before him.

Strikingly pale beneath her heavy veneer of makeup, Judias, clad in her customary plain white blouse and black tailored slacks, devoid of her usually array of expensive jewelry, strode stoically toward the witness stand to testify for the first time in her own defense.

"Please state your name," Johnston directed his unsmiling client.

"My name is Judias Buenoano."

"And do people call you Judi Goodyear?"

"Yes, they do."

"How old are you?"

"I am forty-two."

"Can you describe to the court and jury what kind of marriage you had with Mr. Goodyear?"

"Okay," Judias responded in a clipped falsetto. "I married Mr. Goodyear in New Mexico on November 21, 1962. I was eighteen. We had basically a good marriage. We had two children."

"Leading up to when Mr. Goodyear went to Vietnam, how would you describe your marriage?"

"We had a good marriage. We had a few disagreements here and there, but who doesn't? You can't live with somebody all the time and not disagree on a few things."

"When he was in Vietnam, did you cheat on him?"

"I had dinner with Mr. Crawford," Judias said hesitantly. "I was a businesswoman. Mr. Crawford, you know—I worked for him. After I actually quit working for him, I still tended to drive cars for him to various cities, if that is what you call cheating."

"Did you have any sexual relationship or affair with any man?"

"Not while my husband was alive, no, I did not," Judias firmly denied.

"What kind of relationship did you have with Mr. Goodyear when he got back from Vietnam in June 1971?"

"A good relationship. I was glad he was home."

"You had living with you this Debbie Sims during that period of time?"

"Debbie came to live with us approximately a month after James went overseas."

"What happened to your husband when he returned home in June?"

"Well, my husband was not feeling well when he got off the airplane. We had a coming-home party scheduled at a friend's house. We stayed about an hour and left. He rested a few days. We went to Hawaii and we stayed there a week. He was ill while we were there. He didn't feel well. We came home and rested a few days. Then we went to visit his family. We visited his sister in Virginia and his father in Pennsylvania. We cut our vacation short because he still did not feel well. I drove home. He rested in the back of the station wagon all the way home. . . . He was real tired. He tried and continued to do things. He was a workaholic. When he wasn't working, he felt bad."

"Did you notice any unusual symptoms about him?" prompted Johnston.

"Well, he tired easily. He was nauseous some of the time. He saw things. His skin started to turn yellow, and his eyes," described Judias dispassionately.

"When to the best of your recollection was it that he couldn't go to work?"

"I'm not really sure, Mr. Johnston. . . . He reported to the base every day up until he went into the hospital."

"When he finally got sick enough to be admitted to the hospital, who took him?"

"They took him from McCoy Air Force Base. However, that morning I drove out with him because I was irritated and didn't think they had been treating him properly. He was having difficulty walking. He saw the doctor at McCoy and they were going to send him back home. I went to the wing commander. I wasn't too nice. My temper got away with me. The wing commander looked at him in the McCoy hospital. He said that he felt James should be admitted to the Orlando Naval Air Station Hospital. They took him."

"During his stay in the hospital, did you visit him?"

"Oh, yes, sir. I went there every time the door opened that I could be there."

"How long was he in the hospital before he finally expired?"

"Three days."

"Did you give your permission to have an autopsy performed?"

"Yes, I did."

"Did you provide any arsenic or anything else that killed him?"

"No, sir, I did not."

"Do you remember joking with Constance Lang about putting arsenic in the macaroni?"

"No, I don't. Let's face it, really, who could remember a conversation fourteen years ago? If there was any such conversation, it was exactly that, a joke."

"What did you do when Mr. Goodyear passed away?"

"I continued to live here in Orlando. I was not myself. I had seizures really bad and I went, well, the children and Connie and I took a vacation, just left. I had to get away. We took a trip out west. We also went to Mexico. We came back in October 1971. I went to the hospital in November. They were checking to see why I was having seizures. I stayed in the hospital a couple of weeks."

"When did you move from Orlando to Pensacola?"

"I bought my house in Pensacola the second day of April 1972. I didn't move in until June first. The people needed a couple of months to get out."

"Do you recall Mary Beverly Owens?"

"I met her twice. I never knew her. Her husband had a house he had built on Pensacola Beach for sale. Bobby Morris thought I might like it, and I met her and her husband at that house to look at it. That was it."

"She described your relationship as being good friends and going shopping together."

"I've never been shopping with Mary Owens in my life."

"Did you have any discussions with her concerning fly bait or arsenic?"

"No, sir. I never had any discussions with Mary Owens, period, other than twice and that is it."

"How is it that you met Bobby Joe Morris?"

"Through Mr. Crawford. He introduced Bobby to Connie and Connie was dating Bobby."

"In June of 1972, what kind of relationship did you have with Bobby Joe Morris?"

"We had a good relationship. We were friends. We had no serious relationship at that time. Bobby lived in my household for a number of years. Another friend lived with us as well. We paid one third and one third and one third of all the bills. We were all good friends."

"Who was that other friend?"

"John Daniel."

"How long did this type of arrangement last?"

"Four years until 1976."

"What did you do during this period of time from 1972 to 1976?"

"What did I do? I took care of my children and my home. In 'seventy-five I went to work at one of the local hospitals in Pensacola. I was not a nurse at the time, but I worked in the nursing department."

"Were you and Mr. Morris in any type of business?"

"We opened a construction company. We laid natural gas and water lines. The company folded in 1975."

"Was it your idea or Mr. Morris's idea to go to Trinidad, Colorado?"

"He didn't go directly to Colorado. He didn't like the job that he had. I did the resumés. He called me and asked me if I would resubmit his resumés to different companies for him, which I did."

"Why is it that you finally ended up in Trinidad, Colorado, with Mr. Morris?"

"My son had gone to Trinidad for a vacation for four days. Mr. Morris didn't send him home, so I went to Trinidad to get my son. I picked my son up and came back to Florida. Mr. Morris asked me to come to Trinidad. He had asked me to marry him at that time. I went to Trinidad in the summer of 1977. We had tentatively planned to get married. We bought a house together. He was sober when I got there. He told me he hadn't drunk for a while. He said he was taking Antiabuse and going to AA. He started drinking again. I didn't marry him because of the fact he had started back to drinking."

"Did you hold yourself out as his wife and he as your husband?"

"Yes, sir, I guess you would say we did. Bobby had to be married in order to get the job at the city in Trinidad, so he told them that we were married. So I went by Mrs. Morris."

"What kind of a person was Mr. Morris?"

"When he was sober, he was great. He was a good person. When he was drunk, he was one person, and when he was sober, he was another."

"Would you call him a good-hearted person?"

"Yes, he couldn't say no to anybody. He would give the shirt off his back. He would buy things he didn't want because he couldn't say no. He went and bought a truckload of watermelons once because he couldn't say no and had them dumped in the backyard. Once he bought life insurance in Pensacola that he had no intention of keeping. He had a number of other policies he had bought and he let the policies lapse."

"The state introduced a number of insurance policies on Mr. Morris which names you as the beneficiary. Do you have any knowledge as to why you would go down and get those policies rather than Mr. Morris?"

"Well, I didn't do that on all of the policies. He told me to go pick up the application and take it to his office. I'm sure any of the gentlemen who are married tell their wives to do things all the time for them. We do things for our husbands or boyfriends or children. I did what he told me to do," said Judias with a coy glance at the jury of ten men and two women.

"Do you recall the day Mr. Morris got sick for the first time and went in the hospital?"

"Well, I had a meeting at the college and I didn't get home until five o'clock. Bobby was ill in the bathroom and the children told me that he was ill and they couldn't get him out of the bathroom. I persuaded him to open the door. Then we took him and laid him on the couch. He was in profound shock, so I called the ambulance."

"Did you work as a nurse at the hospital in Trinidad, or a nurse's aid?"

"No, I was just a student. I graduated in August of 1978. I have an LPN license in the State of Florida."

"Were you required to take courses that entailed the study of certain medications?"

"Physiology, nutrition, pharmacology—it entails the study of medications, that is correct."

"Would you say that you stayed with Mr. Morris in the hospital and did all the things that you would expect a wife to do?"

"Well, of course, yes, sir."

"After he was discharged from the hospital, how long was he home?"

"About three days, maybe. He got sick on the day he went back into the hospital. There again, I came home from school and found him in shock. I called an ambulance. Just a few days. He came home on a Saturday, I believe it was. He died the following Saturday."

"Did you approve the autopsy on Mr. Morris?"

"Of course I did. You know, he died."

"Did you call his mother?"

"Yes. I talked to his mother on several occasions."

"How was your relationship with his mother?"

"Before his death, we saw very little of his mother. When I saw her, she was nice to me."

"Do you recall her testimony indicating that you told her certain incriminating things concerning Mr. Goodyear?"

"Yes, I remember her testimony."

"Did you say those things to Mrs. Morris?"

"No."

"When did Mr. Gentry befriend you or you befriend Mr. Gentry? Tell us something about that relationship," Johnston continued his painstaking examination.

"I met Mr. Gentry in the early part of 1981 at a mud wrestling match," retorted Judias with a long-suffering sigh. "We had a real good relationship. We got along great. We had fun together. We liked to do the same things, you know."

"What is the story on the paraformaldehyde Mr. Gentry found in the Vicon-C capsule? Did you know anything about that?"

"No, I did not. Mr. Gentry had been sick since August with a kidney problem. He had kidney stones. Then I developed a cold. I had nausea and vomiting and diarrhea and a temperature. Then I gave it to the whole household. John picked it up. I was giving the whole family the Vicon-C. I took it myself."

"And when Mr. Gentry stopped taking the Vicon-C, did you protest?"

"No, I didn't protest. I didn't care."

"How is it that you and he went to the insurance agency and took out a half million dollars insurance policy on each other's lives?"

"Okay. We have to go back to August. He was having problems with his kidneys. He needed to go to the hospital. He didn't have any money. He didn't have any insurance. He wouldn't go to the doctor even though I offered to loan him the money. So I suggested that he have some health insurance. We went and we talked to Barbara Corwin about health insurance and also talked to her about a group insurance hospitalization and a group life insurance policy plan for the wallpaper company. He put on airs about how he was a big businessman. She suggested that maybe we might be interested in some life insurance. Before we left, it was half a million dollars life insurance that we both agreed to."

"Do you know what paraformaldehyde is?"

"Yes, it is a chemical. I worked in and around hospitals for a long time and I never saw any there."

"Do you know or did you know in 1982 whether it would be fatal if you took capsules containing approximately one and a half grams of paraformaldehyde?" posed Johnston.

"Yes, sir. I knew it would be fatal like that."

"Are you saying it would be fatal if you took one capsule?" Johnston clarified.

"No. If you look in a standard medical dictionary, there is a chart and it gives only liquid paraformaldehyde, which is thirty-seven percent methanol. It would take a lot more than one gram or half a gram to cause death. I studied formaldehyde. I knew that."

"Have you ever bought any paraformaldehyde?"

"Mr. Johnston, if I ever bought any paraformaldehyde, the state would have it right here on display. No."

"Have you ever bought any arsenic?" Johnston concluded.

"If I ever bought any arsenic . . . they would have found a record of it. It would have been here. No," Judias replied with terse conviction.

"Have you ever been convicted of a felony?" Perry began his cross-examination of the increasingly hostile defendant.

"Yes, sir, I have. Since this witch-hunt started, twice," Judias snapped at the prosecutor with barely disguised resentment.

"Did you ever tell Constance Lang that you were unhappy in your marriage?"

"No, sir, I did not."

"Did you ever suggest using arsenic to poison your husband to Connie Lang?"

"No, sir, I did not."

"Did you ever tell Constance Lang, after your husband got back, that poisoning was one way to end marital difficulties?"

"No, I never did say such."

"So, when Constance Lange testified to those things, she told a lie?"

"That is correct."

"You heard Mr. Crawford testify from that same stand that you are seated in and he took the same oath that you took. Did you hear him say that you were sexually intimate with him while your husband was in Vietnam? Was he telling the truth or was he telling a lie?"

"Mr. Crawford was telling a lie about being sexually intimate while my husband was in Vietnam. It was afterward, not before."

"Afterward?"

"After my husband passed away."

"How soon after your husband passed away were you sexually intimate with him?"

"Maybe a month."

"So Mr. Crawford lied also?"

"I don't know that he lied. I think Mr. Crawford just was confused in time. After all, it has been fourteen years. Mr. Crawford, I am sure, had many girlfriends," Judias replied archly.

"Do you recall whether or not Mr. Crawford was at your husband's funeral?"

"No, I don't recall if he was or not."

"After your husband died and you got your life insurance proceeds, did you go out and buy a sports car?"

"Yes, I did."

"So Mrs. Lang was right about that. Did you trade that sports car in and get a Cadillac?"

"No, sir, I did not."

"So, she lied about that? That is one truth and two lies?"

"Two lies and one truth, right."

"You heard Mrs. Lang testify that you told her you were in love with Bobby Joe Morris and you wanted to marry him when she was dating him. Was that the truth or a lie?"

"That is the truth."

"What made you fall in love with Bobby Joe Morris so quickly?"

"He's a nice guy." Judias shrugged.

"Do you recall Mary Beverly Owens's testimony concerning what happened at the grocery store?"

"I recall, Mr. Perry. I heard it," Judias rejoined testily.

"Do you recall her saying that you told her first of all to take out more insurance on her husband?"

"Mr. Perry, I never talked to her. Period."

"So she would be telling a lie also?"

"It appears that way."

"Now, when did your relationship with Bobby Joe Morris develop into something more than friendship?"

"It is really hard to say. It just developed over the years."

"When in the scheme of things did you find out he was an alcoholic?"

"I knew it all along. He would drink a fifth of VO in maybe eight hours. He drank beer on a daily basis."

"Did he ever get violent, whether he drank or not?"

"Yes. He would throw things at you."

"Like what?"

"Anything he could get his hands on, such as his empty beer can or a full beer if he had it in his hand. He would pull my hair occasionally."

"Did he ever strike you with his fist?"

"No, with his open hand in the face."

"Would it hurt?"

"Yes."

"How often would he do this?"

"Oh, maybe twice."

"Did he ever mistreat or abuse any of your children?"

"Yes. He didn't abuse James. They were buddies."

"Was Michael living with you at that time?"

"No, sir."

"Now, that leaves Kimberly. How did he treat her?"

"He scared her. He would pull her hair sometimes and he would grab for her and she would scream and run."

"Did he sexually abuse Kimberly to your knowledge?"

"No, not to my knowledge."

"Your daughter said he did. When did she first tell you about that?"

"A few days ago."

"Now, do you recall the testimony of the insurance fellow that came to the house and took the application on Mr. Morris? Was Bobby Joe home that night?"

"Apparently not."

"Did you make any phone calls concerning insurance?"

"I don't remember."

"Do you remember going to the insurance agency on December second to inquire about insurance policies?"

"I didn't go there to inquire. I picked up what I was told to retrieve."

"Did you ever tell any of those insurance people that Bobby Joe was too busy to come in?"

"I didn't have to. He did."

"How much money did you collect when Bobby Joe died?"

"I'm not sure of the exact figure. It was seventy-something-thousand dollars. Mr. Perry, you have the figures."

"After Bobby Joe died, did you open a business in Trinidad?"

"Yes, I did. I had the same type of business I opened in Pensacola, which was a beauty salon."

"Did you use paraformaldehyde there?"

"No, sir."

"Did you use any arsenic?"

"No, sir."

"You didn't put arsenic in James Goodyear's food or drink?"

"No, sir."

"Didn't you also give paraformaldehyde to John Gentry?"

"Not to my knowledge, I did not. If I did, it was an accident."

"Did you tell John Gentry, ma'am, that the half million dollars' worth of insurance didn't go through?"

"No, sir, I did not."

"So he lied also?"

"I don't think John really remembers what happened. Just like he didn't remember that I had loaned him money. John has a problem remembering exactly what happens."

"And Constance Lang is untruthful?"

"It has been a long time, Mr. Perry. I think maybe Connie is bitter because I took her boyfriend away from her."

"And Mary Beverly Owens is just a liar?"

"She is just a liar."

"Lodell Morris is just a liar too?"

"Yes."

"But the three men that you had been with, you stood to gain financially from each of their deaths, didn't you?"

"That is correct."

"And those three men all came in contact with poisoning in some form or another, didn't they?"

"That is what the state has presented, Mr. Perry. I don't know that for a fact."

"James Goodyear had bad luck, didn't he?"

"I don't know what you mean by bad luck. Explain yourself, please," Judias demanded icily.

"Didn't James Goodyear have bad luck by dying from arsenic poisoning?" Perry asked facetiously.

"I don't know that my husband died of arsenic. You say that, Mr. Perry."

"Bobby Joe Morris had the same kind of luck, because he died of arsenic poisoning too, didn't he?"

"You heard the testimony about that," Judias spat, her dark eyes flashing daggers at the feisty prosecutor.

"John Gentry nearly met the same fate too, didn't he?"

"No, sir, he did not!"

That Tuesday afternoon, the First Circuit Court of Appeals upheld Judias Buenoano's conviction for the drowning murder of her son, Michael Goodyear.

On Thursday, October 31, Belvin Perry delivered his closing argument. "The evidence shows that Judi Goodyear wove her web, a web that did not contain the environment, a web that did not contain Agent Blue, but it contained Agent Judi who systematically eliminated Sergeant Goodyear. James Goodyear had bad luck, and there sits his bad luck, Judi Goodyear," Perry concluded, pointing an accusing finger at the defendant.

Johnston spoke to the jury, beginning his final summation. "Nobody loves you when you're down. Everybody is against you. . . . The State has not presented any case beyond reasonable doubt that Mr. Goodyear died from arsenic poisoning. . . . The state has not proved the case, and the verdict you should return based on that is not guilty. . . ."

The jury retired at 1:11 P.M. to begin its deliberation whether Judi Goodyear was guilty of the first-degree murder of her husband, Sergeant James E. Goodyear. The statute of limitations had expired on any of the lesser charges of second- or third-degree murder.

At 5:53 P.M. the jury returned. "Your Honor, it is going to take a little time before we can come up with a verdict. It is going slow, but we are progressing," the foreman informed Judge Thompson. Retiring to the nearby Harley Hotel, the jury continued its deliberations through the rainy Halloween night.

It was not until the following afternoon, November 1, 1985, that the jury, having deliberated a total of ten hours, returned its verdict: "Guilty of murder in the first degree as charged, so say we all."

Judias closed her eyes and covered her face with her hands as the ten men and two women of the twelve-member jury each rose to affirm individually his or her verdict. As she was led away, Judias, her stony composure finally broken, collapsed into bitter tears.

"She is definitely worried about getting the electric chair," Johnston somberly told the gathering reporters.

23

May God Have Mercy

Detective TED CHAMBERLAIN leaned back behind the wheel of his white Ford 4 x 4 pickup truck on the bright and early Thursday morning of November 2, 1985. He relished the exhilarating sense of freedom he always felt when he cruised along on I-75, Florida's boundless scenic turnpike. He sped north on the wide-open highway, homeward-bound toward Pensacola.

What he needed more than anything right now, Chamberlain told himself, were a few fast laps around the track in his newly rebuilt number 45 stock car. Driving straight through the over seven hundred miles up the middle of the Florida peninsula from Orlando to Pensacola, he'd make it back just in time for the weekend rally at Five Flags Speedway—one of the last meets of the North Florida racing season. He had held second place all the way in his last race, until he hit that oil slick in the far-end hairpin curve and spun out in the last lap. Eight-year-old Bradley, cheering him on from the front row of outdoor bleachers, had taken it harder than he had. There was always another race, he'd told his young stepson. Maybe next time he'd be the first one in, Chamberlain assured himself, reaching for his pack of extra-long dark More cigarettes on the cluttered dash.

Chamberlain had spent the last twelve days and nights sequestered in an Orlando Howard Johnson Hotel on a spartan expense account as a guest of the State of Florida, smoking more cigarettes, drinking more beer, and eating more stale room-service sandwiches than he would ever care to remember.

The subpoena from the Orlando state attorney's office had arrived on August 20:

> You are hereby commanded to be and appear before the Circuit Court at Orange County Courthouse in Orlando the 21st day of October, 1985, at 9:30 A.M. to testify and the truth to speak on behalf of the State in a certain matter pending before said Court where the plaintiff is the State of Florida and the defendant is Buenoano, Judi A.

Chamberlain planned to be there with bells on to see the look on Judias's face when the jury found her guilty for the third and, he hoped, last time. But he never got to the witness stand. Each day from the beginning of Judias's trial for the first-degree murder of James Goodyear, he anxiously waited by the phone in his hotel room to be called to Orlando's monumental courthouse, and each day his testimony was postponed. On the tenth day, Chamberlain received word from prosecutor Belvin Perry that James Johnston had agreed to the admission of the State's similar-fact evidence concerning the attempted murder of John Gentry by poisoning on the condition that Chamberlain not appear in the courtroom. Apparently Johnston feared his client's emotional reaction to the very sight of the man she held personally responsible for the "witch-hunt" that had resulted in her repeated arrests, trials, and convictions.

Disappointed that he had not been able personally to execute his final role in the long and complicated process of bringing a serial murderess to justice, Chamberlain was, after all, satisfied with the verdict. He had been free to leave on Monday after the state rested its case, but he hadn't driven all the way to Orlando not to be there when the jury returned from its final deliberations on the murder of James Goodyear by arsenic poisoning. He'd have driven a lot farther to witness the final verdict of guilty as charged for Judias Buenoano.

It was just as well he hadn't taken Jerri along, Chamberlain reminded himself with a familiar sinking sensation in his gut. He wondered seriously if she would be there when he returned. She had stood at the front door the morning he left and told him that if he went to Orlando without her, she wouldn't be there when he got back. She had a look of determination he had never seen in her before. He still didn't understand why it had meant so much to her. If she thought he was with another woman, she was crazy. She had to know how hard he had worked on this case. He'd sworn he'd get the bitch, and he had. Jerri had gotten pretty involved with it herself. Maybe too involved, Chamberlain thought soberly.

He hadn't told Jerri about the threatening phone calls he'd received before the trial—muffled juvenile voices imitating a bad Hollywood movie: "If she gets the death penalty, you're dead"—or the dead cat left on his doorstep with a rope around its neck. It was the kind of kid stuff he'd expect from James Buenoano and his teenaged troops. But what had happened to Kimberly Buenoano's former boyfriend, David Lackey, a few months after he had testified for the state in James Buenoano's trial for the attempted murder of John Gentry, was certainly no joke, Chamberlain thought bitterly.

It seemed David Lackey, who had been a friend of James Buenoano's before the trial, became James's roommate not long after James was acquitted on the attempted murder charge. According to James, he came home from work one afternoon to discover that his roommate, David, had shot himself with James's shotgun. There was a suicide note referring to a recent breakup with a girlfriend. James had a tight alibi. He had been at work during the time the coroner's report said David Lackey died. Chamberlain had his suspicions, but there was nothing he could prove. Lackey's death was closed out as a suicide.

After that, Chamberlain began taping the hood of his truck and checking his engine and trunk before starting the motor—just in case. If James Buenoano ever tried to harm him or his family, he wouldn't hesitate to put him away for good, Chamberlain vowed to himself. But there was no sense in alarming Jerri with his suspicions. The last thing he needed to do was make Jerri more of a target by bringing her to the Orlando trial. Why couldn't she just trust him enough and understand that he had to go it alone?

Chamberlain checked his speed and eased off on the accelerator. If Jerri had taken the kids and left when he got back to Pensacola, he knew this time he would let her go. It was better that way. She had always needed more than he had to give. Women, he joked ruefully. Can't live with 'em, and can't shoot 'em.

Lighting up another cigarette, Chamberlain took a long drag and forced his tense muscles to relax as he settled back for the long drive ahead. They might have kept him out of the courtroom, he mused, but he'd make sure he was on the witness list at Judias's execution to give her a last wave good-bye. Chamberlain knew for certain that if Judias didn't receive the death penalty in Florida's electric chair, the state attorney in Trinidad would promptly extradite her to Colorado to stand trial for the first-degree murder of Bobby Joe Morris by arsenic poisoning. The maximum penalty for first-degree murder in the State of Colorado was a choice of execution in the gas chamber or by lethal injection.

Sooner or later, one way or another, the witch was going to burn, Chamberlain thought grimly to himself.

"Starting from my right, moving to my left, will each of you give me your names, please." On the morning of November 25, 1985, the Honorable Emerson R. Thompson, Jr., tersely addressed the defense and prosecution witnesses for the penalty phase of the first-degree murder trial of Judias Buenoano.

Standing shoulder to shoulder in the line of silent witnesses about to be collectively sworn in, John Gentry couldn't help feeling like a suspect in a police lineup. Going the last mile, he had returned to Orlando after testifying for the state in Judias's third murder trial to bear witness one final time as to why she, if anyone, deserved the death penalty. If it weren't for the recurring hospitalizations for the removal of cysts from his kidneys caused by particles of debris from the explosion, he might have believed the events of the past two years were all a bad dream. But there sat Judi at the defense table, as big as life and as cocky as ever. He must have been out of his mind, but he had been in love with Judi, no doubt about it. Maybe in some strange way, he had been an accomplice to his own murder. . . . But these were thoughts he'd have the rest of his life—what was left of it—to ponder. Right now all he wanted was to get the hell out of Orlando, pack up his new family, and head north, as far away from Pensacola and all the guilty associations as he could get.

Having charged the witnesses not to discuss the case, Judge Thompson dismissed them and ordered in the jury. Belvin Perry called John Wesley Gentry to the stand to begin the crucial testimony for aggravating and mitigating circumstances. Afterward, the jury would have to determine its advisory sentence of life imprisonment without the possibility of parole for twenty-five years, or death in the electric chair.

In a weary drawl devoid of bitterness, John Gentry dutifully described the events leading up to June 25, 1983, and the explosion that nearly claimed his life. For a brief moment, Gentry's soft brown eyes dared to meet Judias's across the vast room. There was not a flicker of recognition in her sullen glare.

Assistant State Attorney Michael Patterson took the witness stand to reiterate his testimony on the evidence presented in Judias's trial and conviction for the attempted murder of John Gentry by poisoning and car bombing.

And Assistant Attorney Russell Edgar, unaccustomed to the witness seat, stared straight at the defendant as he soberly delivered a detailed summary of the trial and conviction of Judias for the drowning murder of her son,

Michael Goodyear, and grand theft insurance fraud.

Defense counsel James Johnston had assembled a number of witnesses to testify on behalf of his client as to factors that might mitigate her guilt.

Dr. Michael Radelet, a professor of sociology at the University of Florida, stated that the probability for Judias to commit future violent behavior was likely no greater than that of the general population. Dr. Radelet based his prediction on three basic factors. One, she was a woman. In the United States, female defendants account for less than ten percent of all arrests for crimes of violence. Two, those found guilty of primary homicides, or crimes of violence against members of a primary group known to the defendant, have a lower probability of future dangerousness than those who commit crimes of violence against strangers. Since the people closest to one also cause the most stress, once the loved one is dead, the source of stress is removed, reasoned Radelet. And three, the future environment of the defendant in controlled incarceration substantially reduces the probability of recurrent violent behavior.

Dr. Radelet, a professed opponent of the death penalty, cited a series of contiguous-state studies from 1920 to 1983 that concluded unanimously that there was virtually no difference in the homicide rates between states with and those without the death penalty. A 1978 National Academy of Science investigation concluded there was no evidence indicating that the death penalty had a more deterrent effect than life imprisonment. Dr. Radelet's own study of seven thousand cases from 1900 to 1985 in which the defendants were sentenced to death concluded that in 343 cases the defendants were wrongfully convicted; in 25 of them, defendants were executed and later found to be innocent.

Chaplain Max Jones of the Orange County Jail Ministry testified that since Judias's arrival at the Orange County Jail on October 3, 1984, she had faithfully attended all the religious services and Bible studies they had. He had spoken to Judias during a couple of counseling sessions, and she said that she had asked God to forgive her. Whether Judias was sincere was between her and God, said Chaplain Jones. He had no way of knowing whether or not someone had actually found God.

Chaplain Eddie Johnson of the Orange County Jail Ministry first met Judias in September 1985. He gathered Judias was sincere in her statements to him on religious matters and that she had made a change. She seemed to get along very well with the other inmates, Chaplain Johnson said.

Roxanne Nordquist, a volunteer worker with the Orange County Jail system, had spent about an hour a week with Judias over the last year, getting to know her and counseling her. Roxanne felt there had been a tremendous change in Judias in the time she had known her. Judias was encouraging to the people around her in the prison system and to the other inmates. She felt like she had a call to go into the ministry herself as a woman chaplain. Judias had received a teaching certificate from the International Bible College while she was incarcerated, achieving a 90.8 average. She was working on her associate's degree in Bible study from the Pensacola Bible College. Judias had a natural tendency to reach out to people around her, said Roxanne. One day she was visiting Judias in her cell, and as she came out, there was a girl standing outside and crying. Roxanne went over to the girl and asked her if she could help. The girl said, that's okay, Judi Buenoano is my spiritual mother.

Jan Doxtater, another volunteer in the prison ministry at the Orange County Jail, felt too that Judias had really changed since her incarceration. She was more peaceful, cooperative, and friendly to the other women in jail, teaching and helping them with their Bible studies.

And Kimberly Buenoano took the stand one last time to testify on her mother's behalf.

"I talk to her every single day," Kimberly attested in a small, tremulous voice. "She calls to make sure we're okay, and just to talk to me. Even though she's in jail, it's like she's there with me. Sometimes I need somebody to talk to and she's the only person I've got to talk to. She wants to study and stay in the ministry. Even if she was ever to get out of jail, she would stay in the prison ministry to help people who are in the same position that she's in and show them the light and the way they should go," Kimberly recited with wide-eyed innocence. "She's the best mother in the world. If I ever had any kind of problems, she was right there for me. That's my hardest problem, I don't have her there to help me out. It's nice to have someone pick you up when you fall. . . ."

"We call the defendant." Johnston announced his final witness late that Monday afternoon.

Judias came resolutely forward, and being duly sworn, calmly took the seat to the judge's right. The jury members leaned forward in their seats and stared intently at the inscrutable woman whose life or death they were about to determine.

"Your name is Judi Goodyear?" Johnston quietly directed.

"Yes, my name is Goodyear. Judi Buenoano is my legal name," Judias replied levelly.

"How old are you?"

"I am forty-two."

"Where were you born?"

"Quanah, Texas."

"You have been in jail how long?"

"Almost two years."

"Have you done anything in jail that would improve your skills in any area?"

"Yes, sir. I have been studying in prison ministry. I've been working on an associate's degree in Ministry, and I have my teaching certificate in Bible subjects. I teach inside the jail. I teach on a one-to-one basis. I teach in groups. I do a lot of counseling with young inmates, encourage them to call their parents. I give them a word of hope. We pray. I teach them about the Bible. A lot of them don't know what love is. They're down, and I kind of try to give them a bit of life and let them know

God loves them and there's hope," Judias rattled off with self-assurance.

"All right," Johnston intervened. "Have you turned to accept God as your savior?"

"Yes, most definitely."

"When did you do that?"

"In August of 1984."

"What prompted that?"

"My son," Judias replied tersely, offering no further explanation.

"And do you feel that you would like to continue that?" Johnston prompted awkwardly.

"Yes, I would continue, even if I was set free. I would continue to work in the ministry and in prison ministry, either in jails or prisons. There are so many young girls who need the help. It deters homosexuality. When you teach them about God, they learn that they can depend on someone else, that there is a different type of love and different type of friendship, which is a Christian friendship, and that deters homosexuality within jails and the prison system," Judias explained with an air of authority.

Belvin Perry approached the witness stand with one question on his mind.

"Did you kill your son?"

Judias blanched, unable to respond over her lawyer's strenuous objections.

Judias was so overwrought that court was recessed till the following morning, at which time counsels would present their closing arguments.

"She comes before you asking for mercy," Belvin Perry told the jury on the morning of November 26. "But this proceeding is about justice. . . .

"She tells us she found God in August of 1984. Maybe that is true, but where was God in her life in 1971, as she poisoned her husband to death and watched him die? Where was God in her life in 1980, when she drowned her son and collected the insurance money? Where was God in her life when she tried to murder John Gentry, and when the single dose of poisoning and when the double dose didn't work, she tried dynamite? I submit to you that the God in her life at that time was Mr. Green, Mr. Money. Each time that somebody died or stood the chance of dying, she stood the chance of collecting. John Gentry, more than half a million dollars. Her own flesh and blood, between eighty and one hundred thousand dollars. And her husband, twenty-eight thousand dollars plus sixty-four thousand dollars in VA benefits. . . . The Book of Numbers says, 'If he smite him for peace or instrument of iron, so that he die, he is a murderer, and the murderer shall surely be put to death.' The Book of Romans, New Testament: 'Being filled with murder who knowing the judgment of God, that they which commit such things are worthy of death.'

"There is always the question of mercy," Perry conceded, "but what mercy did she show? None. For back in September of 1971 she took a life, and back in 1981 she took a life, and in 1983 she tried to take another life. She showed no mercy, and she deserves no mercy. I submit to you that your recommendation not be based upon emotion, not vengeance, not pity, not sorrow, but based upon the law which we all have agreed to live by, that the defendant deserves under the law the ultimate sanction for the crime that she committed."

An uncomfortable silence hung in the air as Johnston stood to deliver his final plea for the life of his client before the grim-faced jury.

"The grand architect of the universe, in his wisdom, will ultimately judge this defendant. The grand architect of the universe will say, Judi, you shall not enter the kingdom of heaven, but you shall burn eternally in the fires of hell. God will make that decision, but only God knows whether this lady is truly repentant and only God knows whether or not he will forgive her. But looking back upon history, the God that I know is a merciful God, a forgiving God. . . ."

Johnston took a long breath. "Last night, when we went back to the motel room," Johnston confided to the unmoved jurors, "I said to my wife, here is a guy, I think his name is Rudolph Hess, who was convicted of some of the most atrocious crimes known in the twentieth century, the deliberate murder of thousands of innocent children, and some merciful person recommended that that man, for his sins, spend the rest of his natural life in jail. How is it that if man can show that kind of mercy, the state could get up here today and say, well, what you really ought to do is burn this lady in Raiford, when the crimes she's been charged with are infinitesimal compared to the crimes of Rudolph Hess.

"What do we know about this thing called capital punishment and whether or not someone should live or die? We know in this case that this lady has been an asset to other inmates. I guess the two most horrible places in the world to be are jail or a hospital. This lady, if all the convictions stand, has got 25 years to serve. She's got twelve years to serve, and then, if you spare her life, she will have another twenty-five years. That, I believe, is sixty-two years. She will never get out of prison, unless she is pardoned by the governor or some other miracle happens. If she simply saved one wayward soul in those sixty-two years of jail, your decision to give her life would be well worth it. . . . They say that the best preachers are those who have lived the worst life, who know the most suffering, and God knows this lady knows some suffering, internally and externally.

"If she is guilty in God's eyes, let God mete out the appropriate punishment to her. You spare this lady her life. That's not really too much to ask, because if God can forgive, why can't man also forgive? Mete out an appropriate punishment to her of life under man's law."

Johnston turned away from the jury, sadly believing his words had fallen on deaf ears.

"Clarence Darrow was right," he muttered to himself as he rejoined his wife and Judias seated stiffly at the defense table. "There is no justice in or out of the courtroom."

At 11:45 A.M. Judge Thompson excused the jury to vote on their advisory sentence. The jury returned two hours later, having reached its decision over lunch.

"The State of Florida versus Judi A. Buenoano, also known as Judi Ann Goodyear, Advisory Sentence," the clerk read. "A majority of the jury, by a vote of ten to two, advise and recommend to the court that it impose the death penalty upon the defendant."

At 4:20 P.M. the afternoon of November 26, 1985, following a two-hour court recess and the dismissal of the jury, Judge Emerson Thompson called the defendant forward.

Judias, flanked by Johnston and Perry, stood leadenly before the Bench.

"Mr. Johnston, on behalf of your client, do you have any legal cause to show why sentence should not be pronounced?" droned the judge.

"No, Your Honor," Johnston replied miserably.

"Do you want to say anything?" Judge Thompson coldly addressed the defendant.

"I didn't ever kill anybody, Judge Thompson," Judias blurted, the long-unshed tears streaming freely down her face. "It was an accident with my son. I didn't kill my husband, and I didn't bomb Mr. Gentry's car, and that's the truth. I've never, to my knowledge, ever harmed anyone meaningly. I ask the court to spare my life, and I will try to contribute as much to the prison ministry as I possibly can contribute. I just ask you for mercy."

Unmoved, Judge Thompson pronounced the sentence without hesitation.

"It is the sentence of the law and the judgment of this court that you, Judi A. Buenoano, also known as Judi Ann Goodyear, for the murder of James E. Goodyear, be committed to the custody of the Department of Corrections, and at a time to be fixed by the Governor of the State of Florida, you shall be put to death by means of electrocution. . . . May God have mercy on your immortal soul."

Judias was led away, handcuffed and weeping, to the solitary confines of the Florida Division of Corrections to await the issuance of her death warrant.

Whether Judias, like the men she preyed upon, had at last become a victim of her own ambition and greed, or whether she was, as she claimed to be, an innocent victim of an imperfect justice system, no one can know for certain, but she.

Epilogue

FOLLOWING THE IMPOSITION of her death sentence on November 26, 1985, Judias Buenoano was held alone in a single cell on death row at the Broward County Women's Detention Center in Pembroke Pines, Florida, to await the issuance of her death warrant by Florida Governor Bob Martinez.

Judias having been declared totally indigent, her trial attorney, James Johnston, requested that he be appointed her continuing legal representative by the court. Judge Emerson Thompson promptly granted Johnston's request. Over the next three years, Johnston filed numerous motions through the Florida state courts appealing Judias's conviction and death sentence. All of the appeals were denied.

On June 23, 1988, the Florida State Supreme Court unanimously upheld Judias Buenoano's conviction and death sentence, rejecting her attorney James Johnston's argument that her crime was not severe enough to warrant the death penalty.

On April 12, 1989, Judias's newly acquired defense attorney, Robert Wesley, argued before the Florida Executive Clemency Board that her death sentence should be commuted to life and she should be taken from the seclusion of death row and placed in the general women's prison population, since her alleged violence had been directed toward men only. Judias's clemency plea was denied by Governor Bob Martinez and the six Florida cabinet members of the Executive Clemency Board.

In November 1989, the Florida State appeal process having been exhausted by her attorney, Judias's first death warrant was signed by Governor Bob Martinez. Twenty hours before she was scheduled to be executed on January 25, 1990, Judias was granted a permanent stay of execution on her first death warrant by the Florida State Supreme Court. On April 5, 1990, the Florida State Supreme Court ruled that Judias had been correctly sentenced to death, despite arguments by her defense attorney, Robert Wesley, that she had been inadequately represented by her former trial attorney, James Johnston.

On May 17, 1990, Florida Governor Bob Martinez signed Judias's second death warrant, imposing the sentence of death in Florida's electric chair to be executed on some day of the week beginning noon Monday, June 18, 1990, and ending noon Monday, June 25, 1990.

Judias was transferred from her death-row cell at the Broward County Women's Detention Center to the death watch cell beside the execution chamber at Florida State Prison near the North Florida town of Starke to await the hour of her execution, scheduled for Tuesday, June 19, 1990, at 12:01 P.M.

Once again, the Florida Supreme Court stayed Judias's execution, postponing it for two days in order to hear arguments from Judias's state-appointed attorneys that execution in Florida's electric chair would be unconstitutionally cruel and unusual punishment. Citing the botched May 4, 1990, Florida execution of Jesse Tafero, in which a synthetic sponge placed beneath the electrode of the skull cap caused the electric chair to malfunction, lowering the voltage to a torturous level of ninety to one hundred volts over a period of six minutes, during which time flames shot from under the headpiece, Judias's lawyers argued that she would be burned alive in Florida's sixty-four-year-old electric chair.

On Thursday, June 21, Judge Patricia Fawsett of the Federal District Court in Orlando issued another stay of execution to hear arguments from Judias's lawyers.

On Friday, June 22, the stay was lifted and the Governor of Florida reset Judias's execution for Monday, June 25, at 12:01 P.M.

On Saturday a three-judge panel of the United States Court of Appeals for the Eleventh Circuit in Atlanta, Georgia, issued Judias an indefinite stay of execution. She had outlived her second death warrant to return to her death-row cell at the Broward County Women's Detention Center. On July 27, 1990, the same day that Anthony Bertolotti became the twenty-third male to be executed in Florida's electric chair since the resumption of Florida's death penalty in 1979, Judias's latest appeal was filed before the Eleventh Circuit Court of Appeals on the grounds that Florida's electric chair continued to function improperly.

Judias, one of five women currently on Florida's death row, sits in her tiny cell equipped with a small black-and-white television set, alone with her thoughts except for an occasional visit from the prison chaplain, and awaits the signing of her third death warrant by newly elected Florida Governor Lawton Chiles.

Judias has yet to admit to any of the crimes of which she remains convicted.

HERE IS AN EXCERPT FROM ONE OF THE CASES IN *WHO KILLED PRECIOUS?*, A ST. MARTIN'S TRUE CRIME PAPERBACK COMING IN MAY:

BEHIND THE BLEAK STONE WALLS OF ATTICA CORRECTIONAL Facility in the seclusion of upstate New York waited prisoner 78-A-1976, known as Son of Sam.

How to explain him? In the words of poet William Wordsworth?

> *Heaven lies about us in our infancy!*
> *Shades of the prison-house begin to close*
> *Upon the growing boy.*

Born out of wedlock on June 1, 1953, he was the son of a Long Island businessman named Joseph Kleinman and a waitress named Betty Broder Falco. Himself named Richard David Falco, he was put up for adoption because his mother could not keep him. Taken in by Nat and Pearl Berkowitz and renamed David Richard, he grew up painfully aware that he'd been adopted and showed evidence of being phobic and feeling rejected. Never very good in school or at making friends, he created for himself a concealing veneer made up of braggadocio, boastings of sexual conquests that had never happened, and a bullying toughness. In his youth he set many fires in empty lots. Bizarre fantasies entertained him. He began to think about being possessed of demons. Shrieking, they beckoned him to the conquest of women by killing them.

His first weapon had been a knife, slashed and stabbed into a woman he'd encountered on Christmas Eve 1975 where he lived in a sprawl of urban anonymity called Co-op City in the Bronx. Half a year later he drove to Houston, Texas, where with the help of an old Army buddy he purchased a Charter Arms Bulldog pistol. Its big bullets dug out of the flesh of the ten women and men he shot over the next thirteen months would give him one of the catchiest of the colorful names so fancied by headline writers of the New York tabloid papers: the .44-Caliber Killer.

In a very short time, this drab, soft-faced, overweight nonentity had transformed himself into a feared figure that struck in the darkness and terrorized the world's greatest metropolis. He made up names for himself: Wicked King Maker, the Chubby Monster, the Duke of Death. Then an even better name came to him, scribbled down on a piece of paper in his crude, unlearned hand and sent off to New York Police Captain Joseph Borrelli, who'd been on TV calling the unknown killer a hater of women:

> I am deeply hurt by your calling me
> a wemon [sic] hater. I am not. But
> I am a monster. I am the "Son of Sam."

Later he would claim that orders to kill came from a dog owned by a neighbor of his in Yonkers, Sam Carr. Its barking, Berkowitz maintained, was the way a demon communicated with him, urging him to prowl the streets looking for fair game. "The wemon of Queens are prettyist of all," he wrote to Borrelli.

In 1981 the Son of Sam was prisoner number 78-A-1976 and about to be interviewed by Special Agent Robert Ressler of the Federal Bureau of Investigation. In the file on Berkowitz was a psychological profile that had been worked up at the height of his shooting sprees by New York police, doctors, and social workers. It described Son of Sam as white, male, quiet, a loner, and ordinary-looking, someone who worked in a regular job but harbored a seething resentment and animosity toward the world and himself. In psychiatric examinations after his arrest, he'd proved the latter point—page upon page of the psychiatrist's report was filled with hatred.

He resembled the photos taken of him while he was being processed after his arrest—a dumpy figure with a silly smile on his face. That grin, Berkowitz had said later, was just amusement at the sight of hundreds of cameramen scrambling and fighting and falling all over themselves to get pictures of him. "I never expected anything like it," he said. "I guess I smiled. So right away they began saying, 'Ah, you see, he's smiling. He's happy he did it.' I guess that's what everyone thought."

One writer looking at that smile thought the smirk was not that of one who despised his audience, as many journalists had charged, but was the smug and self-satisfied response of someone who was very shy but was suddenly discovered to have done something amazing.

Was he happy about what he did?

"After the shootings," Berkowitz said, "I thought I might weep for some of the people I killed. But I couldn't. It was all puzzling, you know. You hear so much news about victims, all those sob stories. Women in tears. After a while you don't feel anything at all." In a talk with his court-appointed psychiatrist, Dr. David Abrahamsen, he had shrieked, "I don't want forgiveness. Who needs that?"

How did he carry out all those shootings?

They took from several minutes to an hour. The first had taken twenty minutes. This time was spent stalking and watching. He'd walked around the block several times. Checked alleyways. Looked up to windows of all the apartment buildings to see if anyone was looking out. As for the couple in the car whom he'd decided to shoot, he hoped they would drive away. The second murder was quicker, about ten minutes. "I could have waited longer, but I was anxious. I wanted to get it over and then head home," he said. Shootings of Valentina Surani and Alexander Esau in the Bronx on April 17, 1977, took much, much longer. He had been cruising about six hours and was headed toward Yonkers on the Hutchinson River Parkway service road when he saw two heads over the seat of the car. He drove around a corner and parked, than walked to the couple's car, dropped a note at the scene, and opened fire. On June 26, his seventh shooting, he'd stalked out an area of

Queens for hours before he saw Judy Placido and Salvatore
Lupo. "I saw them and just finally decided that I must do
it and get it over with," he said. His final attack was on
July 31 in Brooklyn. He'd come from work, had a snack
at a diner, checked out Queens, where he found no one
to interest him, and moved over to Brooklyn. The lovers
he watched late that night were Stacy Moskowitz and
Robert Violante. Seeing their passionate kissing, he had
an erection. Minutes later, when they were back in their
Buick, he recalled, he "just walked up to it, pulled out the
gun, and fired into the car on the passenger's side. I fired
four bullets. I really wanted the girl more than anything.
I don't know why I shot the guy. But they were so close
together."

Highly organized, plodding, patient, and methodical, he
had in the course of a year and a half stabbed or shot
seventeen people, killing six, paralyzing one woman, and
blinding a man. "You just felt very good after you did it,"
he said. "It just happens to be satisfying, to get the source
of the blood. I had a job to do and I did it. I came through.
I know that 'Sam' was relieved."

Berkowitz talked about how he'd been influenced by
demons. "I used to watch horror movies on TV. Everything from *Dracula* to *Godzilla*. The monsters haunted me.
I couldn't sleep. I'd have to have the light on. The monsters
planned to take me over even when I was a kid. I'm almost
certain that they're the same ones who got me later. I think
I was born so they could take me over."

The worst of these demons took the form of Sam's
dog.

To Ressler, the dog was nothing but Berkowitz's way
of denying responsibility for his acts. Impatient, he cut
Berkowitz off. "Don't hand me that bullshit about the dog,
David," he said. "I'm not buying it."

Through the infamous smirk, Berkowitz said, "You're
right."

The demons were a lie. He'd invented all of it and had
been amazed at the attention his story got.

Having swept the monsters, demons, and "Sam" aside, Ressler turned to genuine fantasies. Berkowitz said he envisioned himself sexually as a superb lover who was passionate and well endowed, with abundant stamina, able to please a partner by giving her multiple orgasms. Most often his sexual fantasies involved oral sex.

What did he imagine when he was a child? As a kid when he played soldier he always took the part of the German. "I always wanted to be the guy who got shot down. When you play war, you know, the Germans always lose."

In the real world of winners and losers, of punishment to fit the crime, Berkowitz did not stand trial. He pleaded guilty. But he turned his appearance in court for sentencing into a show. Handcuffed and guarded by five burly officers, he peered into the spectators' section and saw the mother of Stacy Moskowitz, his last victim. He broke into a singsong chant: "Stacy is a whore, Stacy is a whore. I'll shoot them all." As court officers struggled to restrain him, he bit one and twisted the head of another. In this furious final outburst Dr. Abrahamsen saw Berkowitz attempting to "maintain his status as the star of the show."

Son of Sam's sentence for his crimes added up to 547 years.

On July 11, 1979, Berkowitz was attacked by another inmate at Attica and badly slashed. Refusing to name his assailant, he instead looked on the incident as justice for all his own crimes. In a letter to Dr. Abrahamsen, he explained, "I've always wanted punishment, the punishment I deserve—I love being punished. So, this was it. I've been trying to expiate my sins for so long."

THE "SON OF SAM" CASE—ONE OF THE CASES COVERED IN *WHO KILLED PRECIOUS?*—COMING IN MAY FROM ST. MARTIN'S PAPERBACKS.